I KNOW WHY SHE STAYED

KASEY ROGERS &
K. J. HARROWICK

Cover Design: K. J. Harrowick
Interior Design: K. J. Harrowick
Edited by: Vicki Lowry and Justine Manzano

Library of Congress Control Number: 2024909495
ISBN (Hardcover): 979-8-330227-85-3
ISBN (Paperback):979-8-869313-82-9
ISBN (Ebook): 979-8-869313-83-6

FOREWARD

I was haunted by my own childhood trauma well past my thirties. Bad memories played on repeat in my head, and as frustrated as I was, I still couldn't change my family of origin's dynamic. Around my abusive parent I froze. I fawned. I was the queen of silent agreement while seething for days. But all of that changed when I wrote my story down. Suddenly, I didn't have to carry my pain anymore—it lived between the covers of a book. And I walked away from my father entirely. By writing down his actions, I could see that I wasn't being a drama queen/whiner/ exaggerator (insert your family's favorite term for minimizing your pain here). I could see that I didn't have to stay in the relationship any longer. It was bad enough.

But for me, it was not just in writing that I found release, but in hearing from readers that I wasn't crazy, that it really was that bad, and that I wasn't the only one. That it didn't need to be worse to justify my trauma. And it was in reading other people's stories that this feel was cemented—sometimes it is easier to see the trauma in others than it is in our own lives. It is in reading that we find validation. And in I Know Why She Stayed I had that experience, over and over. I did not know the term, "economic abuse" but I have suffered from it. It is that shared experience that gives us words and power, for if we can name it, we can mourn what we lost, allow ourselves to feel rage and finally release our pain and say, "never again."

Lara Lillibridge, author of *The Truth About Unringing Phones: Essays on Yearning* and *Girlish: Growing Up in a Lesbian Home.*

DEDICATION

To all the women who never escaped.
Who are still trapped and seeking refuge.

We know why you stay.
You are not alone.

DEDICATION FROM KASEY ROGERS

Resilience is knowing that you are the only one
that has the power and the responsibility
to pick yourself up.

~ Mary Holloway

For the Beans.

DEDICATION FROM K. J. HARROWICK

To my niece, Destiny.

You almost made it.
You fought so hard to escape.
Life took you first,
but you'll live on in our hearts and the smiles you left behind.

and

For Chia-Yi Lee (Alice).

You kept me glued together through all of it.
I will forever be grateful for
your kindness and encouragement.

MAP OF LOCATIONS

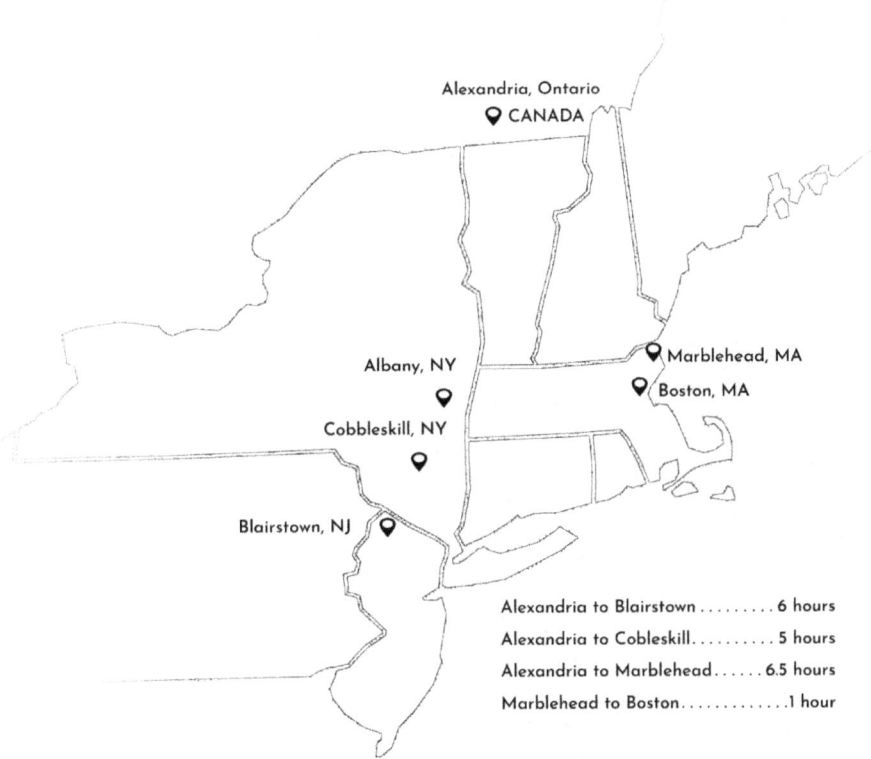

Alexandria, Ontario
CANADA

Marblehead, MA

Albany, NY

Boston, MA

Cobbleskill, NY

Blairstown, NJ

Alexandria to Blairstown . . . . 6 hours

Alexandria to Cobleskill . . . . 5 hours

Alexandria to Marblehead . . . . . . 6.5 hours

Marblehead to Boston . . . . 1 hour

PART 1

SEEDS OF DOUBT

"March on. Do not tarry.
To go forward is to move toward perfection.
March on, and fear not the thorns,
or the sharp stones on life's path."

~ Khalil Gibran

CHAPTER ONE

A Reluctant Farewell

August 30, 2010 Alexandria, Ontario, Canada

The red light flashed on the answering machine. I saw it blinking from the bathroom where I stood drying off from my shower. I wrapped a towel around my body and crossed through the door to the desk in the room. My hand hovered above the play button. Mentally, I listed the reasons I didn't want to listen to the message. Most likely, my husband, Phillip, left a message to ask when I was leaving Alexandria. However, after twenty-four years of marriage, I knew that the questions he asked and what he really wanted to know were two different things. While the question might be, "When are you leaving," he wanted to see if I'd finished packing. I wondered why he always seemed to think haranguing me would make me work faster. What it did, in reality, was piss me off. I stood there, debating whether to listen to the message at all.

I'd been alone for a few days after taking our twins, Jack and Lucy, to Vermont. My brother Jake and his wife Meredith were caring for them for the week while I packed to move back to the States. I thought maybe Jake had left the message, so I pushed the play button. I heard Phillip's familiar voice, heavy with recrimination.

"Well, I guess you've already left to go to Jenny's. Funny how you always have time to spend with your friends. Don't bother calling me back tonight. I'm sure you'll be staying out late. Well, I have to get up early tomorrow because I work for a living. Call me tomorrow when you finish packing, so we...."

I erased the rest of the message without listening to the end. It would only be another reminder of the countless times during our marriage when

Phillip insisted my desire to attend any social function was selfish and that doing so made me a terrible wife and mother. Those hurtful words had prevented me from going to baby showers, birthday parties, and countless other events I had wanted to attend. This latest ploy didn't work now because I'd learned it was another way he tried to manipulate me.

"Screw him," I thought, and flipped the answering machine, the bird, as I walked into the room to get dressed.

I sat down and slumped across the mattress that served as my temporary bed. I berated myself for telling Phillip in an email earlier in the day that I planned to go out in the first place. I should have known how he'd react. I was thankful I didn't tell him everything. Jenny arranged a farewell dinner on my behalf and had invited several mutual friends. She'd also suggested I bring my laundry and spend the night. I did that frequently when Jenny's husband traveled.

I looked down at Chubby Checkers, our small white Bichon-Lhasa mix, lying on the edge of the mattress. He looked up, wagging his tail.

"I'll bet you're looking forward to this evening as much as I am, Chub." I reached over to scratch his head, grateful for his company.

I wasn't used to being alone anymore. I felt untethered without a business to run and my kids to look after. Both kept me grounded and focused on the present. Now, I had too much time to think while I dismantled our life in Alexandria. Questions about the past and the future rattled around in my head.

I wanted to get to Jenny's before everyone else showed up to talk with her about the ongoing saga of my troubled marriage. Things I had been blind to for decades were coming into sharp focus. Recollections of seemingly benign events were called into question and took on new meaning. I wasn't sure who Phillip was anymore. I was starting to think I never knew.

Reaching over, I picked up a small notebook on top of a cardboard box I used as a nightstand. I had spent the last few days packing and never called Jenny to tell her what I'd found under the desk. Earlier in the week, I'd received an email from Phillip asking me to help him recall all the dates of family birthdays and anniversaries. He couldn't locate the notebook where he kept all this information. Then I remembered seeing something on the floor beneath a desk in the office. He must have dropped it there on his last visit, weeks ago.

I was delighted to find that not only did the notebook contain the dates of birthdays and anniversaries, but it also held all his usernames and passcodes. He had a horrible memory of such details. It wasn't long before I logged into his email account and read them without an iota of guilt.

What Phillip had written to various friends and family members left me numb. His tone invoked sheer hostility whenever his correspondence mentioned me. He made claims about my actions or inactions that revealed a resentment built on complete fabrications. Of particular note was an email he sent to his sister, Rachel. Phillip claimed I had squandered all the money from the sale of our house in the States on a "failed" business and that I had refused to follow through in contacting an attorney about our residency status in Canada. I wanted to scream when I read that. How dare he!

None of his claims were true. I had countless communications, in writing, from the Ottawa attorney filing documents on our behalf. I had all our bank statements, including canceled checks to the attorney, that could show he was lying.

Reading this email allowed me to understand that his lies were another form of manipulation. By convincing his sister not to betray his confidence, he knew she would never discuss this with me. His lies were a way for him to exert power and control over us.

Phillip's emails caused me to speculate, and I began to believe he planned to file for divorce once the kids and I moved back to the U.S. He wanted everyone to believe I was at fault for all the problems between us in recent years. The whole matter made me eager to discuss what he'd written in them with Jenny. I hoped to talk to her privately to get her input.

I finished dressing and considered what I should do next, since Jenny suggested I arrive around seven. With almost two hours to go, I considered confronting the piles of packed boxes cluttering the former tearoom, but found it too daunting. With little else to do, I went back upstairs and impatiently waited.

Earlier in the day, I emptied shelves and disassembled various elements of my business located on the main floor of the building. Tomorrow, when I traveled south, I would leave it all behind. Even though the upstairs room was hot and stuffy, I avoided that unpleasantness and stayed camped out in a room upstairs that once served as the office for my restaurant, The 2Beans Café and Tearoom.

Most people assumed 2Beans referred to coffee beans. But our twins were the real inspiration for the restaurant's name. We called them "the Beans" after Phillip, and I saw their first ultrasound. They looked like two little kidney beans facing one another. It was a happy coincidence when it came time to name the restaurant nine years after they were born.

Phillip lost his job as a copywriter in February 2005 when his company in New Jersey merged with another ad agency. Almost every employee, including Phillip, found themselves laid off, which forced us to make some hard decisions.

A year went by and Phillip was still unemployed, so in October 2006, we sold the old Victorian home we had lovingly restored in Blairstown, New Jersey. We moved into a rented apartment close to where the kids went to school and began looking for a way to start fresh.

We'd owned a vacation property in Quebec years ago, and Phillip's lifelong dream was to move to Canada permanently to reconnect with his French-Canadian heritage. He convinced me to purchase the property in Alexandria, Ontario, and we planned to open a family business. I thought reinventing our lives there would bring us closer together. Instead, the move fractured us in ways I never could have imagined.

We moved north at the end of June 2007. Four months after we relocated, Phillip took a job back in the States, leaving the kids and me behind. He claimed we needed the money. I vehemently disagreed because we still had plenty in the bank from selling our home in New Jersey. He expected me to raise our twins alone in a foreign country while I also operated the new business we planned to run together.

Phillip could only travel to Alexandria every few weeks. His visits and our conversations grew shorter and shorter as time and distance came between us.

"Hey. How was lunch today?" Phillip asked when he called each night.

"We were pretty busy," I would reply. I'd give him a brief rundown of the day and then ask, "How about you? Marco keeping you busy?"

"Yeah, I took work home. I have to work for a few more hours tonight. I was hoping I could come north this weekend, but it doesn't look like I'll have time. Traveling six hours each way makes little sense if I can't spend time with you and the Beans. Next weekend, though."

The excuses for why he couldn't come north were always the same, and I believed him when he said he needed to work, but it stung anyway. In the beginning, I tried to hide my frustration.

"That sucks. We all miss you," I would tell him.

"I know. I miss you, too. Are the kids there? I want to say hi," he'd reply.

I would put the phone on speaker so Phillip could talk to them both at the same time. I listened to him ask the same questions every night.

"How was school? Do you have lots of homework? What did you guys do today? How's Chubby?" When the list of banal questions were all answered, and silence filled the air, he'd say "goodnight" and "I love you. Can you put Mommy back on the phone?"

I believed then that the tenderness that came through the phone lines spoke of his loneliness. Back then, it left my heart melting. I both longed for him and hated him for leaving us behind. When I woke in the morning without him, my cycle of anger would begin again as I went through the day without him by my side.

One year had turned into two, and Phillip always had a reason that it made little sense for him to move north or for us to return south.

"How is Marco's business doing? Are things picking up at all?" I asked him often, reminding him of his promise.

He responded, "Once the business is stable, you can all move back. Now is not the right time. We need to be sure my job is secure, and the business has been slow."

It never occurred to me to ask him why he was always required to work on the weekends if Marco's business was so slow.

I grew immune to the loneliness in his voice and the hope that he'd visit. It hurt too profoundly to confront the reality that I had a husband I rarely saw and who our now eleven-year-old twins barely knew. He loomed over us like a distant rain cloud providing a break from the heat, but we knew the drenched earth would soon dry up and leave us all surveying the horizon, wondering when he would appear again.

I complained endlessly about the situation and expressed my anger with him to others. In reality, however, I missed him, and his choices hurt me. He was both the person who knew me best and a stranger. After decades of marriage, we had so much history together. Yet our lives had gone in such different directions.

I can't recall the exact moment it happened, but I suddenly realized I no longer had time to think about Phillip throughout my busy day. I was exhausted from hours of being on my feet. By the time I got into bed each night, the pains that ran down my back erased thoughts of Phillip. We were no longer a couple, with our lives immeasurably intertwined. We were two people who were married to one another, leading separate lives.

At first, he didn't need to be there physically to occupy a large part of my day. The rugs that lined the tearoom floor were the rugs that we had spent hours discussing before we purchased them for the formal parlor in our Victorian home. The antique lights that hung above the tables were the same ones we had selected to adorn our dining room years ago. Family photos and memorabilia brought to mind warm memories when I glimpsed them throughout my day. However, the miles between us couldn't withstand the simple march of time. The warmth of him lying beside me was a thing of the past, and the everyday reminders of him faded during those years we were apart.

All the same, things that were once a part of Phillip and me became part of a different world, one Phillip didn't inhabit. The twins and I had settled into a routine that didn't include him. We adapted and thrived in the place we had thought of as home. We'd become members of a wonderful community while Phillip was just a visitor.

I checked the clock on the makeshift nightstand. It was approaching six o'clock, so I still had an hour before I could reasonably leave for Jenny's house. I picked up Phillip's notebook but avoided rereading his emails for a third and fourth time. Instead, I wandered downstairs to get a cold drink. Grabbing a can of club soda from the fridge, I glanced around the galley-style kitchen that had become my sanctuary. Away from Phillip's constant scrutiny, it was here that I found myself reawakening as my passion for cooking slowly reemerged.

Beginning to cook again had also caused me to realize how much of myself I'd abdicated to Phillip. Rediscovering my culinary flair gave me a sense of joy smothered by the demands of churning out quick meals to feed my family. He always told me any meal that took more than a half-hour to make was a waste of time. Unchained from these demands, the luxury of watching the butter sizzle and brown in a pan to make a roux and other mundane acts of cooking became my elixir.

Standing in the tiny kitchen, my anger boiled over. I feared I would revert to the person I was when I had first arrived in Alexandria once I moved back to the U.S. The self-doubt and loathing faded only when Phillip wasn't there to present his image of me. I realized I had absorbed all the negative messages Phillip had sent me during our marriage when he attacked my character. In his absence, I had regained my confidence.

While I sipped my drink, I imagined dozens of dubious reasons Phillip wanted us to return to the States since this arrangement had suited him just fine for years. Yet, there was a part of me that wanted to go back in time. I yearned to retreat to the days before I had realized that none of the reasons Phillip initially gave me for his living six hours away made sense. I longed to erase the knowledge that he most likely had been lying to me for years. Now that I suspected why he wanted to be so far away, I couldn't shut out the thoughts that forced me to wonder why I hadn't seen it all along.

In March of 2010, he'd taken a new job as a creative director for an ad firm in Albany, New York. I assumed he would happily continue our awkward arrangement of living separately. That wasn't the case. His attitude shifted dramatically, and he began overtly referring to the move north as a mistake and suggesting that it had been my idea. He complained bitterly about missing the twins' childhood and insinuated that because the café wasn't making enough income to live on, it forced him to get a job back in the States to support our family. Then, he did something that thoroughly alarmed me. He opened a separate bank account that I had no access to. He claimed I'd over-drafted our joint statement. At first, I tried to reason with him. After all, he was the one who'd made the unrecorded transaction that hadn't been posted to the account. That led to my assuming we had more funds available than we did. Regardless, he blamed me, and shortly after that, he closed our joint account because he said he needed to "put his foot down because I was financially irresponsible."

In April, he told me he would no longer contribute to paying any of the bills in Canada. He said it was a waste of "his money." The mortgage, taxes, and other building overhead, including all expenses related to his children, were now my sole responsibility. This made me furious, but it opened my eyes. Now I knew he was hiding something—I just didn't know what.

Then Phillip demanded the Beans, and I move to the Albany area. He made no mention of wanting us to move back to the U.S. before he took the job. This made me think that he had been plotting something all along, knowing that the property in Alexandria's overhead and expenses would drain any profit I made from operating the café. It would force me to close the business. Once I moved south, I would have no funds, giving him complete control over me.

At the end of June, I contacted an attorney in Alexandria who convinced me that if Phillip planned to file for divorce, the only way to prevent a messy court battle was to go back south. I was sure he wondered why I was suddenly so cooperative.

Other things struck me as significant signs of his intentions. One night, after he took the job in Albany, he called to tell me he'd found a place to live. He had moved into a single room in an expensive renovated mansion close to his job. This meant the Beans and I no longer had a physical address in the U.S. Not only did this present a problem regarding our immigration status, but Phillip didn't seem the least bit concerned that we had no place to stay if we visited him in the area.

"My room is small, but it's close to work, so I don't have as long a commute anymore. You would love this place. The owner converted a beautiful ballroom into a common area for the tenants. I've been coming down here at night to play my guitar. Man, the acoustics are great."

I expressed concern when he mentioned it cost twice the amount he'd spent on rent previously.

"If it has no kitchen, what will you do about preparing meals? Aren't you going to have to eat out all the time?" I asked him.

"There are plenty of places to eat, and it was the closest place to work that I could find on short notice," he insisted.

"Okay. I get it. I'm just concerned because you told me your stomach acid is worse, not to mention the cost. It also worries me that the twins and I will have nowhere to stay when we come down there."

"I'll get up there again soon," he told me. "Look, I have to get up early. I'll talk to you tomorrow." He hung up abruptly without asking to speak to the kids.

By July, we began mainly communicating by email. Phillip's calls became less frequent, and when he did call, I immediately put the kids on the phone or let it go to voicemail. His tone of voice had changed. He was cold and business-like.

When the time came to look for an apartment for the entire family, he suggested I look online at apartments forty-five minutes to an hour from Albany, claiming the rents would be much cheaper. He evaded my question when I asked why it was now okay to live that far away from work again.

I stood in the kitchen remembering these events. I had always taken Phillip at his word for much of my marriage. Even before we had children, we spent much time apart. But after they were born, he continued to spend much of his time away from me and the Beans. I always assumed our rental properties in another city demanded his attention. However, when I looked back at all the times he was away from us, I began questioning my thinking. My gut told me the miles between us were not the sole reason for his disengagement. I had begun to suspect there was another motive. I couldn't help but recall another time, years before, when we had broken up. His words back then echoed in my mind.

"I've met someone else, Kasey. I'm in love with her."

CHAPTER TWO

Distant Memories

I'd almost completely forgotten about Molly and the day Phillip announced he was ending our two-year relationship, since it happened so long ago. The memories came flooding back, returning me to that miserable day in the fall of 1985. I had walked through his apartment door in Arlington, Massachusetts, a town close to Boston. I had just flopped on his sofa when I noticed the look on his face.

"I think somebody's had a rough day. You should have called me, honey. I would have stopped and picked up a nice bottle of wine. All I can offer you now is a few Tic Tacs I found earlier at the bottom of my purse."

Phillip usually laughed at my attempts at humor, but my remarks did nothing to change the expression he wore.

"Phillip, what's wrong?"

His silence filled the room.

"I've met someone else, Kasey. I'm in love with her."

I couldn't speak. I wiped my eyes, trying to find the reason for my blurred vision. The floors beneath me seemed to move, and I held onto the arm of a chair next to me before I slid into it, unable to stand. With my heart pounding, I gathered my thoughts and waited some time before I trusted myself enough to say something civil while I absorbed Phillip's explosive news.

"I see. Who is she?"

"The new receptionist at work. Her name is Molly."

Phillip had mentioned Molly's name several times since she'd started work a month earlier. I never picked up on anything more than a casual remark about a new colleague. I waited to hear more, but he said nothing.

"I'm assuming we're over?"

He nodded but refused to look at me.

I choked back tears, got up, and walked toward the door. What he said next was beyond comprehension.

"Wait!"

I turned back to face him.

"I don't want to lose you!" he said. "We can still be friends."

I didn't wait to hear more and ran out of his apartment to my car. Driving away, I only made it as far as the parking lot of a nearby convenience store before I needed to pull over. Struggling to find a tissue to blow my nose, I came up empty after searching my pocketbook and the glove box. I saturated the sleeve of my blouse with tears and mucus, humiliated that I had no other remedy. I avoided looking at all the people who passed my car on their way into the store. I kept searching my purse as if I were looking for something deep within the various pockets while I struggled to compose myself. When I could finally drive back to my apartment, I rushed inside, crawled into bed, and locked the world out behind me. I pulled the covers up and lay there sobbing, assuming I'd never see Phillip again. Like so many things, I was wrong.

When Phillip and I met in 1983, he worked as a producer in Boston. I'd scheduled a business meeting for my company, RSVP Communications, to introduce the work of a consortium of producers and directors that my partner Gerry and I represented. I wanted to learn more about the company Phillip worked for so I could persuade them to use RSVP's creative talent within their agency.

A handsome young man approached me when the elevator doors opened to the lobby of the ad agency. Phillip introduced himself and reached out to shake my hand. His engaging eyes and friendly demeanor left me taken aback.

During his presentation, he exuded confidence. I wanted to know more about him. I glanced around the room for a way to check my appearance, hoping my lipstick was the right shade and the bobby pins in my hair were holding it in place. I smoothed my dress and avoided looking at Phillip's crooked smile too closely.

Weeks later, I contacted him about joining my company as one of our producer/directors. It was merely an excuse to contact him. Soon, we began working together to develop small film projects.

My friends kept asking me if I was interested in him romantically. I insisted I wasn't. But something about him made me look forward to seeing him. Our projects soon became an excuse to be with one another. I enjoyed spending time with this talented and funny man.

What I appreciated most about Phillip initially was how different he acted from many of the men I'd worked with in the past. I always seemed to work alongside this fraternal pack of grown boys who barely recognized their female colleagues as co-workers. Many of the women I worked with got smaller projects and lower salaries. Phillip, however, treated me more seriously, both personally and professionally.

One of the reasons I started my own business was I got sick to death of being just as skilled as my male counterparts without getting the credit for my work. It seemed like I only got positive feedback when I wore something that showed off my figure. I'd hear the whispers and tried to laugh off the uncomfortable banter my male co-workers called jokes.

"Hey, where's your sense of humor?" my male colleagues frequently asked.

As a single woman, I was often passed over for promotions in favor of male co-workers because they had families to support.

I started my own business to get away from a company where men had the right to say and do despicable things, and I was expected to go along.

By the time I met Phillip, I found it so refreshing to work with a guy who never displayed these horrible, misogynistic tendencies—at the time. He treated me like an equal back then, and I couldn't help but admire him.

As our working relationship grew, we pooled our financial resources to option the T.V./film rights of a book by local writer Art Meyers called Ghosts in America and Where to Find Them. I acted as producer, while Phillip directed, and we co-wrote the pilot episode, with Art acting as the pilot's narrator.

We had scheduled the film shoot for a weekend in early September of 1984. It was a cold and rainy day. We were shooting the film at two locations. First, we set up in a graveyard and, next, at an inn with a restroom haunted by the ghost of a woman.

Things went haywire all day. We ended our graveyard shoot early because of heavy rain. Then, our fully-charged batteries failed when we tried to use them to power the camera to shoot a scene in the attic of the inn. While shooting a scene in a meeting room, Phillip attempted to do a white balance on the video camera. He ended up recording a shadow between the camera and the wall only inches away. We were all spooked by the day's strange events, and most of the footage we recorded was unusable.

The owner of the inn provided us with dinner at its in-house restaurant. Before our meals came, I hurried off to use the restroom, the one rumored to have ghostly sightings. Shortly after I used the toilet, something startled me so much that I screamed.

The camera guy knocked on the bathroom door.

"Are you okay? We thought we heard a scream."

"I'm good. There was a huge spider. It scared me. Nasty creature. The size of a quarter," I fibbed. Embarrassed, I came out of the restroom and sat down, convinced I had covered up the truth about what had occurred.

Phillip and I had driven to the shoot together, so he drove me back to my apartment after we wrapped up for the day. When we arrived, he parked in the driveway and turned to me with a knowing smile.

"Okay, Kasey. What happened in there?" he quizzed me.

I hesitated for a moment before telling him.

"All right. Busted. If you tell anyone about this, I'll kill you, got it? Well, I accidentally wrapped my underwear around the toilet seat. When I went to get up, the seat came up, too, and as I pulled up my undies, it crashed onto the enamel bowl. I thought it was a ghost."

He started to laugh so hard I laughed, too. At first, I thought he was making fun of me, but then he looked over and pulled me toward him.

"I've wanted to do this for a long time," he said, kissing me.

We went upstairs to my apartment and started a new chapter of our relationship.

After we began officially dating, our romantic and creative goals became wholly intertwined. We discussed moving to New York City, where we planned to produce independent films together. At the time, I worked for a company near Boston, because my business had folded when my former partner and I had creative conflicts. I didn't like the job, so we decided I should look for work in Manhattan first, and Phillip would move down shortly after that. But before that happened, our relationship ended and he started dating Molly, a divorced woman with a young child.

My heart broke. Not only was I losing the man I'd fallen in love with, but I was also losing one of my best friends and my writing partner. Gone, too, were our dreams of moving to New York City. I'd already started sending out my resumé to secure a job before Phillip quit his full-time position. When he ended our relationship, I felt like I'd lost my world. In many ways, I did.

I didn't realize until he broke up with me how much Phillip seemed to complete me. I couldn't console myself. My entire life fell apart. I picked up the phone dozens of times to call him, but didn't dare to dial his number. I found myself going to a second-run movie theatre in town and watching sad, romantic movies so I had an excuse to cry. I didn't realize at the time, but there was another reason for my fragile emotional state.

More than a month passed when Phillip called me out of the blue. I tried to control myself when I heard his voice. He told me he was in Los Angeles, where he'd gone on vacation. Just like that, he announced his relationship with Molly had ended, claiming it was a huge mistake.

His voice moved me, but I questioned why he assumed I would be so willing to accept him back into my life. I wasn't sure if he wanted to resume our romantic relationship or reconnect as friends. I didn't ask the hard questions, and instead, we chatted about safe subjects like work and movies. But we talked for hours. By the time I got off the phone, I knew I still wanted to be with him.

When he came back from Los Angeles, he arrived at the door of my attic apartment with a bouquet of roses and asked me to forgive him. I let him in and made dinner, grappling with a way to tell him my big news.

"So, speaking of awkward timing, I have something to tell you," I started, trying to find the right words.

"Did you get that job in New York?"

"Not exactly." Finally, I blurted it out. "I don't know how this happened, but I'm pregnant. I mean, I know how it happened. Shit, you know what I mean."

Phillip was quiet for a long time.

"Say something, Phillip. I need to know what you're thinking."

"Well, it's not the news I expected. What happens here is your decision, but I am hoping you'll decide not to have an abortion. It's the whole Catholic thing. Other than that, Kasey, I don't know what to say about the situation."

I moved the food around on my plate. I didn't press him, knowing the news was a shock. I'd had weeks to process everything. He'd only had a few minutes, so I let him be. He left shortly after that without saying much. I cried endlessly over the next few days when I didn't hear from him. When he finally called, he didn't even bring up the subject.

I was riddled with guilt, believing I had ruined Phillip's life. It didn't occur to me then that we were both responsible for the situation and this life-altering news affected me, too. Regardless, humiliation overtook me. The religious upbringing of my childhood made me believe that unplanned pregnancy made me a bad person, and I was ashamed that, despite taking birth control, I still got pregnant. I fell into a state of constant anxiety, struggling to decide what to do.

Long before this happened, I knew I didn't want to answer to a man. I had wrestled control of my life away from my father. I cherished my independence, and I was determined to avoid what I saw as the pitfalls most women face once they leave home. I even refused to learn how to type, fearing it would mean I would only be considered for secretarial positions or office work. I frequently joked that if I married, it would be in my eighties, and I'd have kids in my nineties. Marriage and children meant relinquishing control over my heart's desires.

As the youngest of seven children, I watched my mother struggle to gain independence from my father, which made a big impression on me. I didn't want to be overcome with the bitterness I sometimes saw in her. She had eight pregnancies, carrying a child for most of her twenties and thirties. She finally got her driver's license in her forties, and got a part-time job as a cook in a nursing home when I was around ten. I feared marriage and children would make me dependent on a husband. I was unwilling to give up my cherished independence.

When I faced the decision of what to do about the unplanned pregnancy, however, I found myself very conflicted. I assumed I would be raising the child on my own and struggled with the idea of what being a single mother would mean. I never dreamt of weddings or motherhood growing up. I couldn't see myself following the same path as my mother, who had little control over the direction of her life.

I couldn't see myself having an abortion because, deep inside, I kept imagining myself with the baby. Finally, I decided I wanted to keep the pregnancy, despite the circumstances, and was determined to raise the child on my own since Phillip seemed to have walked away from the relationship yet again.

When he called weeks later, he seemed cold and distant. It surprised me when he said he wanted to go out to dinner on the weekend. I assumed he wanted to meet someplace neutral so he could break up.

We met at a steak house not far from where I lived. Shortly after we ordered dinner, he looked across the table. I held my breath, expecting the worst.

"Kasey, I've been thinking about asking you this for a while but—will you marry me?"

I was in shock.

"Gee, Phillip. I do love you, and I do want to marry you." It was true. I did want to marry him. "Honey, I don't want to start a marriage feeling like the only reason you want to marry me is that I'm pregnant. You broke up with me because of Molly, and now you're suddenly willing to commit to marriage? I have to think this is more about my being pregnant than it is about our relationship." And that was precisely how I felt. He reached across the table and took my hand in his. He looked me in the eyes and pleaded his case.

"Kasey, the fling with Molly was a terrible mistake. It happened. But when I went to L.A., the only one I thought about was you. I missed you. I didn't miss her. There was an attraction with her, but it's over. I called her before I called you that night because I wanted to be with you. That was before you even told me. We have a chance for a life together. I know that now. I've considered asking you to marry me even before you told me. Honest. The pregnancy just hurried things along."

I wanted to believe him, but deep inside, I had doubts. We always talked about life together, but he never mentioned marriage once. Still, that night, I accepted his proposal. We agreed to get married after the New Year.

In January of 1986, we said our vows before a justice of the peace. I was several months pregnant at that point, and it seemed like he wanted to raise a child. He moved into my attic apartment, and we started our life together.

The cracks in the relationship started soon after that. The biggest one was that Phillip refused to tell anyone other than his sister Rachel that we were married. While he told his close friends and colleagues at work, he kept the rest of his family in the dark. Phillip wouldn't even tell them we were living together. Instead, he told layer upon layer of lies to conceal his secrets.

The awkwardness of this was detrimental. I'd told my friends and family members that we'd gotten married. I didn't tell them why but knew they'd figure that out soon enough. It was hard to keep track of who knew we were married and who didn't.

I was having serious doubts that he had really been planning to ask me to marry him. My anxiety and guilt magnified as weeks passed. Phillip made excuse after excuse for keeping our marriage hidden. Whenever I brought up the subject, he acted like I was making a fuss over nothing.

In February, right before President's Day weekend, we were out buying a gift for his mother's and grandmother's birthdays. We were heading to his parents for a big celebration since my birthday and Phillip's birthday also fell on the weekend. When we got in the car, I finally mustered the courage and asked him the looming question.

"Are you planning on telling your folks we got married?"

"You don't know my mother very well," he told me. "This news will ruin the weekend. I'm already the black sheep of the family. I'd rather not contribute to my already shocking reputation," he told me.

I reasoned that he knew them better than I did, but it bothered me.

Months passed, and still Phillip refused to tell them. When I was almost five months along, I had a routine visit with my OB/GYN. I'd been feeling poorly and had little appetite. The doctor ordered an ultrasound, which revealed I had miscarried and he did an emergency D and C procedure.

The day was a blur. I remember calling Phillip to come to get me at the hospital. We were both distraught. He took the next day off of work to stay with me. The shared experience didn't seem to move us closer or tear us apart. We seemed to ignore the emotional toll by moving past it without any discussion. This became a familiar pattern to our conflicts.

Whatever Phillip felt about the loss of the pregnancy, he kept it to himself. The whole matter became a dark moment in our relationship, one we never discussed. There was only one sign regarding his grief. The tiny booties my friend Dawn had knitted for me, the ones I'd kept on my dresser, disappeared one day. I never saw them again.

A new sense of guilt festered in me. I believed Phillip blamed me for miscarrying, or for the pregnancy itself. I blamed myself, too. Was it something I did or didn't do that triggered the miscarriage? I tried to convince myself that I was hardly ready for the responsibility, but was outright sorrowful, too.

After the miscarriage, there were unspoken emotions that lived on in the tiny apartment. We still had the same intense physical attraction, but we were much more reserved since the unplanned pregnancy. Trying to make sure I didn't get pregnant again, I not only kept using a diaphragm, but I started using the Pill, too. Still, he questioned me every time we made love.

"Is it safe?"

His question astonished me. Did he think I knew exactly when I ovulated? I had trusted that my birth control methods were working. It angered me that he insinuated I should be able to assure him that I wouldn't get pregnant.

He continued to avoid telling his parents we got married. I couldn't understand why telling his parents the truth had been so daunting. I started to believe he was somehow ashamed of me, which wreaked havoc on my self-confidence. I believed that, at any time, he could decide to end the marriage if I gave him a reason. At some point, and without much fanfare, I somehow went from being his girlfriend to being his fiancé. When we visited Marblehead, where his parents lived, I removed my wedding ring and put on my engagement ring.

Phillip's concealment of our marital status from his family also meant keeping our two families apart. My family and friends became secondary in all matters related to things we did as a couple. It had set up a dynamic in our relationship where I was erased. My traditions and experiences weren't a part of us. I assimilated into his world to accommodate his lie. He said, "I love you," but what did that mean if he couldn't even tell his parents that we got married and why?

Our expectations for the future seemed to hang solely on the creative nature of our relationship. Moving to New York became even more of an urgent goal. All Phillip and I talked about was where, when, and how to move to Manhattan so we could further our careers in the film industry. These were safe subjects that raised few of the emotions we'd buried.

I happily agreed to pave the way for both of us since I'd lived with my parents for a short time in Brooklyn years before. We again discussed the idea that I should try to get a job in New York City first, and once I was established, Phillip would quit his job and move there.

In the fall of 1986, I landed a full-time job at an animation company in midtown Manhattan and rented an apartment in Brooklyn. Phillip moved down months later and maintained his lie, telling his parents we were living in separate places.

Another complication emerged soon after he joined me. Phillip wasn't working. Phillip relied on his savings to "establish himself" as a film director. He always spoke of being the next Joel Coen or George Ramos, directors who started making low-budget films that catapulted their careers. He relived his glory days as the young up-and-coming Boston director who created a commercial news insert series. The inserts his company made featured a prominent Boston actor who spoke of consumer and safety tips. After a disagreement with his partners, the company dissolved, and he moved on to the ad agency where I had met him. I couldn't understand why he wouldn't take any job to show off his skills to those who could help him move up the ladder.

"I'm not going to work as a production assistant, Kasey. Forget it. I'm sorry if you don't think I'm more talented than that."

"Phillip! No one believes in you more than I do! But you can't expect a job directing in New York immediately. The markets are completely different. I see all these young guys your age working as producers or editors, making great money so they can build their director's reel. It takes time to break into this market. You need contacts and a reputation."

"Yeah, I'll get right on that."

I didn't mind our awkward arrangement most of the time, because I loved him. Phillip made me laugh, and we had great fun together exploring New York City and dreaming of the days ahead when we were both established in our creative careers. But in many ways, I didn't feel like we were married. Our relationship seemed almost like a "friends-with-benefits arrangement."

Looking back, I realized that my inability to confront him about money established an imbalance in our relationship. I believed he felt trapped back then and stayed with me because he needed my help to further his career. In the early days of our marriage, it made me try harder to please him. I thought if I proved I was worthy of his love, he'd love me the way I loved him.

Waiting to head to Jenny's, I began to perceive that doubt plagued my marriage from the start and that I should have confronted Phillip long ago. However, I was too afraid to hear the truth as time passed, so I ignored our problems. I didn't know then that buried feelings would linger and color our relationship for years to come, leaving me assuming things about our relationship that would eventually haunt me. I was just beginning to grasp the full extent of the past's impact on my marriage to Phillip.

My recent revelations haunted me. If we divorced, I would be presented with another set of problems. The job market had not recovered from the recession, and without the café, I no longer had a way to support myself and the Beans. Phillip had ruined our credit, and I feared his lies could result in my loss of custody. There were problems on both fronts of life, with or without him.

Phillip wasn't going to make the process easy. I could already tell by what he'd written in his emails to friends and family that he blamed me for much of our dysfunction and portrayed himself as the injured party. Additionally, I knew divorced women rarely recover financially. In my case, my lucrative career in New York was long over. Even if I could someday return to Alexandria and keep my restaurant, I knew the expenses for the building were mounting, and repairs often exceeded the income I made from the business.

His refusal to contribute to these expenses meant I had little in the bank at the end of each month. So, when I returned to the States, I would have no money to reestablish myself or care for the Beans.

I finally understood my mother's decision not to leave my father decades ago. She was so unhappy about his decision to move the family to Western New York so he could attend Bible school. My mother complained bitterly about moving away from her family and friends, but my father made many decisions in their marriage.

I realized that you're not just leaving a husband or wife when you leave a marriage. You're leaving all the entanglements marriage involves. It means giving up more than a spouse. You're giving up a way of life. The language of marriage is we and us and ours. Years of living together blend the boundaries of family, finances, and memories. There is little individuality anymore. Where one ends, the other starts. This homogenous creation is difficult to separate, like the yolk from the egg white.

When my mother thought about leaving my father, she struggled because it meant leaving a large chunk of herself behind. So she stayed. For her, it turned out to be the right choice. She seemed to reconcile herself to this new experience and adjusted to the change. But unlike my mother, I grappled with a host of different issues. My father loved my mother, and she never needed to question his fidelity or commitment to their relationship.

In those early days of our marriage, I offered Phillip reasons to stay in the relationship. While my intention was to be supportive, it fostered an unhealthy way of using money as a tool to get what I wanted: a husband who would love and appreciate the sacrifices I made. However, my acts gave him even more control over me.

Suddenly, I realized that back then, Phillip had kept secrets from those he loved the most during our more than twenty-five years together. That made me believe Phillip was keeping secrets from me.

It was finally almost seven o'clock. I opened a can of cat food and separated the contents into two bowls before placing them on the kitchen floor for our two Maine Coon cats, Duncan and Felicia. With that out of the way, I gathered items I would take to Jenny's and placed them on a table by the front door.

I went upstairs to get my overnight bag, and Chubby tagged along. He patiently waited while I gathered my belongings so we could leave. The look on his face expressed his love for me: unwavering, complete, and forgiving.

I didn't want to rush up and down the staircase, so I closed Chub in the office, knowing he'd be unmanageable once he sensed it was finally time to go. He frantically scratched at the door while I carried my bags downstairs. When I had everything together, I grabbed his leash off its hook and went back upstairs to open the door for him. He looked crushed, thinking I'd left him behind.

As he rushed down the stairs, I dropped his leash. I picked it up and noticed the reflection in the window at the bottom of the stairs. I could see all three rooms that comprised my former business. To the right was the tiny galley-style kitchen, stripped of all the equipment. It looked naked now that the cupboards were bare. Ahead of me was the entrance to the café. Other than the counters that still held the cappuccino machine and coffee grinder, it was also empty. To the left, the once elegant tearoom was piled high with boxes and trash bags to be discarded. It was a reflection of my life, which was in total disarray. I left for Jenny's, thankful I had something else to look forward to instead of the whole scene I was leaving behind.

CHAPTER THREE

Time for Wine and Whine

"Come on, Chub. Let's go."

I locked the café door and left for Jenny's, looking forward to the evening with friends, trusting it would lift my spirits. I put Chubby in the front seat, hoping he'd behave. He had a bad habit of trying to climb on my shoulders while I drove. The kids were usually there to prevent him from advancing toward me. When I was alone, however, he had a sneaky way of waiting until I wasn't looking, then he'd lunge toward me. The sudden movement startled me and he'd almost caused me to go off the road more than once.

I thought about the long drive I faced the next day. I would be transporting two angry cats and a devious dog for hours by myself. The van itself was barely roadworthy. I couldn't determine fuel levels or speed due to a faulty instrument panel. I started thinking about whether I should see if my friend Jody would board Chubby for a few days at her kennel.

I drove down the gravel laneway to Jenny's house. Vast fields of grasses, wildflowers, and trees of various sizes lined either side of the drive. White balls of Queen Anne's Lace offset the deep pink flowers of the milkweed in bloom. Long, dusky green stems of mullein with delicate, yellow petals could be seen interspersed with the thin stragglers of miterwort poking out of the chaotic array. I took in the familiar scene, trying to remember every detail as a reminder of good times.

Jenny's small, brown, bi-level ranch was about a quarter of a mile from the road. Chubby tried to get out before I even stopped the car. Unable to climb over me, he retreated, hung his head out the window, and barked at Lacy, Jenny's aging black lab. I opened the door, and he jumped over me, chasing Lacy down the expanse of the backyard.

The house sat on fifty acres of wooded land with large, lush lawns surrounding the house. The manicured areas had towering blue spruce, dogwood, and eastern redbud trees. The magenta, heart-shaped leaves of the redbud would soon start to fade, but they created a lovely border. An aging barn stood near a small pond off to the right. A large beaver pond meandered across the very back of the property.

The smell of fresh-cut grass filled the air. The dogs dodged Jenny's riding lawnmower parked near a storage shed. Seeing them disappear into the bushes made me smile. I left my overnight bag and laptop in the car but gathered the bag of food I'd brought for the occasion.

Climbing the steep, wide steps of the back porch, I found Jenny sitting there, talking with Carole. It was a familiar scene. Carole, Jenny's no-nonsense, snarky but brilliant neighbor, spent as much time on Jenny's back porch as I did.

The expression on my face must have given away my mood. Jenny and Carole met me halfway up the steps. Carole took the bags and disappeared into the kitchen. Jenny walked over to the table, where there were several bottles of wine and alcohol. I needed no encouragement to join her. She gave me a gentle hug. I looked away, knowing she understood the night would be difficult. Her wry smile spoke of her acknowledgment of my emotional turmoil.

I knew the occasion would be fraught with a range of emotions. I'd been through this exact scenario too many times in my life. I used to believe it was possible to maintain friendships at a distance, but my past informed me not to be optimistic. There would be earnest promises to stay in touch, and, for a while, those promises would be kept. But life has a way of filling in around us. The one leaving is soon replaced with new people or experiences. They are fondly remembered but forgotten over time. I'd learned the hard way to write names in address books with a pencil because even the closest friendships don't weather distance easily.

"Looks like someone could use a big ole glass of wine!" she said, handing me a large glass of chardonnay without asking.

"Make it a bottle, and now we're talking," I said with a lame smile.

Over the last three years, Jenny and I had confided in one another about our marital woes. Having experienced the break-up of a marriage on multiple occasions, she was able to offer advice. She schooled me on how to handle the situation. Her input helped because I believed my marriage was heading in that direction.

Jenny and I crossed the porch and took seats next to Carole. I caught them up on the events of the last few days, then began telling them about Phillip's notebook.

"I couldn't believe it. I wish he'd jotted down his bank account information. I don't even know how much he's making in this new job. Of course, he's hounding me about getting the packing done. He completely ignores that I had the kids and a business to contend with up until a week ago. He's sitting in an air-conditioned office, writing advertising copy. He thinks it's nothing to pack in this heat."

"Has he offered to come up and help you?" Carole asked.

"Nope. He said he would come up last weekend but then called me and told me he had to work."

"Do you think that's true, or is he making excuses?" Jenny asked.

"Who knows? I don't know what the hell is going on down there. And I still have one last catering job tomorrow. Thank God Kate offered to do all the baking. Phillip was furious that I agreed to take the job, but I need the money since he refuses to pay any bills up here."

"What? When did that happen?" Carole asked as she grabbed the crudités off a nearby table and offered me some.

"Jeez, he did that months ago. Yup. He opened a separate bank account when he took the job in Albany." I gnawed on a carrot loaded with dip.

"Gee, Kase," Jenny cautioned. "That's not a good sign."

"I've only met him a few times, but he always seemed like such a nice guy," Carole added.

"I know. That's the problem. He is a nice guy. Or at least he can be. None of this adds up," I told them. "That's why I'm convinced he's looking to divorce me, and he's trying to get custody, too."

"Well, I agree he's up to something... but do you really think he wants custody?" Jenny added, frowning.

"It sure seems that way. Maybe I'm reading too much into things, but why would he try to make me look financially unstable and lie about where our savings went? Plus, he knows how vulnerable I'll be without a job once I return to the States. He doesn't want me back there because he misses me. The kids, maybe, but not me. That's for sure."

"Well, we could always throw him in the beaver pond!" Jenny said with a smile.

"Why didn't I think of that? Problem solved!"

We raised our glasses.

"To the beaver pond!" We all cheered.

I pictured the acres of marshy wetlands and Jenny's beaver pond. Throwing someone in the beaver pond was the Canadian version of sending someone to sleep with the fishes. We all touched one another's glasses of wine and cheered again.

"Wait! Who's going in the beaver pond now?" Lisa asked as she approached the massive row of bushes framing Jenny's back porch.

"Hi, Lisa. Phillip, of course!" I said jokingly. Like many of my customers and friends, she'd met Phillip. She climbed the steps carefully, holding a platter of lemon squares and brownies.

"What did I miss?" she asked. I made room for her platter on the table before responding to her question.

"Well, I'm pretty sure my marriage is over," I told her. "For some reason, Phillip seems to resent the life I've built here. He's convinced moving to Canada and opening a café was all my idea."

"But that's not true! It's all sour grapes. It's too bad it never worked out for him here, but he can't blame you."

"He can and does." I heard the gravel of Jenny's driveway crunching. Moments later, Betty poked her head around the corner. I grabbed the antipasto she was carrying while Lisa took the bottle of wine.

"What did I miss? I heard you all talking!" she asked.

"Kasey was filling us in on her troubles with Phillip," Lisa said, looking my way.

"It's the same old story," I assured Betty. I took her antipasto into the kitchen to place in the fridge.

My cavalier attitude belied my deep concern. I shuddered at the thought Phillip would try to get custody of the Beans. I had grave doubts that he had any idea what it took to work full-time and care for them. Once, he scoffed when I told him it was hard to work all day and always be available to address the kid's needs. He'd told me repeatedly, in dozens of ways, that he didn't even consider owning and operating the café work.

Then, there was another issue that bothered me even more. What if Phillip was having an affair? Would he come clean and tell me? How would the twins react to his new life? The Beans were so shy around new people. I couldn't imagine a scenario that would be good for them. They already resented him for forcing us to move after we'd promised them that we were moving for the last time when we left the States.

I returned to the porch carrying a bowl of hummus and a platter full of naan bread I'd taken from the fridge. Lisa and Betty were talking and turned to me, prepared with questions from our earlier conversation. Lisa seemed skeptical that my concerns about the custody issue were as serious as they were.

"So, do you really think he would try to get custody? They've lived with you, here in Canada, for what, three or four years?" She took a slice of naan and dipped it in the hummus.

"I honestly don't know. But I think that's why he's trying to guarantee I'll have no means of supporting the kids. And he's lying about things to his sister. You wouldn't believe the horse crap he's feeding to her in his emails. The man is up to no good."

"Wait! How do you know what he said in an email to his sister?" Betty asked. I smiled and let them speculate.

"Let's just say Phillip's not the only one who's up to no good."

"Hey, ladies! We're here to party. Betty doesn't even have a drink yet!" Jenny reminded us, pouring her a glass of wine.

Jenny and Carole approached the table and started chatting with Lisa and Betty. I ducked inside the house, pretending I needed to use the washroom. I really just wanted a moment to myself. I wanted to enjoy the night, but it was hard not to think about the future. Without a job or any other source of income, I would have to trust Phillip to support us. But since he'd already abdicated his financial obligations in Canada and wasn't supporting the Beans, I had no assurance he'd do what was right.

A few more of our friends joined us as the evening progressed. When we'd had enough of the appetizers, I went into Jenny's kitchen to make our main entrée, my famous "Tuscan Chicken." I had no idea if this dish was Tuscan, never mind Italian. I called it that for lack of a better name when I served it at the café. The tang of the vinegar and honey had almost an Asian flavor. I suppose the balsamic vinegar inspired the name. Plus, anything that sounds Italian sold well at the café.

Like many chefs, I hated to use recipes. I drew my culinary inspiration from what I found in the fridge or while cruising the aisles of the grocery store.

I knew Jenny's kitchen almost as well as my own. I grabbed a large skillet out of her pantry. I began to relax, away from conversations laden with heavy questions. I hummed to myself while I removed the chicken breasts from the fridge. The tension melted as I pounded each breast into thin medallions, seasoned each portion with generous amounts of salt and pepper, and seared the medallions in olive oil before adding minced garlic.

Removing the nicely browned chicken, I turned up the heat, then added balsamic vinegar and honey to the hot pan. The flavorful bits of chicken and garlic loosened from the bottom of the skillet, and soon, I had a thick brown sauce that smelled rich and fragrant. I returned the chicken to the pan in small batches, coating each piece with the tangy mixture. I turned each piece, and the chicken became a mahogany brown. Standing over the stove, inhaling the savory scent of chicken, I thought again about my relationship with Phillip and acknowledged that there were problems I ignored.

About a year after we moved to Brooklyn, Phillip received a letter from his sister that got him to finally consider resolving the awkward situation about our semi-secret marriage. One day, when I got home from work, he came out of the office and told me about a letter he'd received from Rachel. She had grown frustrated because she and her boyfriend Dennis wanted to set a date for their wedding.

"Well, what are we going to do?" I asked him.

"I think the only way around this is for us to get a divorce, and then we can get remarried in the Church sometime after their wedding."

"What? Phillip, that's insane! Why can't you tell them we got married?"

"You don't understand my family dynamic. I'm the screw-up, Kasey. I didn't get a normal job and stay in Marblehead. I constantly live in my sister's shadow. I don't want to add to my parents' disappointment in me. Telling them we married more than a year ago would add to their belief that I'm a failure."

I was furious.

"Well, first of all, I don't see that. Your folks love you and would understand. But they're not my parents. You can tell them whatever makes you feel comfortable, but I'm not getting a divorce unless we're really getting divorced. It's a complete waste of money, so we're either staying married, or it's over."

"What do you recommend?"

"The same thing I've recommended for the last year, Phillip. Just tell them and get it over with."

That pissed him off, and he pouted for days.

After he told his folks we were engaged, Phillip said he wanted to wait before setting a date so he wouldn't upstage his sister's wedding, so we were in limbo for another year.

It seemed like he would never resolve the matter. But, he offered a different suggestion sometime after Rachel and Dennis married.

"So what I'm thinking is, we go to another county in Massachusetts and take out a marriage license."

"How can we do that? We're already married."

"I've done some research, and I don't think they can easily check the records. We just pretend it's our first marriage, and since we are already married to one another, it won't be illegal or anything."

Regardless of how ridiculous it was, I relented because it would allow us to move forward and end the charade.

Phillip announced at Christmas of 1985 that we planned to get married the following summer. By that June, we would already be married for three and a half years. We got a marriage license and reserved a date for a wedding at Saint Elizabeth's in Marblehead.

His parents generously offered to pay for the wedding, and Phillip accepted. He no longer had a savings account to pay his bills, never mind being able to contribute to the expenses of the wedding. I was in an awkward position because, in many ways, it wasn't my wedding. I couldn't ask to do things as I would have liked to since his folks were paying for the wedding. The two of us had a massive fight when I complained to Phillip one day.

It started when I casually said, "I thought it would be nice to have something other than white tablecloths and napkins."

"Well, if that costs more than white linens, forget it. I'm not asking my parents to pay for anything more. You could ask your parents to chip in."

"Sure. I'll call them right now and ask them to pay for part of the wedding they know nothing about. Yeah, that will work, telling them their thirty-three-year-old daughter is getting married to the man she's already married to. Should I send them an invitation to attend the wedding, too? How about my brothers and sisters? Are they all invited?"

"Screw you, Kasey. All I said was I didn't want my parents paying for napkins."

"No, Phillip. You said I should ask my parents to chip in. Do you understand how insulting that is under the circumstances? I can only have a few of my most trusted friends attend our wedding because I know they will keep our secret. I'm not allowed to invite even one relative because that would mean revealing the lie we've been trying to maintain. So, no. This isn't about napkins. It's about you spending thousands of dollars of your parent's money because you don't have the balls to tell them the truth."

I left the apartment and didn't go home until late that night. It was the first of several nights I stayed away because I refused to apologize. Eventually, the tension eased, and once again, we buried the root cause of the argument.

When the wedding day arrived, it was surreal. We played the part of the happy bride and groom. I gave my friends knowing glances; they were troopers about going along with the charade. When it was over, it didn't change anything. We still had a secret to keep, and nothing we did would make that disappear. We drove to Florida a few days later for our honeymoon. When we stopped to see my parents, I couldn't help but feel like I'd betrayed them.

Given the current financial crisis I was facing in Canada, I realized how often similar situations had occurred earlier in our marriage. I'd relinquished control over the purse strings too often throughout our relationship. I knew the first step would require me to regain my financial independence from him once I left Alexandria, but I couldn't figure out a way to address the problem immediately.

I heard my friends laughing out on Jenny's porch as the sunlight faded in her kitchen. I was just placing the last batch of chicken on the large serving platter when Jenny came in to see when the main course would be ready. She called the others to come grab the side dishes in the fridge, and Betty held the door while I carried the hot chicken outside to the table and placed it on a trivet.

Conversations swirled around me as we all ate. I kept my mouth full, so I wouldn't have to say too much. My problems had seemed to dominate the conversation earlier, and I feared it was getting tedious.

I gazed at the lovely and kind faces of the women around the table, chatting with one another while I ate. I tried to absorb all the details and nuances of what made them so important to me. I had had many close girlfriends in the past and some friends that remained close even though distance prevented us from seeing one another frequently. These women were different because they had made me a part of their community. Because I had moved so often, I'd only experienced that feeling of belonging as a child. The love and support these women provided made me feel like I had contributed to something as a whole. Moving from place to place as a teenager, I never had that sense of belonging. Alexandria was a place where I mattered somehow.

By 9:30 that evening, many of our friends had left since they had to work in the morning. Those that remained gathered dishes and brought the leftover food inside. "Anyone up for coffee?" Jenny asked. Murmurs of approval indicated we were.

"I am if you have anything to add to it!" Lisa quipped.

I still needed to wash and dry my laundry, so I headed downstairs to the basement to grab my things from the van. I exited the basement door. The most beautiful magic was on display. Hundreds of fireflies lit up the night sky, twinkling like a gathering of magical faeries. The scene captured my feelings for this place. I stood in awe, unable to move, as I took in the dreamlike quality of this special quiet moment, bringing me a sense of peace and tranquility. I vowed to myself that I'd somehow figure out a way to return to Alexandria with the Beans, the place we all thought of as home.

The spell was broken by the roar of laughter coming from inside. I smiled. The sound was an antidote to my angst. These women believed in me when I failed to believe in myself. They knew I could be a total goof and would laugh with me and share my humor. They accepted me, warts and all.

I gathered my laundry from the van, loaded the washing machine, and then headed back upstairs, planning to tidy the kitchen. The aroma of the coffee wafted through the air. Jenny stood at the cabinet, grabbing a few empty mugs. She handed them to me so I could take them into the living room.

"When you come back, can you get the Bailey's out of the fridge?" she asked, placing a pitcher for the cream next to the sugar bowl.

"That's why I love you," I turned to her and winked. "You know what I want before I do."

I poured some liquor into my mug and settled into an overstuffed chair by the fireplace. I hardly needed another drink with all the wine I'd had earlier. I justified it, knowing it would be a long time before I would have another chance to be this carefree.

Betty took a seat on the couch, coffee in hand; Jenny, Lisa, and Carole joined us in the living room. My mind wandered as I listened to snippets of conversation from around the room. After a while, I excused myself and checked if the laundry was ready for the dryer.

I passed the guest room and looked longingly at the king-size bed. I wished I could climb into it and go to sleep. Jenny's guest room was much more comfortable than the mattress on the floor in the stuffy room above the café. I resisted the impulse and went to put the clothes in the dryer.

I needed to check my email, so before returning upstairs, I went into the guest room, with Chubby at my heels. While I arranged all the pillows at the head of the bed against the wall, Chubby jumped onto the bed and promptly fell asleep. I grabbed my laptop off the nightstand, hoping it would power on—a damaged input jack made that an iffy proposition.

My last official catering job was early the following day, and then I would have to leave. My client Lise had responded with a headcount for breakfast, as promised. Phillip had emailed me as well. I waited to read that because I knew it would ruin my evening. Instead, I sent Kate the headcount so she could start baking in the morning.

Kate was one of my former employees and a dear friend who had worked with me over the last few years. Kate and Sharilyn had been my two longest employees, with Sharilyn starting with me shortly after I opened the business and Kate coming on board about a year later. The three of us were from different backgrounds but got along famously. We seemed to bring out the best in one another, with each of us contributing different skills to the operation of the café.

Kate came from a large, middle-class Irish family with strong connections to the community. She had dark auburn hair, a flawless complexion, and deep-set green eyes. When she wasn't working at the café, she was a fitness instructor, and her body reflected her commitment to a strict workout routine.

Sharilyn, on the other hand, came from a hard-working, blue-collar family who married the love of her life at a young age. They raised two daughters, who were now adults. She was attractive with a pixie-ish haircut that framed her face. Her upbeat attitude always cheered me up. She wasn't as skilled at cooking or baking as Kate, but she was so good at everything else that she more than made up for her lack of culinary skills. These two women always had my back, especially now that life had become complicated.

From the moment we assembled in the kitchen each morning, the three of us would chat as we prepared to open the restaurant. Music in a range of styles played in the background. We had a routine that allowed us to complete our tasks while chatting about whatever was going on in our lives. Once we opened, Kate waited on tables, Sharilyn assembled the previously prepared foods for each order, and I ran between them, doing whatever needed to get done.

Kate had gone through a divorce shortly after we opened. She carefully planned everything before she made her move. She read books, talked to friends, and had a network of support before she filed for her divorce. I admired her tenacity.

When we discussed my situation with Phillip, she said, "Take the emotion out of it. You're allowing Phillip to have all the control because instead of confronting the problem, you're trying to confront your emotion as well." Try as I might, I couldn't wrap my head around how to do that, and I would agree with her but never managed to adhere to her advice.

I heard the activity from above, so I knew it was time to rejoin Jenny and the others upstairs. I shut off my computer, ignoring Phillip's email. "Let him wonder what I'm doing for a change," I thought. Before I could get off the bed, Chubby snuggled closer to me. His gentle breathing made me smile. I wished I still believed I was married to someone just as faithful as my furry companion.

When I returned upstairs to join my friends, I realized something I'd almost overlooked. All my friends had been through a divorce, except for Carole, who had never married. They had survived their ordeals and even thrived in the aftermath. As evidenced by the laughter and gaiety around me, they were through with the anger and bitterness of their dysfunctional relationships.

I began to feel better knowing I would be able to look beyond these dark days someday. If I had known then what was to come, however, I'm not sure I would have had the courage to leave Alexandria the next day.

CHAPTER FOUR

Out of Excuses

Even though Jenny's guest room was much cooler and more comfortable than the room above the café, I found it difficult to sleep that night, and I woke up early the next morning feeling drained. My almost daily routine of three years of waking up by seven each morning was a hard routine to break.

The client wasn't expecting me to deliver the catering order until 10 a.m., but I left anyway since Jenny and I said farewell the night before. I wrote her a note thanking her for a wonderful evening and left as quietly as possible.

As I left Jenny's, I thought it might be a good time to purchase some fresh fruit and two large containers of yogurt for the last catering job I'd do for my business. Throughout the years, there have been weddings and Christmas parties, social events, and office parties. It was the most profitable part of the café's services but also the most demanding. I had gained an excellent reputation around town but competed with other caterers who had developed their clientele over decades. Despite this, I'd cultivated both small and large corporate clients.

When I got to the parking lot at the grocery store, I looked to see if anyone I knew was around. I didn't want to talk with a former customer, someone I knew from the kids' school, or one of the many friends I wouldn't have a chance to say goodbye to personally.

Then I realized I couldn't possibly know who was inside based on the vehicles in the lot because I had no idea what type of cars or trucks they drove. I knew my customers by the tea they drank or how they took their coffee. I would often bring a pot to their table before they even ordered. I ensured I had plenty of Jade Garden for Sharon and Earl Grey for Glen.

Mrs. Spicer preferred Lemon Ginger; if I had none, she would most likely order the Orange Spice Black tea. Lisa always ordered a latte, and Mary drank her coffee black but her tea with milk.

The emotional landmine that awaited me at the grocery store left me heading to a farm stand that sold fresh fruit and produce in the small town south of Alexandria. I backed out of my parking space to head down the 34 toward Lancaster. I justified this as an act of emotional survival, reminding myself that by going to the farm stand, I didn't have to leave Chubby in the car while I shopped.

When I returned to the café, I turned on the aging Rancilio Espresso Machine. The water heated in the double boiler. I made a cappuccino with an extra shot of espresso because I needed the caffeine boost to get me through the next few hours, and I poured the remainder of my beans into the grinder. The angry sound of the beans being crushed by the blades matched my mood. Tamping the freshly ground coffee into the portafilter, I wished I was doing anything but packing to leave. I didn't bother frothing the milk in the stainless steel cup but poured it directly into the largest mug warming on top of the machine.

"These will have to be packed, too," I thought, watching the foam building in the mug. In the early days, I struggled to get the milk to cooperate. Now, I could do it in my sleep. I poured the espresso into the mug and wandered into the tearoom, followed by Chubby.

With a few hours to go before delivering the catering, I started taking decorations off the wall, teapots off the shelves, and wrapping the glassware in bubble wrap. Every item had a story. I had found the delicate teapot at the thrift store, St. Vincent de Paul's, a block away from the café. It wasn't very practical, but I thought it would look nice on one of the shelves. One day, Kate ran out of the teapots we kept on top of the espresso machine. We kept them there because they stayed warm, since pouring a hot beverage into a cold cup or pot was counterproductive. Kate grabbed this very teapot off the shelf and, without checking, she used it to make tea. I'd never considered it more than a decoration, so I'd never cleaned it properly before setting it on the shelf. Kate delivered the pot of tea to the customer, only to have the woman she served call her to the table moments later.

"Are you charging me extra for these flies?" she asked Kate. We all had a big laugh. Almost all of my customers were so good-natured. This one appreciated my offer of lunch on the house!

Those were the types of memories I packed that day; so many laughable memories of things that had happened over the years. Each time I placed an item in a box, it seemed like I was burying a piece of myself in the depths of the stiff and unyielding cardboard.

I had changed so much since I'd opened my restaurant. In Alexandria, I thrived on a pace and had a sense of well-being that had eluded me for so long. The work I did to establish my restaurant and reconnect with my artistic side brought out the best in me. I worked long hours and often struggled to balance the needs of my kids and myself. Yet, the experiences had restored a part of me that had become lost before we moved to the north. I knew I must remain strong but feared I could lose my sense of self once again.

With the morning sun streaming through the windows, I stopped packing and called Jody about taking Chubby for a few days. Chub was so attached to me that I knew it would be hard for him to be left behind. But I also knew how dangerous his habit of suddenly trying to climb on my shoulders could be. Of course the twins would be upset when they found out I'd left him behind. But, I would explain, it would also give the three of us the perfect excuse to return to retrieve him and say goodbye to their friends. They would warm to the whole idea.

I tried to imagine my encounter with Phillip once I arrived at the new apartment in Cobleskill, New York. The trip was about a five-hour drive from Alexandria, and I calculated that if I left before 8 p.m., Phillip might still be awake, and I'd have to spend time alone with him. I started thinking more and more about going as late as possible to avoid interacting with him. If I arrived late and unpacked the van the following day after he left for work, I could head to Vermont to get the Beans before he got home, thus avoiding seeing him altogether.

I knew eventually we would have to come face to face, but having the Beans with me when that occurred would be more comfortable. I needed time to adjust to the situation and knew that when I spent time alone with him, I would be vulnerable because he'd manage to find a way to push all my emotional buttons. But he couldn't sabotage me if I was a moving target.

I dialed Jody's number, but the line was busy, so I went into the kitchen to make a light breakfast before I assembled the fruit platter. I cut the strawberries and thought of how much my daughter Lucy loved them. Jack seemed more partial to blueberries and watermelon. I hoped the twins were enjoying their time with Jake and Meredith.

Before I dropped them off, they had been having a rotten summer. All the talk of moving and leaving their friends behind was too much for them.

Only three years ago, we'd torn them away from their home in the U.S., and now we were making them move again. I worried about the instability. I knew how they felt all too well. The Beans still believed their close friends would remain close. They thought everything would be the same when they came back to visit.

I hated that they were reliving the part of my childhood I'd vowed to avoid with them. Since selling our home in Blairstown, New Jersey, in 2006, we had moved three times. They had been reluctant about moving to Canada, but they had adjusted and made friends. They were a part of the small community, and they were being torn, once again, from the place they thought of as home.

I carefully cut a small watermelon, pineapple, and honeydew and placed the uniformly cut pieces of fruit around the pineapple leaves to form a colorful pattern before adding the grapes and strawberries, interspersed with the melons, to create an attractive arrangement. I made decorative rosettes out of a pint of strawberries and used the leafy green top of the pineapple as the center of the platter. I was pleased with how it looked and knew it would be well received, especially with the basket of Kate's yummy baked goods to round out the presentation. I covered it with wrap and stuck it in the fridge until I had to leave.

Looking at the clock on the stove, I saw I still had time before I needed to pick up the miniature coffee cakes and banana muffins Kate was baking, so I tried to reach Jody again. This time, the call went through. Not only did she offer to take Chubby, but she also offered to let him stay in the house with her and Brice so he wouldn't be in the kennel with the other dogs. Her offer eased my guilt about leaving him behind.

When I went to pick up the baked goods from Kate, I had to hold back a wave of emotions the moment she opened the door.

She gave me a quick hug. "Do you have time for coffee?"

"Not really, but I'll make time. I'm already exhausted from packing."

I walked into the foyer of her home and spotted the beautiful arched mirror that once hung in the tearoom. She bought it from me when I struggled to pay the bills the previous month. I'd begun to sell things because I needed the money. It looked as beautiful as it had in our tearoom. I was glad it went to her, because it held so many good memories.

When I told Phillip about it, I justified selling it to her, saying we couldn't fit everything in the apartment he'd rented in Cobleskill, New York, and most of our belongings were going into storage. I didn't want to reveal how desperate I was for money since he seemed determined to keep financial matters secret from me, too. He hadn't said anything about the mirror but put his foot down over items like our antique sleigh bench and a stained-glass window that had once hung in our old Victorian home in Blairstown.

"How's the packing going?" Kate asked. I followed her into the kitchen.

"Argh! I've been at it for two days and feel I could spend another month without finishing. Whatever I get done will have to be it until I come back. I need to get to Cobleskill with the cats before I pick up the Beans in Vermont. I want the kids to have a chance to settle in before school starts. Most of what I'm packing is going upstairs in the office or into storage.

"Why wasn't Phillip here this weekend helping you?"

"He said he had to work, of course. Or that's what he claimed anyway. It's like he thinks I should be grateful he came up to help move all the heavy stuff."

"Don't let him off the hook. He should be here helping you," Kate reminded me.

"You're right. Of late, the only thing Phillip's good at is offering excuses."

I sat at her farmhouse-style table that stretched across her kitchen. I imagined her and her new husband, Jason, having meals there with their blended family. She pulled a familiar brown bag of 2Beans coffee stamped with my business logo from her cabinet.

"I think I wiped you out of the rest of your coffee. I don't know what I will do once this is gone," she lamented.

The coffee was a specialty blend crafted just for the café by a local coffee roaster. I'd tasted various combinations of coffee beans for days before deciding the smooth but dark blend of beans with a velvety taste was the right one for my business. It made excellent espresso, too.

"I'm sure Yves would be willing to roast some for you if you bought it in bulk. He's a good egg. I can give him a call before I leave, if you want?"

"Would you? It's just one of the things that's hard about closing. You're going to be missed," she said, measuring the coffee as we chatted.

"I know. I ran into four people at the grocery store while buying some cleaning supplies a few days ago. They were gobsmacked I'd closed. I could barely get out the door without sobbing. I don't want to leave."

"I know. Maybe you can work it out and come back?"

"I'd love to, but it might take a while. Phillip's putting me in a very precarious position financially. I've been selling everything I can to make ends meet. He won't contribute anything toward the bills up here now. He claims it's a waste of his money. I'm so broke I wouldn't have gas money to Cobleskill if it wasn't for this catering job. Suddenly, the café, the building, and everything related to Canada is my responsibility."

"Have you pointed out to him that's abandonment?"

"I doubt he sees it that way. Right now, I'm playing nice. Or at least I'm trying to. I don't want him to realize how alarmed I am about what's been going on or that I suspect he's going to try to divorce me. He's had more time to put a plan in place than I have. If we do end up in court, I can show them how I was completely responsible for the Beans and everything else once he moved back to the States."

"Are you sure that's all it is? I know you've told me you hate confronting him."

"You're right, but that's not it. I'm trying to figure out what Phillip's doing before I act. A good friend of mine taught me that."

She smiled and nodded.

"Well, Sharilyn and I have been talking, and we might have come up with a way for you to keep things going up here. What if she and I took over the healthy school lunch program?"

I started the healthy school lunch program shortly after I opened the café. Alexandria was a farming town, and the schools were built at a time when kids still went home for lunch. When my kids showed me the order form provided by their school to order lunch, I was dumbstruck at the lack of choices and the cost. That's when I learned that the five area elementary schools didn't have cafeterias, so they ordered food from area restaurants.

At the school they attended, a bagel with cream cheese from Tim Horton's was considered a lunch, and it cost two dollars and fifty cents, with most of that money going to finance other programs at the school. I created a PowerPoint presentation and sat before the boards of the French and English schools, pitching my healthy school lunch program. Within a year, I provided the five area elementary schools with lunches. It kept me afloat when business slowed, like when the town spent two months tearing up the street in front of my business.

"You guys would do that for me?"

"Well, you'd have to pay us, of course, but maybe we can figure out how to do that. Did you send the letters to the schools yet, telling them you were closing?"

"No. I haven't had a chance."

"Well, think about it. Maybe that will help keep the door open until you can come back."

"I will. The only hitch is Phillip's pressing me to sell the building, too. I could always rent a separate kitchen," I told Kate.

"That's an idea! It will all work out. You'll see," she assured me.

Kate poured the coffee, and we chatted for a while longer about more pleasant things before I left. Her suggestion gave me hope that maybe coming back wasn't such a crazy idea after all.

Returning from Kate's, I picked up the fruit platter and yogurt from the café before delivering the food to my client at the bank, only two blocks from the café. Lise met me at the back door with a cart to carry the food upstairs, and handed me an envelope with an enclosed check to pay for the catering. I tucked it in my purse and hugged her. Turning quickly away, I swallowed hard.

After depositing the check, I headed back to cram what remained of the life I'd built in Alexandria into cardboard liquor boxes. I had no more excuses to stay in Alexandria.

I tried to focus on packing, but the August heat left me exhausted. I took a break and went into the office to do a little snooping on the internet. Thinking about Molly and the time Phillip broke up with me decades earlier forced me to consider again that Phillip was having an affair.

Once online, I Googled "signs your spouse is having an affair." Several articles suggested the signs of a cheating spouse were staying out late, showering more frequently, losing weight, and having an increasingly hostile attitude. Among other clues, Phillip had recently lost weight and his hostility was apparent. But if he was having an extramarital affair, he didn't have to worry about staying out late or showering more often because I was never there to witness this behavior.

I spent some time determining what steps I would need to take if Phillip made his move. Once I got to Cobleskill, I realized I might not have much time. I scanned sites like Barnes & Noble for books Kate recommended when she went through her divorce, knowing I couldn't afford to buy them but could perhaps get them from the library. I would hide them or read them at the library without checking them out. It wouldn't be the first time I'd hidden things from Phillip.

In 1990, Phillip wanted to move out of the New York City area. We began looking at properties in Western New Jersey because properties were more affordable than in areas surrounding Manhattan. Initially, I balked because he worked from home, and I commuted into the City each day. I finally agreed to give it a trial to see if I could cope with all the traveling, and we rented an apartment in the town of Blairstown, leaving me to commute via bus or to drive the two-and-a-half-hour trip each way to work. I made the most of it by working on writing the libretto of my musical on the long bus rides to and from Manhattan.

Three years later, when Phillip inherited a small sum, we finally agreed to purchase a home. By then, I was so used to the commute, I agreed to look in that area. We bought an old Victorian in 1993 and settled into a life that revolved more around renovating the property than pursuing our creative goals.

Phillip and I had been married for over a decade when I began doing things behind Phillip's back. It started with little things, like buying something I wanted that I knew he wouldn't have approved of if I'd asked before purchasing it. The fact he required me to get his permission set me off. I earned most of the money, but he got the final say in how I spent it.

We'd agreed early on to always discuss purchases over a hundred dollars. But that seemed to only apply to me. Whenever Phillip wanted a new piece of film equipment for his lackluster business or the tools required for renovating the house, it was never discussed. Whatever he bought, he considered it a necessity. Whatever I bought was wasteful.

Per usual, I never had the guts to call him on it. I recall buying a comforter on sale and hiding it in the attic. When sufficient time passed, it magically appeared on our bed.

"Don't you remember when we bought this?" I asked him. He faked remembering and accepted the plausible explanation that he'd forgotten about the purchase.

I started getting bolder and bolder because he never caught on. Clothing and household items miraculously appeared. I even bought a new 9x12 rug for our bedroom. Since we were doing major renovations in certain areas of the house, I'd blend things into the piles that remained in unused rooms, so when we unraveled the mess in the room, things were there, and he just assumed they were there all along. He never said a word, even when he helped to lay the rug on our bedroom floor.

This became a pattern, and I was emboldened by keeping things from him. It made me resent him more because I had convinced myself that he made me do these things. But even though I knew it was wrong, I continued to go behind his back.

I found myself getting angry and annoyed with Phillip over other things, too. After more than ten years of marriage, rafting down the Delaware River, going to movies, antiquing, or dressing our cats in hats to take funny pictures of them wasn't enough anymore. I'd grown tired of the insulated life the two of us had.

I tried varying our routine, but circumstances made it difficult. If I wanted to go out with my friends in Manhattan, it didn't make sense to have Phillip travel two and a half hours from the home in Blairstown to join us for dinner or drinks. However, the only friends I had where I lived were casual acquaintances I chatted with on the bus, so I rarely socialized with anyone in the very place I lived. My life was so disjointed. I was caught between two worlds and neither one fulfilled me anymore.

The only thing I found fulfilling in those years was working on my musical. I'd been plugging away at the project for over a decade. I'd workshopped the show in Manhattan several times and had recorded a demo of the music in the studio. I finally found a producer who wanted to produce it in his small theatrical venue in Soho. He brought a director/choreographer on board who loved the project. Everything seemed to be coming together. But shortly after we started raising money for the production, we learned the older actor we had cast as our leading man had cancer, and the funding that we'd secured went out the window.

I became increasingly disillusioned with the whole theatre scene in New York City. Despite all my progress, I started to doubt my work would ever reach the stage. After struggling for years, my dreams began to disappear.

Phillip, however, still clung to the idea that someday his career would be solidified, and financial success was right around the corner. He reinvested almost every dime he made from his company into his business; however, success never came. It wasn't his talent that held him back—it was his lack of understanding of how networking played a large part in who got hired for lucrative jobs in the film industry.

He repeatedly lamented, "I refuse to kowtow to morons. Their mommies and daddies buy their way into the industry, and they don't know squat about how to direct or produce. And you want me to hang out with these people so they'll give me work? Fat chance."

Around 1996, he got a short gig with the production company I worked for in the City. For whatever reason, he didn't complain about using my connections. The scenario that played out after that led me to recognize one of the many underlying problems within our relationship.

When he got hired, Phillip commuted into the City each day instead of working from our home in New Jersey. He started looking for a room in Manhattan, so he didn't have to deal with traveling by bus to the City, though I had commuted five hours each day, round trip, back and forth to our home in Blairstown, for ten years.

He rented an expensive room on the Upper West Side of Manhattan where he could stay each night he had to be at work. I stayed there sometimes, but it was a tiny room and very uncomfortable for two people to share the twin bed.

The whole situation made me furious. I found myself glad I didn't have to see him when I got home or worry about making us dinner. Without him there, I had more time to think about the fact that it seemed like, in Phillip's mind, his time and needs were always so much more important than my own.

"Are you staying in the City tonight?" he asked me one day when he called me at work.

"No, someone has to go home and feed the cats."

"Well, I have an early day tomorrow, so call me when you get home."

"You bet."

He didn't even hear the sarcasm in my voice. He seemed utterly oblivious to the fact he was a complete prima donna. I hung up the phone, seething, but never mentioned that I, too, had an early day.

All this reinforced my belief that my needs would always be secondary. Phillip's double standard and my inability to broach the problem led to my mushrooming anger. My friends were tired of hearing about it and suggested I confront him. I balked but knew they were right. I grappled with hating myself for being too weak to do anything and hating him for being too blind to see how unhappy I was.

One day after that, I had lunch with a friend from work who announced she was pregnant. For years, I had focused so much on my career, ignoring my growing desire to start a family. Her joy-filled news made me realize the depth of my despair.

As I approached forty, my desire to have children became more urgent. However, Phillip wouldn't even talk about starting a family. Whenever I brought up the subject, he came up with one insane excuse after another. He even told me once that it would be unfair of us to have a child since his sister Rachel and her husband were having difficulty conceiving. All this led to more arguing, and I found more excuses to spend time away from him.

I became determined to approach the subject with Phillip rationally. I practiced what I wanted to say all the way home on the bus to avoid blowing up like I usually did when my frustration boiled over. When I got home, I delivered my speech.

"You know, honey, if we're going to start a family, we need to start thinking about that soon because the clock is ticking."

"I've had a long day, and if you think we're going to discuss this, forget it." With that, he left the room. I followed him into the dining room, where he poured himself a scotch. He stopped and looked at me.

"What don't you understand?" he asked without waiting for a response. "If you think we're going to do a Dave and Beth, that is not happening." He ignored my gaping mouth and finished pouring his drink, then headed upstairs to his office, where I heard him slam the door.

I was gobsmacked. My close friend Beth had given up her teaching career to stay home and raise their three kids. Her husband, Dave, supported her decision, but Phillip refused to have children if it meant I would quit my job to raise them. I went after him, storming up the stairs, and pounded on the door.

"You know what, Phillip? Screw you."

"Back at you, Kasey."

This time, I left the house and by the time I got back, he was snoring on the couch. The following week, he stayed in the City. Whenever we talked on the phone, the tension between us was apparent.

For months after that incident, I was a complete bitch any time we were together. So much so that he began making veiled threats.

"If you don't change your attitude, you'll see what happens."

"Yeah? What's going to happen, Phillip? Are you threatening to divorce me?" I scoffed at him.

"Don't think I haven't thought about it. You've been a complete asshole lately."

I turned and looked at him, calling his bluff.

"Just remember, Phillip. You have a lot more to lose than I do."

I walked out of the room, feeling smug. I'd finally given him something to think about. If we divorced back then, he would have been forced to get a full-time job to cover his expenses. I relished the thought of him panicking, afraid he would leave me.

Gone were the days I rushed home because I wanted to see him. At that moment, I no longer cared if he stayed. Those feelings became more deep-seated as months passed, and we avoided being in the same place at the same time.

After he finished the gig in Manhattan, he gave up the rented room so he was home more. On a rare Saturday morning when we were both home, I heard him come into the kitchen while I made breakfast. I was tired of all the fighting, and when he seemed in a good mood, we started chatting casually about our plans for the day. I don't recall why, but I mentioned that I'd missed my period. This caused Phillip to fly off the handle.

"So you got pregnant anyway? Even though we talked about this months ago? This is how you get what you want, Kasey. You do things even if I say no."

"I never said anything about being pregnant, Phillip. I said I missed my period. That happens to women sometimes, especially those my age. But, gee, I'm so happy to know you think I would intentionally get pregnant," I said as caustically as I could.

"Well, it's not the first time you got pregnant on me."

His flash of anger revealed what I'd suspected all along. He thought I got pregnant on purpose. At that moment, I regretted ever trying to prove I was worthy of his love and commitment. Gone were the days when I played the martyr. For more than a decade, I had put his every desire before my own, and, in that moment, I confronted the reality that my actions bolstered his belief that his heart's desires were, in all ways, more important than my own.

I'd been suppressing my longing to start a family for years because he said we had to wait until we were financially stable. So I waited, never asking, "How much stability do we need?" When those words flew out of his mouth, I knew his excuses were about so much more than financial stability. It was about his need to maintain a lifestyle, one where he got to pursue his career goals without any interference.

I left the room without commenting because really—what could I say? He must have known I wasn't pregnant. We had barely had sex during the few times we were home at the same time. I believe he said that to hurt me. It did. All the feelings I'd pushed back came to the surface. This time, I didn't shrink back and shove them away. I realized I was just as responsible for the situation as he was. He took full advantage of my insecurities, but I let him.

After that, I finally gave in to my deepest longings and began exploring fertility options without him. If Phillip wouldn't even discuss having a family, I began considering a divorce and entertained the idea of trying to get pregnant through the means of a fertility doctor or adopting a child on my own.

Knowing that the window for conceiving a baby was rapidly closing, I became frantic. I started looking into the subject of in vitro fertilization, especially since one of my colleagues, years younger than me, was going that route.

I began staying in Manhattan later and later, telling Phillip I had to work late. This was mostly true because I had changed jobs with the ad agency and went from a broadcast business manager to the sole business manager of the agency's new interactive, or new media, department.

Because the internet was so new, I'd jumped at the opportunity, but there were many more responsibilities. Knowing this, Phillip never questioned my revised schedule. But sometimes, I stayed late to get information on all the ways older women were successfully getting pregnant. I read extensively on the subject and reviewed the success rates of a fertility specialist who had an office not far from Blairstown.

My boss at the time seemed to realize that my newly developed skills as an Interactive Business Manager made me a hot commodity. He must have heard I was being headhunted by other ad agencies looking to establish their own interactive departments. But, still, I was shocked when he offered me a twenty-thousand-dollar performance bonus contingent upon documenting the workflow of the agency's new interactive department.

Fate had finally intervened in my favor. Once I got the bonus, I could actually afford to pursue very expensive fertility treatments. But, more importantly, he'd offered me a staff position, which meant I would get health insurance as an employee instead of paying out the hefty monthly premiums for minimum coverage, like the insurance Phillip and I had at the time. Most ad agencies at the time hired freelancers as full-time personnel even though they worked in long-term positions. Having a staff position was a huge boon.

One weekend morning, I stood at the stove making breakfast when Phillip came up behind me. He put his arms around my waist, which caused me to stiffen.

"What's wrong?" he asked me, trying to kiss my neck.

"What's right?" I replied, and shook him away.

"Not this again," he said in a teasing manner.

I wasn't going to allow him to joke about my feelings, so I continued making my omelet, allowing the uncooked eggs to get firm.

"So, you're going to ignore me?" he said, stroking my hair.

"I'm not ignoring you, Phillip. I'm making breakfast," I replied sharply.

"Are you making me some?" he asked, continuing to make light of the moment.

Then, I ignored him. I finished making my breakfast, poured myself a cup of coffee, and headed into the dining room. A few minutes later, he followed me.

"Why?" he asked, taking a seat at the table.

"Why what, Phillip?" I said after swallowing the eggs in my mouth.

"Why do you want to have kids?"

I sat there, stunned, unable to think. Were we actually having a conversation without shouting at one another?

"I don't know. I just do."

"That's about the most honest answer you've ever given me, Kasey. Okay, what if we were to do this?"

I turned to face him.

"That's it? You're agreeing to start a family?"

"I guess I am. So now what?"

I almost fainted.

When we finally committed to try to conceive, I was forty-one years old. I told Phillip we should immediately make an appointment with a fertility doctor because time was of the essence. He never asked why I already had names and information available, or why there wasn't a long wait to see one. That's because I'd already made an appointment.

Trying to get pregnant seemed to change everything. Suddenly, we were this happy couple, totally in love and planning for the future. I couldn't wait to get home each day. All we talked about was our latest "production." It felt like the old days, when we wrote screenplays together and talked endlessly about how to accomplish our goals.

During this time, Phillip acted kind and loving, especially when he needed to stick me with needles containing the powerful drugs the doctor prescribed, or when the effects of the large-scale hormones affected my moods.

We got pregnant in the first round of in vitro. We went for blood tests, and the results showed we might be having twins or even triplets. We held our breath, waiting to hear back. When the doctor's office confirmed we were indeed having twins, we breathed a sigh of relief because the doctor had warned there was a chance of conceiving multiples in vitro. We danced around our kitchen, singing and laughing. Every negative thing he had ever done or said seemed wiped away in the moment.

Even in those happy days, when our relationship seemed to be mending, we never took the time to deal with the dysfunction of our marriage. Once again, we buried all the issues. Our decision to try to have a baby made them magically disappear. Now I realize none of it ever went away. It was still all there, hidden right below the surface.

CHAPTER FIVE

Emergency room

On the 24th of March, I was scheduled for a routine check-up. I stayed home from work that day, as I still traveled to Manhattan three times a week for work and telecommuted the other two days. It became increasingly uncomfortable to sit on the bus for hours and get on a crowded subway for the trip to downtown Manhattan. Thankfully, my assistant Dana could carry on when I wasn't in the office. Working from home allowed me to get things done without the stress of traveling daily, but I wanted to work as far as possible into my pregnancy.

Phillip had found a freelance job writing advertising copy for an agency in Morristown, New Jersey, an hour from Blairstown. He was offered a full-time staff position several months into the gig. We were both making good money and looked forward, with excitement, to this next chapter in our lives.

At the appointment, the doctor said the ultrasound revealed baby A (Lucy) was no longer thriving. Her weight had stagnated, and the doctor feared she might not make it to the end of my term. He told me I needed to deliver the twins, even though they would be five weeks premature.

I called Phillip on his cellphone and gave him the news.

"Are you sitting down?"

"Yeah, what's up?"

"They want to induce labor and said I should report to the hospital tomorrow or Thursday."

"Woah! We don't even have cribs set up yet!"

"I know, but I don't want to risk losing another pregnancy, so I want to go in tomorrow, okay?"

"Sure. Whatever you want. I'll let my boss know when I get off the phone."

A nurse gave me some Pitocin to induce labor around seven o'clock the following evening. I expected contractions to begin right away and was anxious about the anticipated pain. Phillip waited, equally anxious, beside me. Using the TV remote, he flipped through the various channels to find something to take our minds off the unknown ahead. As the night wore on, I tried to sleep and became irritable as the nurses entered and exited the room, checking my vital signs.

"Just relax," Phillip told me when the latest nurse left the room.

"So much easier to do when you're not the one about to give birth to twins."

I closed my eyes again and tried to rest but found it impossible to ignore the irritating noises from the machines that whirled around me. The cacophony of alarms, whistles, and buzzers overwhelmed me with each pitch, rhythm, and frequency, demanding I focus on what they were signaling, contributing to my inability to rest.

I finally managed to fall asleep when a nurse came in, probing my arm with a needle. "I can't get any sleep!" I complained.

"Honey, you're about to become a mother. Get used to it," she told me with a sardonic smile.

Throughout the next day, Phillip did his best to distract me. He told me stories I'd already heard and made silly jokes. When hours passed without any signs of contractions, he once again searched for programming on the television that might interest me and frequently refreshed the bucket of ice chips, the only thing I could have by mouth. He held my hand and gently kissed my fingers, trying to keep me calm, especially once I told him I felt a noticeable tightening below my abdomen.

In the late afternoon, I started having contractions. The nurse told me they were going to prepare an emergency room in case the doctors needed to do a C-section. Despite the waves of searing pain that accompanied each contraction, I fell asleep between each one, alarming the nursing staff, who thought I was fainting.

My regular doctor checked on me before she left for the evening and told Phillip that since I had only dilated five centimeters, he might want to go to get dinner.

A new doctor came on duty about fifteen minutes after he left and checked my cervix.

"Let's have a quick look before I go have dinner," she said, lifting my hospital gown. "Well, this isn't what I expected! You're almost ready to deliver," she told me. "Unfortunately, now we don't have time for any medication or epidural. Let's get you to the emergency room."

Phillip came back into the room as they were wheeling me away. She told him what was happening, and he turned gray. I was terrified. Everyone around me was talking in hushed voices, and I felt powerless to do anything to protect the children who were about to enter the world. I quietly sobbed as they moved me to a gurney, and the doctor had interns look under my hospital gown while she commented on my condition using words I barely understood. One intern gasped at the size of something, causing me to panic. My frenzied mind wanted to know what was happening, but I couldn't articulate my concerns, so I obediently let them do whatever they thought necessary.

"Push, now!" my doctor commanded. I did so with utmost determination. I held my breath and focused my entire willpower on expelling Lucy from my body. Praise and encouragement kept me from collapsing even when I believed what I tried to do was impossible. Phillip stood beside me and squeezed my hand, but I shook it off as it distracted me.

At 7:12 p.m., Lucy passed out of my body, but I heard no cry. I panicked, grabbed Phillips's hand, and looked at him to answer my unasked questions. I knew something was wrong but didn't know what. Then, the doctor told me Jack was breech.

"You're not going to like me for this, but I have to reach up and try to turn him. Otherwise, we might have to take him by caesarian."

Phillip stood off to the side, trying to comfort me. The anguish in his eyes told me he was distraught. Minutes passed, and I could feel the doctor's hands reaching deeper and deeper inside me. The ripping pain increased every inch she penetrated, seeking out Jack's tiny legs to pull him down the birth canal. I heard an audible sigh from below.

"Got him," she told us. I couldn't see her, but imagined she smiled.

Eleven very long minutes later, she grabbed him by both legs and gently pulled him out. I heard him cry. The smiles and sense of relief were palpable. Everyone I could see seemed visibly relieved when the doctor finally delivered Jack.

"Do you want to hold him?" she asked, placing him on my chest without waiting for an answer. The warmth of his body melded into mine. His red, wrinkled skin was covered in a white fuzzy coating. He let out an angry cry, balled his hands into fists, and shook them, demanding to know why I wanted him to leave my womb. It reminded me I hadn't heard the same from Lucy. My concern grew over the whereabouts of my daughter.

"Where's Lucy?" I demanded to know.

"Lucy's APGAR score is low. We took her to the Neonatal Intensive Care Unit as a precaution," she said matter-of-factly. While this news was meant to be reassuring, I began to sob, frightened we were going to lose her.

"But I didn't even get a chance to say hello."

Within minutes, they took Jack to the Neonatal Intensive Care Unit of the hospital. The pain from the 2nd-degree vaginal tearing set in, and the doctor told me it would require some stitches. Once they addressed it, they wheeled me back to the hospital room without being allowed to see Jack again or meet Lucy.

Phillip spent the night, reluctant to leave us behind. The next day, though, we were able to have Jack with us in my hospital room while Lucy was required to stay behind in the incubator.

Phillip seemed like a new man. He was so attentive to both Jack and me during those first days. He held Jack tenderly and teared up when we left Lucy behind after each visit to the NICU. Although tiny, four days after her birth, Lucy was strong enough to join us in my hospital room.

We took them home at the end of March. The temperature had reached an unusually high eighty-six degrees. Seeing people in shorts and t-shirts passing us in the hospital hallways was surreal. The heavy winter clothes I had for the twins and me were left in the suitcase. Instead, I dressed them in lightweight, matching striped one-piece outfits that were too big for their bodies. We placed them in car seats made just for preemies and drove home in a comfortable silence.

We walked up the front steps of our house, each carrying one of our Beans. Our neighbor saw us and called over to us.

"Getting prepared? It will be here before you know it!"

Phillip and I just looked at each other and laughed.

"Actually, they arrived early! Come take a look," I responded.

She climbed up the porch steps and looked at Jack and Lucy.

"They're beautiful!" she said.

"I know," I beamed.

As expected, life changed dramatically over the next few years. I was still trucking into Manhattan three days a week, even though I'd left one agency to work for another. I was now an interactive business manager for J. Walter Thompson's new division. I got my new boss to hire Dana, who worked with me at my previous employer, and together we established the business process for the department. Initially, I had a lot of responsibility and couldn't take much time off, but eventually, I could work from home several days a week, and then I cut back even more. My skills were in high demand back then, and I made more money working three days a week than I had been working five.

But life was far from rosy. Even cutting back on the number of days I commuted into Manhattan did little to keep me from being overwhelmed. The first year of the Beans' lives remains a blur. I remember almost nothing from those sleep-deprived months when I had little time to eat, sleep, or even shower. Jack had colic, and I carried him in a sling. Lucy was very content and earned the nickname of *Angel Baby*. But while Jack was colicky and frequently cried, he developed more rapidly than Lucy in most areas except speech.

Lucy said her first word at eight months and could count to twenty by the time she was thirteen months. She could recite whole passages in books, which made her look like she was reading them. But she didn't start walking until she was eighteen months old. On the other hand, Jack hit all his milestones right on time. Once he outgrew the colic, he became more content, even though he still hated being put down for a nap.

Watching the two babies grow and develop simultaneously enabled me to observe their burgeoning personalities. However, I became concerned about other observations. For example, Lucy cried whenever she heard loud noises, even laughter. She seemed to panic when she saw bright lights. She screamed when I put her on the changing table, so I changed her on the floor. Jack exhibited none of these behaviors.

When I tried to discuss these matters with Phillip, his reaction upset me.

"It's in your head, Kasey. They're both fine. You're just a worrier," Phillip told me.

"But when I take them to playgroup, she's not even interested in playing with the other kids," I reported. "She is totally content playing by herself."

"So what? Maybe she doesn't want to play. Did you ever think of that? You create problems to get attention. What's wrong with you?" he fired back.

I couldn't even respond. Phillip came home each night long after the kids were in bed, yet believed he knew better than I did about these matters. I knew I was right, so I kept exploring the issue and ignored him.

At a well-baby visit, I expressed my concerns to our family doctor. After observing her, the doctor too had concerns and suggested getting early intervention to help her. When I told Phillip, he responded with comments that implied I had forced the doctor to draw his conclusions.

As the Beans got older, I observed more things that caused me to comb the internet. It wasn't just at playgroup sessions that social interactions were difficult for Lucy. Jack would naturally interact with the other kids at swim class or any other group activities, but Lucy always stayed by herself. The only child Lucy interacted with was Jack, who would sweetly check on Lucy occasionally. He would reassure himself she was okay and then run off to play with his pals.

While I got Lucy some therapy to help increase her gross motor skills, that didn't help with the other things that alarmed me about her socialization skills. All these things made me increasingly uncomfortable being two and a half hours away from my children. I knew these years were critical in terms of their development. But any time I mentioned my concerns, they were rebuffed by Phillip.

Things came to a head when the Beans were about eighteen months old, and I came back from Manhattan to find my usually happy son clinging to Lydia, the twins' babysitter. He wasn't crying, but he was utterly listless. I looked at her questioningly.

"How long has he been like this?" I asked Lydia.

"All afternoon," she responded, handing Jack over. I took him in my arms, and he barely reacted to me.

"Why didn't you call me?"

"I tried to leave you a message, but your voicemail is full."

"Okay, sorry." I felt horrible.

I'd never seen Jack like this. He was always bubbly and energetic. I held him tightly, rocking him back and forth, and kissed his forehead to see if he was hot.

"You can take off," I told Lydia. "I'll see you tomorrow."

"Let's go upstairs, buddy," I said, trying to soothe him.

This was the third childcare arrangement we'd had. The first was a childcare center that charged two hundred dollars per week per child. The Beans got sick for the first three weeks, and we still paid for the care they weren't getting. On top of that, it cost fifty dollars per half hour when a parent was late picking up a child. Since I commuted by bus, that occurred frequently. I paid double because the fee was per child.

The second babysitter was so inept that she fed them soy milk that had been in a bottle on the kitchen counter and had fermented. She also threw away expensive cloth diapers because they were *too poopy*.

Lydia was a delightful woman and a former teacher, and I didn't hesitate to leave the Beans with her. Similar situations caused me too much anguish. I hated the idea of them always being cared for by someone else.

I sat in the oversized chair in the twins' room for a moment, watching Lucy in the playpen. Jack clung to me and continued to be unresponsive. For some reason, I checked and noticed he had a soiled diaper. I carried him over to the changing table and carefully unbuttoned the wool diaper cover. His diaper was full of a loose stool, and his bottom a blistering red. Phillip came upstairs and into their room a moment later.

"Don't get your coat off. We're taking Jack to the emergency room."

Somehow, Lydia had missed Jack's horrible diaper rash. His inflamed bottom was a scarlet red, and he cried when I touched it. It might have occurred right after she changed his diaper, or it was a simple oversight. Regardless, I was livid.

Until that moment, I had gone along with Phillip's reasoning that we needed two incomes. He saw nothing wrong with us being hours away from our children. That day, however, I realized I couldn't do it anymore. The next day, I gave notice at work.

The cracks in our relationship became chasms overnight. "How could you do that?" Phillip yelled when I told him I'd quit.

"It was easy. I should have done it after the Beans were born. I won't be two and a half hours away from our children anymore, especially when they're this little. They need a parent close by," I screamed.

"Oh, of course, that parent is you."

"Are you saying it should be you? Are you kidding me? You have to call me three times if I leave them with you to go to the grocery store. Who noticed that Lucy had developmental issues? The only reason I could get her help was that I had flexibility in my work schedule. Those appointments alone took months to get. If I had to pick and choose when I was available, I would never have been able to get an appointment. Don't worry, Phillip. I'll find a job here so you don't have to support us alone."

"You're never going to earn the same money out here. You know that!"

"So that's what's important here? Not the welfare of our kids? It's always my paycheck that matters most to you, isn't it?"

"You can manipulate this any way you want, Kasey, but not having the income to support them makes you the selfish one. I'm sure you've been planning to leave your job from the moment they were born. You do whatever you want, and I have to pick up the mess from your half-assed decisions."

"Really? How many failed businesses have I had?"

The moment those words came out of my mouth, I regretted saying them. I knew the devastating impact of thoughtless words when Phillip made insensitive comments to me. This was a low blow because his company folded years ago when his former partner embezzled all their money on top of the film and office equipment. He only had a few freelance jobs in almost three years until he took the job as a copywriter at the agency in Morristown, NJ, right before the twins were born.

I tried to ease the tension.

"Look, I'll put out some resumés and get a job out here. You're making a good salary now. We have plenty of money saved, too." He was still furious with me, but I didn't back down and wasn't surprised when he didn't speak to me for days.

At first, I didn't see how unbalanced things had become once I stopped working full-time. I was too busy trying to work several part-time jobs and keeping up with the twins and housework to notice how much had changed regarding the dynamic of our relationship.

I was doing some housework before the kids got up, and Phillip wandered into the kitchen, asking if I'd made breakfast.

"Not yet. How about you make it for a change," I said half-jokingly.

"I'll wait until you're done, thank you," he said in a tone that reflected annoyance.

"Well, it's going to be awhile. It's hard to get housework done while the kids are awake," I told him.

"I'm going to run to grab something at Dunkin," he replied.

"Phillip, you eat something from there five days a week. Can't you wait for a little while so I can get the dishes done? I didn't say I wouldn't make you breakfast," I responded.

"I have stuff to do, so I don't feel like waiting," he told me.

"Well, this is my stuff to do. And while we're on the subject, why is it that when you were home alone, we could afford a housekeeper, but now that I'm home alone with the Beans, that's off the table?"

"What housekeeper?"

"What do you mean, what housekeeper? Have you forgotten about Lynette?"

"No, I haven't forgotten. Look, Kasey. Don't blow this up. I can easily count the number of times Lynette came to clean."

"What are you talking about? She came here once a week for years!"

"I'm not doing this, Kasey. You exaggerate everything."

"How am I exaggerating?"

Soon, the morning turned dark. He ignored my questions, so I pressed because I knew I wasn't the one exaggerating.

"So, she only came occasionally? Really? And was that you who had meals on the table when I came home each night?" I said, becoming impatient. "You spent your time shopping for groceries and doing laundry all those years? Did you empty the litter boxes and pay the bills? You were the one doing that the whole time? Gee, I thought it was me."

"There you go again. You're pretty pathetic. Why is this even an argument? I can't be expected to come home from work and do housework, so forget about Lynette. As it is, I spend all my time working to support you and my family."

"Need I remind you that you only took a few freelance jobs in almost three years before the kids were born? Why was it okay to pay for someone to clean when you were home alone? And secondly, how can you forget I supported you for years?"

"This is so typical. I worked my ass off renovating the house during that time, and you're here complaining. What do you have to do all day? Oh, don't bother to answer that because I know the answer. We're not discussing this anymore. You were the one who wanted to stay home. Deal with it." He left the house and didn't come back until noon.

Arguments like this persisted. Phillip claimed I exaggerated or outright lied about the past even when I had proof to the contrary. He used a common phrase, "I wish I had recorded what you said because I'd play it back so I could prove you're lying." Or sometimes he claimed, "You don't even hear what you just said."

There were times I started thinking it was all in my head. When he wasn't home, I'd dig through records to prove I wasn't losing my mind. I had canceled checks to show that Lynette came each week, yet his accusations made me question myself, always putting me on the defensive. I began to believe something was wrong with me. I started to think I couldn't trust that the words I thought I spoke were the words that came out of my mouth.

Phillip tried to trip me up by instructing me to repeat exactly what I'd just said. According to Phillip, this would prove his point. When I couldn't recall the precise words I'd used previously, he claimed it proved I lied.

This became a source of anxiety when we argued. I would try to remember the exact words I used so Phillip couldn't make these accusations. It made me hesitant to engage him in any argument because I couldn't recall every word I'd uttered and then parrot them back to him. Even if I pointed out that he couldn't do it either, he turned the tables and said I was now trying to manipulate him.

When I got a part-time job designing and maintaining a website for a local realtor, he became kinder because he hoped it would lead to a business we could develop together. While the income helped, it didn't compare to the weekly paycheck I once made. Since I only had the most basic coding skills, I needed his help to do the more advanced coding. He was a natural coder. But, I stopped asking for his help after he told me I was faking my lack of knowledge so he would have to do the work.

Once I wasn't contributing as much to the household income, Phillip wanted me to account for every dime I spent. But, at the time, I didn't care. Exhaustion overtook me and I could barely manage to get through the day. I was scared because my energy levels had become so depleted that I began to suspect something was wrong health-wise.

I finally acknowledged how bad it was when I couldn't find the strength to push the Beans' carriage home from a small park only two blocks away. I called my neighbor and asked for help. When I mentioned this to Phillip, he snapped.

"Don't tell me about tired. You're not the one who has to leave for work at 7 a.m."

"No, I don't. I just get up two or three times at night to deal with the kids. Do you remember I got up each morning to be on the bus at 5:30 for twelve years?" He shook his head, insinuating that I had exaggerated again.

All the years I supported him so he could develop his career were erased or forgotten. So were the promises that I could relax once he was established and have time to pursue my career goals. I didn't even care about "my career" anymore. I just wanted him to support my decision to stay close to home to care for our children. Yet, he refused to acknowledge all of my contributions to his life, not just the financial ones.

I went to bed as soon as the Beans were asleep to combat my fatigue. If I heard Phillip come up the stairs, I pretended to be asleep because I knew he'd be angry with me for not waiting up. Sometimes, he sat down on the bed.

"Hey, what's up?" he asked one night.

"Not much, I just have a headache," I lied.

I knew if I told him again about my incredible fatigue, it would lead to an argument or an accusation, so I avoided the subject.

"It's all in your head," Phillip told me repeatedly.

"I left some dinner in the fridge for you to microwave. I'm going to try and get some sleep."

I began sliding into depression, thinking maybe Phillip was right. His snide comments that I was lazy or inept played repeatedly in my mind. Self-doubt crept in, and I allowed him to take more and more control of our lives without questioning his decisions. I began seeing myself through his eyes, and what I saw wasn't pretty.

When I told my friend Shannon about feeling lethargic all the time and unable to focus, she convinced me that a trip to my doctor was warranted no matter what Phillip thought. I didn't tell Phillip I planned to see my doctor and almost canceled the appointment, feeling foolish.

Once there, I recall feeling ashamed for even being there, wasting her valuable time over something insignificant.

"Maybe it's because I'm too old to be the mother of such young kids," I half laughed with embarrassment. "Phillip thinks it's all in my head." She rolled her eyes and asked me to describe what I experienced.

"It's like every ounce of energy has been drained from my body," I told her and began to cry. "I'm a high-energy person. At least, I used to be. Now I can't function some days. I'll start out feeling fine, and then it's like a battery has died, and there's no power left. I've started limiting what I do with the twins because I often can't finish what I started. I think something is out of balance somehow. I think something is wrong."

"When did this start?" she asked while poking and prodding my neck.

"I don't recall exactly, but it's been over a year. The first time I remember it getting really bad was when I had to call someone to help me get the twins back home because I couldn't push their carriage."

She stopped and looked at me. As my regular physician, who I'd seen for years, she must have noticed the change in my demeanor.

"This is not in your head. Without more tests, I can't say exactly what's wrong, but this isn't something imaginary. I will have one of the nurses get you an appointment to see a specialist. We're going to figure this out," she assured me.

After seeing the specialist, tests revealed I had several benign tumors that were affecting my parathyroid glands. That caused my calcium levels to drop dangerously low, causing my severe fatigue. I was relieved to learn it wasn't all in my head, but angry that I was harangued and characterized negatively by Phillip over these real physical problems. Not once did he apologize. After surgery, I recovered with the help of some supplements to compensate for the lack of calcium.

The slow erosion of my confidence didn't bounce back just because I felt better. However, the experience made me realize how much I conceded in my marriage now that I wasn't earning more than Phillip. I had absorbed all the negativity Phillip spewed at me since leaving my job. A part of me even clung to Phillip's vision of who I was or wasn't. I had relinquished so much of my control to him while I had suffered from the unexplained exhaustion. Regaining any measure of confidence remained difficult.

The man who I once thought treated me as an equal controlled almost every aspect of my life. I no longer had much, if any, input into the decisions within our marriage. Instead of confronting him, I did what my mother did. I adapted to the new dynamic of our relationship.

CHAPTER SIX

What to do About Chubby?

It was one in the afternoon, but I couldn't force myself to continue packing. Exhaustion set in and I needed to get some sleep so I could make the trip to Cobleskill safely. Still, I had a hard time drifting off. I tried to keep my thoughts on the Beans and wondered what they were doing and if my brother enjoyed having them there. He always kept them entertained. I imagined them playing some of the invented games Jake had played with his own two girls when they were young. A made up game called Louie Prima ball, became a favorite. Jake's wife Meredith had played with her siblings when growing up in the house where they now lived, and he convinced the Beans it was an official Olympic sport and that they were, in fact, world champs. He proved it by creating a homemade certificate, then printed and framed their award to present to them. They were still at an age where they believed anything an adult told them.

As I drifted off, I couldn't help but think about the startling events that had unfolded in recent years. Selling our home in Blairstown was unsettling enough. I thought our old Victorian, where we raised our children, would be where Phillip and I would grow old together once the Beans left home.

Then, I remembered the long conversations the kids and I had driving back and forth from Cobleskill to Alexandria. They pelted me with questions about why we were moving. I didn't want them to be in the middle of a tug-of-war between Phillip and me. I tried to be honest but left out as much as possible about why we were moving again. It bothered me tremendously that I'd already broken my promise to them that they wouldn't have to move again if we moved to Alexandria. I had believed it at the time. I never imagined things would take the turn they did.

The sound of banging startled me. I woke abruptly from my nap. The noise came from downstairs. Someone was pounding on the café door. It took me a minute to get my bearings. I stumbled to get dressed, then rushed down the stairs. But by the time I reached the door, no one was there. I saw a car pulling away but didn't know if it belonged to whoever had come to my door.

Meandering into the kitchen, I looked at the clock on the stove and was shocked to see it was approaching five o'clock. I'd slept for hours and never took Chubby for his walk. I grabbed his leash from the hook near the door and locked up, hoping the black flies would be kinder than usual when we ventured out to one of the trails that surrounded the lake a block from the building.

When I returned from my walk with Chubby, I began packing the van in earnest. A little after seven o'clock, I returned inside and started hunting for Duncan and Felicia to get them into their crates. They were nowhere to be found. I searched everywhere. I shook the treat bag, opened a can of cat food, and did everything I usually did that brought them running. I didn't blame them for hiding because I wished I could hide, too.

I went upstairs, thinking they might wander out if I wasn't around. Chubby followed me up the stairs and jumped on the mattress. I noticed how matted and dirty he looked. Handing him over to Jody, looking so grubby, would have been embarrassing.

"Hey, Bud! Come with me. I know a tub with your name on it." The tub was full of dirt and grime after washing him.

By eight, I knew I had to decide whether to leave or head out in the morning. I was still tired but knew I couldn't delay the trip forever. Even though the thought of being out on the road by myself late at night concerned me, I planned to head out as soon as I located the cats.

My growling stomach reminded me I hadn't eaten since breakfast. I reasoned that the cats might come out of hiding if I went to Tim Horton's to grab a bagel and cream cheese. I brought their crates into the bathroom upstairs so that once I found them, I could close the door to prevent them from escaping. About ten minutes later, I headed to the local Tim Horton's Coffee Shop with Chubby in tow.

I finally got back about a half hour later and found the cat food in the kitchen gone. I headed upstairs, hoping for the best. Both cats were now asleep on the mattress. They looked up at me as though I were the enemy who had come to bring them before a firing squad. I corralled them into their crates. They yowled and complained while I packed the last of my belongings. I went over to the desk to retrieve the picture I kept there of the Beans, placed it inside my suitcase, and reluctantly began to leave.

Suddenly, I became overwhelmed at the thought of having Chubby stay behind. Somehow, having him with me kept the loneliness at bay. I again considered calling Jody to delay my trip by a day. But I thought it would be rude to change plans late at night when she was waiting for me. So, with all the pets in the van, off I went to hand over my faithful companion.

I arrived at Jody's a little after nine. She and her husband Brice had a farm in the countryside outside Alexandria. They bred small dogs and had a kennel next to their house. Jody hailed from the U.S. but had moved to Canada decades before. She and Brice were a terrific couple. Just like almost everyone else I met in Alexandria, I met them through the café,

Even though she'd offered to let Chubby stay in the house with her and Brice, I stalled, reluctant to leave him. Internally, I reasoned that he would be in good, loving hands, but I held onto his leash. I didn't realize just how attached I'd grown to him. When I finally let go and began walking away, he yipped and whined, accusing me of betrayal. Climbing into the van, I could hear his plaintiff howls. I almost turned back at the end of her laneway but kept going. I would have been embarrassed for anyone to see I was crying so hard.

A profound loneliness crept into my heart as I headed toward the border. I drove south toward Cobleskill and had hours to think about the future. I was tired of starting over every few years. I longed for a home and a place where I could feel settled. I wanted that place to be Alexandria. At one point, Phillip had wanted that, too. I knew I would make new friends, but the constant upheaval left me feeling defeated.

Knowing that Phillip could soon exert even more control over my life than ever before made me distraught. Even worse, I feared the isolation. The friendships I'd developed in Alexandria had sustained me. However, once I moved to Cobleskill, cultivating new relationships would be a point of contention. Phillip told me the desire for friendships outside our marriage was unnatural. Even before we had children, he constantly discouraged me from socializing. I struggled to understand why. I knew the gathering at Jenny's only happened because he wasn't in Canada.

What was so mystifying was that Phillip was outwardly a friendly and engaging person. He eagerly kept up with his former classmates and friends from high school. But he rarely interacted with those people regularly because they were so far away. Before we got married, Phillip loved to socialize. We organized enormous parties at a local state park to play Capture the Flag and had BBQs, or went with friends to listen to bands or comedy shows. But they were usually events shared with his friends. We saw my friends and family over the holidays, or not at all.

His attitude extended beyond going out and socializing, to phone calls as well. Any time I called a friend from home, it frequently became an issue after I got off the phone. Phillip told me my call to them had taken too much time. Depending on who I was speaking to, he even told me my friends were using me somehow.

He called these relationships "selfish" and "harmful" to our marriage. He called me immature for even wanting them. I got around it when I worked in New York because he wasn't a part of that social life. However, events like an office Christmas party or joining another couple for dinner became problematic as time passed. After these evenings ended, a fight would ensue. He always framed his complaint similarly: "We have too much going on to spend time socializing." Phillip's to-do list was a revolving excuse to avoid spending time with anyone other than his friends or his family.

After we had children, Phillip attempted to isolate me even more. It was easier to do that when I no longer had my life in New York City to shield me. Back in Blairstown, all the people I associated with were casual acquaintances, except for my friend and neighbor, Shannon. She was a godsend, especially when the twins were little. She came over frequently to help with the kids when I needed a break. As they grew, the twins called her Auntie Shannon and her husband Uncle Vince.

Phillip liked Vincent but barely tolerated Shannon. He told me he found her too outspoken and opinionated. The longer we were married, the more I realized he believed that about many women he worked with or for and that Phillip was quite the chauvinist. He repeatedly claimed his female colleagues only got where they did by "sleeping with the boss." I questioned how he thought I got ahead.

Other situations made me realize his attitude toward women was consistently negative. It was tough to ignore after something happened one weekend while Phillip traveled for a business trip. Shannon offered to help me paint our dining room. I thought it would be a lovely surprise for Phillip.

"How could you do this behind my back?" he screamed at me.

"Phillip, I thought you'd be happy, for Christ's sake! It looks amazing. It's one less room you have to contend with doing. Why are you so mad?" I shouted back at him. He wouldn't speak to me for days after this happened. Instead of being pleased, it had led to an ongoing battle about "priorities" and my friendship with Shannon. He told me we had painted it "without his permission." He said Shannon was "unqualified" to paint our dining room. This was absurd because she and Vince had renovated the bed-and-breakfast they owned in our historic neighborhood entirely on their own. Shannon could paint without using painter's tape to prevent getting paint on the ceiling. But, in his mind, she wasn't qualified.

When Shannon and I painted that room, his fury was over the fact I had taken control of something he considered his domain without consulting him.

"Is that because she's a woman?" I asked him, point blank.

"Screw you and screw Shannon, too," he said, storming out of the house.

From that point on, he spoke ill of Shannon.

Anything related to the house was under his complete domain and done at his discretion. Once, when I complained about an unsafe light fixture with exposed wiring right near a shower stall in the bathroom. He scoffed at my concern. It didn't get fixed for years, even though it would have taken less than half an hour. The fact it made me nervous seemed to please him.

I believed Phillip feared that anyone from the outside could weaken his influence over me. While I did have a few friends in Blairstown, somehow, if they didn't meet his approval, socializing with them was a major flash point. It had become so commonplace that I didn't have the perspective necessary to see any of it until I moved to Alexandria, and I no longer needed Phillip's approval.

I finally pulled into the driveway of the new apartment in Cobleskill at about one o'clock in the morning. I stopped for a moment before heading in. The cats were yowling to be let out of their cages. I knew exactly how they felt.

Phillip told me he'd leave me a key in the ashtray of our Elantra. I grabbed it before carrying the cats in their cages to the apartment's back door, hoping it would work in the lock. It was unsettling to enter an apartment I'd never been to after midnight. After opening the door, I put the cats inside, hoping they wouldn't wake Phillip. Then I grabbed my suitcase and their litter box from the van. The crunch of my footsteps on the gravel of the driveway unnerved me as I looked around to ensure I was alone. The noise seemed too loud for my small feet to be making. I hurried inside.

With the door unlocked, I attempted to locate the switches to turn on the lights. Unable to find them, my eyes began to adjust to the darkness. With only the moonlight from a window in the door to guide me, I passed a set of stairs that I assumed led to the second floor. I stepped cautiously beyond the mudroom and found a bathroom to the left. A small night light illuminated its unadorned interior. The only evidence of use was a single toothbrush and paste haphazardly placed in a glass on the vanity.

Beyond the bathroom, I found another empty room. One would have to pass through this room to get to the toilet. I wondered which twin he envisioned would have to use this as their bedroom. My nose wrinkled at the musty smell from the carpeting as I traversed the room.

To the right, I found the kitchen. It was empty, too. The lack of a table or chairs made me think that Phillip ate in front of the TV each night when at home. I entered the living room, where I found our couch and the television perched on a kitchen chair.

"Bingo," I thought.

The door to another room off the living room was closed. I heard the rumbling of Phillip's snoring coming from within the room. I couldn't figure out why he chose to sleep there as he'd told me the largest bedroom was on the second floor. I searched for the smallest of signs of welcome to my new home. A blanket, a pillow, or something to provide even a modicum of comfort. There were none.

A caterwaul reminded me the cats were still in their crates, so I returned to the bathroom and set up their litter box before I let them out of their cages. They looked grateful to be out and quickly disappeared into the night. Without unpacking or even brushing my teeth, I returned to the living room, lay on the couch, and quietly wept before sleep overtook me.

Phillip had left by the time I woke up the following day. I never heard him leave. I wandered inside the now open room where he'd slept. A pillow and a light blanket were on one of the twin's beds. He'd placed a small TV on top of a dresser we'd used in Jack's room. Phillip's jeans also hung on a hook on the back of the door. I checked the dresser drawers and found a few pairs of underwear, some T-shirts, and another pair of jeans. There were no other signs of his belongings or the rest of his clothing.

After using the bathroom, I wandered around to look closer at the place in the daylight. The layout was strange. While advertised as a three-bedroom, besides the bedroom where he'd slept, there was only the room between the kitchen and mudroom, making it awkward to use as a bedroom. After climbing the steps to the second floor, I found our antique Victorian bed in the largest bedroom. It was disassembled, with the headboard and footboard leaning against the wall. The drawers to the matching dresser were piled up on top of the mattress on the floor.

I desperately wanted some coffee, so I hurried back to the kitchen to find the cabinets were almost bare. A few plates, bowls, and glasses were on the lowest shelf of the cabinet closest to the sink. There were some Tastykake Powdered Mini Donuts, a jar of peanut butter, and a loaf of Wonder Bread on the counter. I found a pint of milk, an open bottle of red wine, and a half-eaten burger and fries in a to-go container in the fridge

I knew Phillip had a habit of stopping at the closest Dunkin Donuts for coffee and breakfast each morning. I assumed this hadn't changed. It didn't surprise me. Famished, I thought about picking up a few groceries before unloading the van, but realized I had no money to spend on groceries. This made my new reality abundantly clear.

Welcome to your new home, I thought.

Our agreement to move to Canada was the result of several unforeseen events in our lives. In 2005, Phillip returned from work and headed straight for the liquor cabinet before delivering the bad news.

"They let go of a few more people today. I might have to start sending out resumés."

"What positions are they cutting?"

"It seems across the board. I think I'm safe for a while, but the risk is that if I wait, there's less chance of finding any positions open at another agency. You know, you could send out resumés, too," Phillip told me.

"Not this again!" I replied and went into the kitchen to fix dinner.

I wanted to remain close to home and stubbornly resisted Phillip's attempts to make me feel guilty about quitting my Manhattan job. However, I worried when he came home, unable to eat due to his persistent acid stomach and his self-diagnosed IBS. He managed his symptoms with over-the-counter medicines and some changes to his diet.

"Honey, can you pick up some Tums?"

"Are you out of them already? Do you think you should see Dr. Powers?"

"I can't take time off right now. Can you buy me more Tums or Rolaids?"

"Sure. I'll run out now. Is Mexican food okay for dinner? I picked up some stuff to make burritos."

"Yeah, did you get the mild salsa? I can't handle the medium anymore." With his hectic schedule, he ate an enormous amount of fast food. I often suspected his diet contributed to his stomach problems. Regardless, he would get angry if I offered to prepare lunches for him to bring to work.

Everything fell apart in the beginning of February.

"Hey, what's up?" I asked when he called my cellphone.

"I just got escorted out of the building. It was the most humiliating thing I've ever experienced. I'm on my way home."

"I'm so sorry, Honey... drive safe. Love you."

When he came home that evening, devastated, I just held him for a long time. For weeks, they'd been laying off more and more personnel. He thought if he worked harder, stayed later, and took work home, he would magically escape the layoff.

"Well, I guess I can pour myself a double scotch tonight because I don't have to work in the morning."

"Look, it stinks. But we'll be okay. Something will turn up."

It didn't. Soon, the fighting began again, as we tried to hang on to our very different solutions to this urgent problem.

By the spring of 2006, we had blown through most of our savings, trying to stay afloat. Our monthly COBRA payment alone was more than our monthly mortgage: over twelve hundred dollars each month just for health insurance.

We discussed selling the two rental properties we owned in Scranton, about a forty-five-minute drive from our home in Blairstown. I thought this would be best because they were losing money. Phillip said we should keep those and sell our lovingly restored home. I disagreed vehemently. By that time, however, he had grown accustomed to having the final say in decisions. The financial stress led to long, extended arguments, since we had two mortgages for the rental properties, on top of our personal expenses.

"Why can't we sell the income properties?"

"That's my retirement."

"Don't you mean *our* retirement?"

"Yeah, whatever. We'll get a lot more money for this than we'll get in Scranton. Those places still need work."

"Exactly. We should sell one and cut our losses. This is our home, Phillip."

"If we sold this, we'd have money to invest there and have rental income."

"Where are we going to live if we sell this?"

"Well, if you would start looking for a job in New York again, we wouldn't have to have this conversation."

"No."

"Why not?"

"We have discussed this, Phillip. Asking me repeatedly won't change my answer. I don't have the same connections in the business to secure the type of job I once had. When I left Interactive Production, Netscape was still around. The industry has changed, Phillip. Why do you keep pressing this issue?"

"You're just stubborn. You could find something."

"And so could you."

We each dug in on our positions. I understood all too well why Phillip didn't want to commute each day, but he was the one who wanted to buy the properties that left him busy on the weekends. He'd already missed so much of the kids' lives. If he got another job, it would take him away from them each day again. In the seven years since they were born, he had rarely had time to spend with them.

There was the practical side of the issue, too. Phillip had little interest in the day-to-day tasks of operating a household. Whenever he was asked to perform housework, he complained that he had other things to do. Or he did the chore so poorly, I'd stupidly jump in. I fell right into the trap of doing it all myself, unwilling to confront the angry mood that chores inspired in Phillip.

My various part-time jobs weren't enough to sustain us, and we finally ran out of options. Although I was reluctant, I went along when he suggested we put our house on the market. It sold six months later.

We rented an apartment in a town a short drive from the kids' school, where I taught computer skills two days a week. The Beans were now in third grade and flourishing in every way. They had friends, and I hung out with some women I worked with at the school. It wasn't a perfect life, but it was far from horrible. Phillip spent so much time away completing the renovations on the properties in Scranton that I didn't have to contend with his unpredictable moods.

He stayed home on weekends and played with the kids. We'd crawl into bed and speak about our more modest dreams of running a business or doing something that would provide financial security and the freedom to be independent of the corporate world. Long gone were our creative ambitions. Our shared dream was to leave it all behind so we could enjoy our time with the twins. It was a modest dream, and one that I learned when we moved to Alexandria was also an illusion.

CHAPTER SEVEN

Oh, Canada

Our decision to move north began with what I thought was a casual conversation. One weekend, he confessed that he'd been looking online at real estate. As we sat on the couch after the kids were in bed, he said, "Hey, look what I found online."

"Where is it?"

"Alexandria,"

"Virginia?"

"No. Ontario."

"Oh, too bad it's so far away! It's lovely! How much are they asking?" I stared at the pictures of a brick heritage building. The wrap-around porch and Victorian features piqued my curiosity. We had previously owned a condo in the Eastern Townships in Quebec but had sold it and reinvested the money in the Scranton rental properties. We'd always discussed buying another vacation property in Quebec one day. I looked over at him, and I could tell this wasn't the end of the conversation. Phillip didn't respond to my question about the price of the building, so I looked up to see why he was silent. The grin on his face was contagious. I'd seen the same expression countless times and I smiled back.

"Okay, confess! What are you thinking?"

He then delivered a speech that sounded like he'd rehearsed it a thousand times. "Well, it's no surprise that I'd like to consider moving north." I took a deep breath because he had talked about this many times.

"I know we couldn't before, but we always said we'd buy another place after we sold our condo in Quebec." I let him continue.

"Remember the place we stopped to eat when we went to Ottawa last summer? The restaurant in that old mill?"

"Yeah, how could I forget? The food was excellent, and I spilled my wine all over the waiter."

"You've always been a klutz," he said, taking my hand. "Well, this place is near the same lake and on Main Street. I want to go up and look at this. I have a good feeling about the place."

"But when would we do this?"

"Maybe we can look when the Beans have spring break? I still have loads of work in Scranton, but I want to do this. What do you think?"

"I don't know, Phillip. It's an odd location for a vacation property, even with the lake. Besides, we can't afford this right now."

"I'm not talking about using it for vacations, Kasey. Let's move there."

"What? Are you serious?"

"I am. This property is in Ontario, so the French language requirements wouldn't be as much of an issue for the Beans in school. Plus, the Ontario government still funds Catholic schools. We wouldn't have to worry about health insurance because they have universal health. So, instead of flushing our money down the drain every month on health insurance, we buy a property like this. Think about it. We could start our own business and do something that would build a future for the Beans. They could learn to work alongside us, and we wouldn't have to deal with other people fucking up our lives to save a buck or two on a salary. I'm serious about this. I think it would be a marvelous opportunity."

"Holy shit, Phillip. This would be an enormous step." My mind raced as he sprung this on me.

"Well, if it works out, we would be able to run a small business and it would give us time to do some of our creative projects. Kasey, I'm tired of missing the kids' lives. I don't want to go back into Morristown, either. I don't mind writing copy for a living, but the commute is brutal. I could see about freelancing from up there. A lot of companies need content writers, and I could help with the business while doing some writing on the side. It makes sense to me. Don't you think it's worth looking into?" He reached over and stroked my hair.

"If you're going to convince me, you'll have to do much more than stroke my hair." We snuck upstairs as quietly as we could and got in bed.

Over the next few months, our discussions continued. I came around to Phillip's arguments as he frequently reiterated the many reasons it made sense to move to Canada. He wanted the kids to continue attending a parochial school. Since they were free in Ontario, we wouldn't have to pay tuition. I also liked that the school they would attend was similar in size to the one they already were. For me, this factor weighed heavily on the positive side. However, nothing Phillip said weighed more heavily in influencing my decision than my concerns about the financial stability of the real estate market in the U.S.

One of my jobs then was working as a part-time mobile notary. This involved going to people's houses to witness borrowers signing second mortgage loan documents. I witnessed the homeowners sign forms on all the lines before sending them back to the lender. Washington Mutual, Citibank, and Chase were just a few of the banks I worked for under the auspices of firms that used notaries who belonged to The National Notary Association.

While working with this organization, I saw a pattern in the loan documents. The income-to-debt ratio of the individuals taking out second and even third mortgages didn't add up. These people didn't make enough income to secure the loans they were approved for by these large financial institutions. I'm no financial genius, but this concerned me long before subprime loans alarmed economists.

"Phillip, these banks are giving people money like candy. I swear some of these numbers make no sense. These people have little to no equity in their homes, yet they are taking out second mortgages for swimming pools and heated driveways." Phillip just scoffed at me, saying I was ridiculous.

What eventually convinced me wasn't about saving on health insurance or tuition. I realized if we put the remaining money we had from selling our house into a Canadian bank, it would be less risky. Canadian banks are far more regulated than banks in the U.S., and are more solvent. Years earlier, when the U.S. had suffered because of the Savings and Loan Crisis, Canadians didn't suffer the same fate. Besides the limited number of banks in their country, their financial institutions are more diversified. I thought having our money in a bank that didn't need to get bailed out might be good.

I also knew that the Canadian dollar was weak against the U.S. dollar. That meant we'd have more Canadian dollars to buy a property. I checked the currency exchange rate daily, and the more favorable the rates got, the more I agreed with Phillip about taking a trip to look at properties. I wanted to get our money out of Dodge because what we had left over from the sale of our house would go a lot further. The biggest bonus, however, was that Phillip agreed to sell the rental properties in Scranton.

One night when he remained home I suggested, "Let's take a trip to Alexandria." He was over the moon.

Alexandria reminded me of the part of New England where I grew up. No one seemed deterred from being outside, despite the unpredictable weather. The spring air was warm on the day we arrived, before turning bitter cold the next. Alexandria also had an unpretentious and inviting feel to it. The main thoroughfare was lined with small businesses, a bank, a gas station, a funeral parlor, and a grocery store. As we passed, someone honked their car horn in the parking lot of a Tim Horton's. A man with a container of coffee in his hand looked up and waved as he recognized a neighbor or perhaps a friend. A dog strolled down the street. It stopped at the schoolyard and glanced through the fence before greeting a small girl clad in a snowsuit. Kids of all ages carried hockey sticks and had ice skates hung over their shoulders. I could easily envision Lucy and Jack joining new friends and enjoying all the outdoor activities many New Englanders also experienced in their youth.

As we approached the building Phillip had zeroed in on, the same charming brick "heritage building" he'd shown me months earlier, my anticipation rose. I grew excited at the prospect of sitting at a table on the wrap-around porch, or finding the right flowering plants to adorn the small front yard. I imagined hanging ferns between the pillars, and pots of red geraniums lining the stairs.

Phillip pulled into the parking lot behind the building, and once he'd stopped, he reached over and squeezed my hand. He got out of the car and opened my door for me, something he hadn't done for ages. A current passed through us that expressed our joint excitement. We embarked on this journey together, and our need for a fresh start heightened our anticipation.

The Beans followed us to the front of the building, and we all climbed the steps to meet the owners in the area they once designated for a bookstore. We shook hands with owners Ron and Carmen, and after showing us the sizeable one-room bookstore, they offered to show us the other two apartments in the main building, and an additional two-bedroom apartment off the rear of the building.

Later in the afternoon, we checked into our hotel room. Phillip and I sat together on one of the beds, comparing thoughts about the property.

"We could see if the tenant in the front apartment would move into the apartment in the rear since it's vacant. That way, we could use her apartment for a business. It's a perfect location, being right on Main Street."

"I was thinking the same thing. The place has so many possibilities."

"We could use the upstairs bedroom for an office for the business. Ron said there was a door plastered over to connect all three first-floor rooms, so we'd have plenty of space once we decide what to do," Phillip told me.

"It'll take time, but if we're living over whatever business we have, it would be easier on the Beans because they could see us even when we were working."

"Eventually we could move to the rear apartment and even put a balcony off the building to have a view of the lake." Phillip wrapped his arms around me and kissed the top of my head.

"I suppose we should think about getting the Beans some dinner, but I hate to go out again. This is so nice," I said, settling into his shoulder.

"How about we order a pizza and see if they deliver?" he suggested.

I frowned.

"What's wrong," Phillip asked.

"You know that stuff like that always upsets your stomach," I chided.

"I brought some antacid. I'll deal with it. Let's call the front desk for a recommendation."

After our visit, we made an offer on the property. Every time the phone rang, we hoped the owners were calling with news that they accepted our offer. We waited weeks. When the call finally came, Phillip took me in his arms. I felt a sense of relief that we would be moving ahead with our plans but sadness at leaving the place I'd called home for so long.

"Let's wait until school is over before telling the Beans and the rest of our friends about our plans to move north," I whispered to him.

"We should wait to tell my parents, too," he added.

Despite our research on how to emigrate to Canada, the process wasn't as easy as we originally thought. We hired an attorney to help us navigate the paperwork.

At the time, we weren't sure exactly what type of business would suit the building, and didn't want to duplicate a more successful venture in such a small town. We crossed off the bowling alley and curling club right off the bat. There were already a few gift shops, a pet store, and plenty of restaurants.

Phillip pushed for the latter because I loved to make things from scratch and could spend hours making a meal. He would open a box, dump it in a pan, and call it a day. I told him the space wasn't suitable for a restaurant because the galley-style kitchen on the first floor barely had any counter space. The electric stove and refrigerator were in rough shape, and not the type of equipment found in any of the restaurants I'd worked in while waiting tables in college and beyond.

One day, as we worked on touching up the paint in the building's front, a woman named Gail, who owned a used bookstore down the road, approached us. Like everyone we'd met, she was friendly and warm and asked us many questions that we politely answered.

"Is it true you're opening a tearoom?" she asked.

Phillip and I exchanged a quizzical look, and before I could respond to her question, he said, "That's the plan for now."

"Well, that is just lovely!" she exclaimed. "I've always thought that a tearoom would do well in a town so rich with Scottish heritage!"

When she left, Phillip looked at me and laughed. "Well, that was interesting! So, this town needs a tearoom? I guess we have to figure out what it takes to open one."

"So just like that, we're opening a tearoom?" I asked him.

"Well, how hard can that be? Besides, you love tea, and I'm sure we can learn enough about it by doing some homework," he added.

"Well, I think we need to do more than a little homework," I told him, a bit dumbfounded at his response.

Thinking back, it seemed like buying the building and working to turn it into an income property was the last time our goals were aligned. We worked all summer to make the place suitable for the business. Everything fell into place once we transformed the bookstore into a tearoom. We adorned it with our best antiques from our former home. We hung our beautiful authentic gasoliers from the ceiling and covered the industrial-looking green wall-to-wall carpeting with our colorful oriental rugs. We left the bookshelves. They were a deep cranberry color and coordinated with the rugs, and they would give us a place to display items for sale, like teapots, coffee mugs, and other related giftware. We painted the walls a rich tan and placed plants and greenery around the room to give it a homey feel. I even scored six solid granite tables with wrought iron bases for eighty percent off at the local Giant Tiger. They made the room look more contemporary while blending with the surrounding antique tables and chairs.

By mid-August of 2007, we finalized some decisions about the business. I handled all the details, such as getting our vendor licenses and other necessary paperwork to make the business compliant with local and regional regulations. Everything seemed like it was coming together. For the first time since the birth of our twins, Phillip and I appeared entirely in sync again.

The apartment above the tearoom was small, but held our huge dreams. Enclosed within the walls were joint ambitions of starting over and having a business we could run as a family. When Phillip and I bought the property in Alexandria, we were happier than we'd been in a while. We were once again a "team," each bringing our unique set of skills to the table. We discussed things and made decisions together. Now, Phillip was willing to listen to my ideas and suggestions, something that had abruptly stopped once he gained control over our finances.

"What kind of food should we serve?" he asked as we approached the store's grand opening.

"It's got to be simple with such a compact kitchen. I think mostly homemade soups, salads, and sandwiches. We should also have plenty of desserts. I want to look into the cost of an espresso machine so we can serve cappuccino and lattes. Those will turn a tidy profit."

"Why don't we get everything from one of those food supply companies? Wouldn't that be easier?" Phillip asked earnestly.

"Phillip! The restaurant right across the street does that. Why would anyone come here if we're doing the same thing? They sell everything from pizza to Chinese food. I see the Sysco® truck delivering prepackaged foods several times a week. We can't compete with a restaurant that's been around for forty years unless we're not only better but different."

"Well, I still think it would be easier to get things pre-made, but whatever," he said.

We still disagreed over things that summer, but it seemed different. In the past my thoughts and suggestions were shoved aside. Nothing I said seemed to matter. With this new venture, Phillip and I had an equal say in everything. In our new life, I was once again a valued member of a team instead of being his sidekick.

"This paint looks fantastic. What a brilliant choice!" He complimented my selection, wrapping his arms around me as we admired our handiwork.

"It goes so well with the rugs, don't you think? I love the granite tables, too. They make it feel more like a café instead of someone's dining room. They're so practical!" In those moments, it seemed like nothing could tear us apart.

Without friends or family close by, Phillip became my sole companion again. He seemed to relish the added attention and not having to fight me over going out occasionally with my girlfriends. We were more intimate than we had been for years. We laughed more easily and enjoyed spending time together, and fell in love all over again. He was once again my best friend.

Knowing that our lives would get more complicated once the Beans started school, Phillip and I worked at a breakneck speed to get ready to open the 2Beans Café and Tearoom. Our lives changed drastically over the summer months as we embraced the challenges of moving to a new country and opening a business together. We drew upon our various skills to tackle each task, acting in concert. Everything seemed on course until late that summer.

"I created a sample catering menu," I told him when he came down from the office and into the café kitchen one day in late August. "I did some research, and most of the local companies offer some pretty basic stuff. I think I can win over some corporate clients with this menu."

Phillip said nothing, so I looked at him and saw he had an odd expression on his face.

"You will never believe who I just got off the phone with!" Phillip told me excitedly.

"Well, I hope it was our lawyer because we still haven't heard back from him," I teased.

"Marco called. He's opening a new company in New Jersey and offered me a job. Isn't that great?"

At that moment, even hearing his old boss's name startled me. It was as if our two worlds had collided, and part of the life we had put behind us seeped through to this new life we were working to create. Knowing Phillip's fondness for working with Marco colored my response.

"That's fantastic! Congrats, honey! He knows you'll have to work remotely, right?"

"Well, not exactly. He wants me to be in the office. I already told him I'd accept the position."

"What?" My jaw hit the floor. "Is he willing to pay for the costs of moving back?"

That's when Phillip told me that none of his former colleagues knew we'd moved to Canada. It was the whole secret marriage situation all over again. I realized Marco had no idea that Phillip had jumped at the opportunity to leave his wife and kids in a foreign country to take a job back in the States. This blew my mind.

"You told me that a restaurant could be a tremendous gamble. I'm nervous that if this doesn't work out, we'll have no income," he maintained. "We're spending a lot to get this going."

"Phillip, I told you that *before* we bought the property. You said we should do it. It was our chance to turn our lives around. We've invested our time and money into opening the business."

"We can still run the business. I can help develop marketing from anywhere, and I'll come home on weekends," he assured me.

My face began to crumble in disbelief at Phillip's assessment of the situation. I squeezed my eyes shut and turned my back, unable to look at him. Leaning against the kitchen counter, I studied the tile pattern, desperate to focus on anything but the words he'd just uttered. He came toward me and gently rubbed the back of my arm. I pulled away and turned to him, trying to find a thread of reason within him.

"So, I'm supposed to stay here, care for the kids, and run a new business on my own? Aren't you the same man who wanted to spend time with his family? Didn't you say you hated missing such a sizable chunk of the Beans' lives? How could you tell him 'yes' without discussing it with me? You get upset if I use the bathroom without telling you that's where I'm going." He stared past me. The pleas in my voice didn't seem to register. "The whole point of moving here was to be together as a family, Phillip. What is the point of doing this if we are not together?"

"I just don't think I should turn down this position. I'll make more than you can make here at the café, and I can still visit. Don't make me feel guilty for wanting to provide for my family, Kasey."

Tears stung my cheeks. I'd failed to reach him. I left the room because Phillip hated it when I cried. He claimed I tried to make him feel guilty whenever tears flowed, robbing me of my honest emotions when I was utterly distraught.

On the one hand, I, too, was afraid of relying solely on the income from a new business, especially a restaurant. I knew of the failure rate of new restaurants. But the whole point of starting over was to reinvent our lives.

When I got myself together, I told him, "This is insane, Phillip. The cost of maintaining two separate residences will eat into whatever you're making. We haven't opened yet. The kids haven't even started school. Why don't we rent this place and all move back together?" He wouldn't hear of it.

The day before Phillip left to resume his life back in the States, he said something that, over time, bothered me more and more. The Beans sat at a table in our newly decorated tearoom, eating dessert. While I brought the dirty dishes into the kitchen, Phillip followed me and grabbed me from behind. I spun around so he could hold me. I was utterly despondent over his leaving.

"I'll miss you, you know," he whispered, holding me close.

"Me, too," I said, trying to keep my emotions in check.

"If Marco's company takes off, I'll let you and the Beans move back to the States, I promise," he assured me.

"Why can't we come back now? We still have plenty of money in the bank. I don't want to do this all alone."

"Look, that's not a smart thing to do. This is a new venture, and who knows if it will take off. If it doesn't, we'll be in the same boat without the money to start over again." Then, with little emotion, he added, "Promise me one thing? Don't start making friends here because we need this business to fly, and I know you, you'll end up blowing it because you'll spend time with your new pals."

Caught up in thoughts of him leaving, I never processed what he'd said. Instead, I just nodded and told him, "Sure."

The next day, he called me from his hotel room and said he'd begun looking for apartments around Blairstown instead of one in Morristown, close to where he would be working.

"But, Phillip, didn't you say you hated the commute? Wasn't that a big reason for moving to Canada?"

"The apartments in Morristown are too expensive," he told me.

He ignored me when I pointed out that the money he spent on gas and the wear and tear on the car negated any savings he might have had by taking an apartment right back where we had just moved from months earlier.

These memories were unsettling. As I sat there on Phillip's couch in Cobleskill three years after the move to Alexandria, with my cafe closed and my Canadian friends left behind, not only did my future appear uncertain, but my past did as well. The time and energy I had poured into my life there felt pointless. I knew that we were never that "perfect" couple. No family is ever what they seem to be on the outside. But now, I questioned the most basic assumptions of our relationship. Were we ever really working together to create a fresh start? Perhaps the move to Canada was part of some plan he had developed so he could lead a double life? He'd introduced the idea of moving north. I accepted everything he told me at face value. The goal was to work together and build a family business. I envisioned us working side-by-side and watching the Beans grow into adulthood. I thought we shared this vision.

On one hand, I was grateful for my time in Alexandria. My time there enabled me to rediscover parts of myself that had been erased ever so slowly. The erosion of my self-esteem happened so gradually; I didn't even realize it had happened until he could no longer scrutinize my every move. Owning and operating the café became an integral part of my healing.

The overarching message from Phillip back then was that I was a deeply flawed person, but he tolerated and even loved me despite my failings. I internalized his perception of me. But while in Alexandria, I finally realized how deeply insecure I'd become.

I couldn't remain married to someone who inspired so much mental and emotional anguish. Phillip seemed to delight in sucking the life out of me. Based on all that had happened recently, I knew I had to figure out a way to leave the marriage and, if possible, return home to Alexandria.

PART 2

Our New Reality

"Do not just slay your demons.
Dissect them and find out
what they've been feeding on."

~ The Man Frozen in Time

CHAPTER EIGHT

Our Lost Boy

September 1st Cobleskill, New York

My brief time in Cobleskill turned upside down within hours of arriving. Before going to Vermont to get the Beans, I checked my email. Jenny had sent an urgent message asking me to call her right away. I used the last of the airtime I had available on my Canadian data plan and called her, only to learn that Chubby was missing. He had gotten loose when Jody took him out for a quick pee before heading into the house the night before. Chub tried to follow me and strained on his harness so hard it broke. He took off into the night and into the woods and fields surrounding her property. I'd traveled miles away by then. After talking with Jenny, I immediately called my brother Jake.

"What's wrong?" Jake asked me when I called. I could hardly speak; I was so upset.

"It's Chubby!" I told him haltingly. "He got away from Jody and is missing," I sobbed, recounting the events for him.

"I didn't even have his tags on," I told him. "What am I going to tell the kids?"

"Calm down. Where are you now?"

"I'm in Cobleskill. I left Jody's late last night. She couldn't reach me because I turned off my cellphone so I wouldn't get roaming charges. My friend Jenny sent me an email because Jody called her to see if she could contact me. It happened just after I left. They've all been looking for him, and there's no sign of him anywhere. Poor Jody is beside herself."

"The kids can stay with us longer if you need them to. Just let us know what your plans are. I won't say anything just yet," Jake said and hung up.

Two other farms bordered Jody's property, and hundreds of acres of corn surrounded her house. To the rear were miles of dense woods filled with predators that would love a tiny dog as a snack. Now, my kids not only had to contend with leaving their friends and school behind, but they would also have to cope with a lost dog. It seemed like a terrible omen.

"Please don't blame yourself!" I told Jody. "I'm the one that forgot to put on his collar after I bathed him!" I told her through tears. "I'll call you in a bit when we figure out the game plan, and you'll be the first to know, okay?"

The original plan for the Labor Day weekend was to have the Beans spend the weekend with Phillip while I traveled to Alexandria one more time to fetch more of our belongings. But I'd revised my plans several times, and with Chubby missing, I wanted to return to Alexandria to find him as soon as possible. I called Phillip at work to tell him the news. He responded with kindness and concern, as he should have.

All the travel, packing, and unpacking left me frizzled. I needed some time to get more sleep, but I couldn't stop thinking about our sweet dog. My imagination was working overtime.

Chubby was the Beans' tenth birthday present from Phillip and me. We'd looked at Labrador and Retriever puppies since Lucy had always wanted that. It seemed wrong to buy a full-bred puppy when so many other dogs needed rescuing, so I started looking into area animal shelters. I was also concerned about having a gigantic dog in our tiny apartment above the tearoom.

One day, Glen, who owned the antique shop next door to the café, came by for his usual cup of Earl Grey tea. His wife, Loretta, bred small dogs as a side business. They had ten dogs of various tiny mixed breeds. Whenever I took the twins to play with their two boys, one dog stood out. His name was Chubby Checkers, and he was a Bichon-Lhasa mix. He weighed about ten pounds, and his sweet, funny personality won us over. Glenn mentioned that Loretta planned to sell him because he was "too big" to breed with her other dogs. I called and asked her to stop by the next time she was at Glenn's, and she came by later that afternoon.

"So, how much do you want for Chubby?" I asked while serving her a cup of tea and a slice of lemon pound cake. Loretta was smart and sassy, and Glenn's perfect foil. I related to her because she held everything together so Glenn could open his antique business while she traveled to work each day. "I'm looking for two hundred," she told me. I gulped. I wasn't sure if this was a fair price, but I didn't have that kind of money available regardless.

She got up from the table and looked around at the various items I had for sale on the shelves. Along with an assortment of coffee—and tea—related items, I also had some handcrafted items, paintings, and jewelry, all crafted by local artists. I had made most of the jewelry when I lived in the States. There were beaded bracelets, necklaces, and earrings on display.

"How about we barter?" Loretta asked.

"Sure!" I agreed. "What are you interested in?" I'd priced the earrings at ten dollars a pair. She selected twenty pairs, turned to me, and said, "Sold!" That's how I paid for Chubby.

Jack and Lucy loved him. So did Phillip and I. Loretta had trained him, and he was so well-behaved. He immediately became an integral part of our family and went everywhere with us. I especially loved bringing him to Jenny's, where he could be off his leash and run with Lacy. The two bound down the mowed part of her back lawn at incredible speeds, with Lacy outpacing Chubby and his short legs. A quick shout or whistle, and they would reappear, begging for a treat or to get a drink of water.

My heart became heavy just thinking about what might happen to our puppy-boy. I knew I would have to do everything I could to find him, and that meant alerting everyone I knew in Canada to enlist their help in our search for him. I emailed all my friends and customers on the café email list and asked if they could look out for our Chubby. My friends and former customers responded, offering their efforts to assist us.

That day, Phillip offered to meet Jake halfway between his home in Vermont and our new apartment in Cobleskill so we could get the twins before heading back to Canada the next day.

The twins and I went up on Thursday with the van, and Phillip came up on Friday after work. We had agreed that the kids and I would pack more of our belongings in our Dodge Caravan, and Phillip would take the van back to Cobleskill and unpack it when he arrived at our apartment. He would leave me with the Elantra so Lucy, Jack, and I could spend time looking for our lost pup over the weekend. In the meantime, we made flyers to post when we arrived. Chubby had now been missing for a day. I didn't want to think about what he was doing to survive.

When we were about ten miles from Alexandria, I pulled over to give a flyer to a woman walking her dog.

"Excuse me. We're looking for our dog, who's missing. Could I give you a flyer?" I asked her.

"Are you searching for Chubby?" she asked.

"Yes!" I replied eagerly.

"My friend Natalie called me, and I'll keep an eye out for him," she said with a smile.

The same thing occurred when I stopped to speak to another two people we saw. They all were searching for him already. My friends, colleagues, and the whole community seemed to be there to help find our pup. It moved me tremendously.

One of Jack's close friends came over to keep the kids company while I searched for Chubby. When I returned to the building later that day, I saw a tiny gray kitten in the parking lot. It had startling green eyes and couldn't have been over six weeks old. I'd seen many cats dodging cars along the main street of Alexandria. I was determined the same fate wouldn't happen to this little thing.

I brought the kitten to the kids playing upstairs in the office. The feisty kitten was an instant hit and kept them amused for the remainder of the day. When we left, I thought I could bring the kitten to Carole since she fed several strays. It was better than being up against the traffic on Main Street.

When Phillip arrived, he helped us search for a few hours, but he believed our search was useless, so we went back and continued packing.

"What are you going to do with that cat?" he asked as I carried a heavy box to the van.

"I don't know; I haven't thought about it," I replied in my distraction.

"That's so typical. You never think ahead about anything," he scolded me.

He was livid. I was beyond caring. I shoved the box inside the van and stormed off to avoid yet another fight. We barely spoke for the rest of the day. It was as though I'd run to an animal shelter and grabbed a kitten to annoy him.

Call after call came in from people asking if I'd found Chubby. Each time the phone rang, I jumped to grab the phone. The Beans looked on anxiously while I spoke to whoever had called hoping they'd found our Chubby.

The disaster underscored what I was losing in the community of people who embraced me enough to look for our dog. The emails I got, the calls I received, and the help from strangers touched me deeply. Throughout my life, I'd longed for this sense of belonging. And now I was leaving it all behind.

When Phillip left to return to Cobleskill, I could breathe again. Lucy, Jack, and I were again free to roam the back roads searching for our dog. We hunted for hours, but no one had seen him. Jody and her neighbor helped us explore the property around her house. But Chubby was still missing.

When the weekend ended, we returned to Cobleskill so the Beans could start seventh grade. We were all crushed that our little guy with curly white fur wasn't with us. But I made sure one little gray kitten was coming along.

CHAPTER NINE

Switching Gears

I pulled into the parking lot at Sacred Heart Academy early on Tuesday with the Beans sulking in the back. The small Catholic school looked more like a modern church than a place for education. They shuffled across the driveway and up the stairs to the school's office. Jack held the door for Lucy and me. I knew he wasn't being polite. He didn't want to be the first to go in. I put on a fake smile as I approached the principal's office.

I delivered the twins, like the sacrificial lambs they were, to Tammy MacKay, a small woman with an engaging smile. She exuded warmth, but the kids weren't having it. They stood like statues in the school office, waiting to be told where to go next.

The office secretary took Lucy and Jack to their class while I spoke with Tammy. She understood the fragility of the kids' emotions, especially having just lost their dog, who had been missing for almost a week. She expressed how happy they were at the small, family-oriented school.

The place had a different feel from other Catholic schools I'd visited. Sacred Heart had more of an unpretentious feel than the previous school my children attended. While there were religious symbols throughout, the building wasn't filled with children lined up in antiquated hallways with stifled smiles and restricted curiosity. The building was modern and less formal because the students didn't wear identical uniforms.

I spoke to Tammy about volunteering at the school since I wasn't employed yet, and she informed me they needed help serving lunches each day. I knew this opportunity could help me get to know others and develop a support network immediately. When I told her my background, Tammy also asked if I would be interested in teaching a film class in exchange for tuition. I jumped at the chance to further connect with members of the school community.

My next mission was to get a phone. It pissed me off that no one could contact me in the States when Chubby first got lost. Phillip had refused to install a landline at the apartment. He wanted to isolate me again from my friends and family, and I vowed I wasn't going to let it happen anymore.

I dug through every crevice I could in the apartment and van until I had about fifty dollars in quarters, nickels, and dimes. I left the pennies at home and hid them for an emergency. With that, I walked into a local credit union.

"I'd like to open an account," I told the clerk.

"Someone can help you with that in a minute. Have a seat." I felt like I'd asked them to be my co-conspirators in a crime because I had already anticipated a negative reaction from Phillip. I held the bag of change close, embarrassed that my life had come to this.

"May I help you?" a woman in a bright red pantsuit asked, approaching me.

"I hope so. I've recently moved here and don't have a lot of available cash. I want to open a bank account with the change I have here and a check from my business account in Canada. Is that possible?"

"Yes. Are you a U.S. citizen?"

"Yes."

"The check might take some time to clear, but the change can be deposited and withdrawn immediately," she assured me.

Once the check cleared, I would have about one hundred dollars in the account, give or take a bit, because of the exchange rate. But, more importantly, I would have enough money from all the change I'd collected to buy a computer device called a "magicJack®," which allows a user to receive or make calls on a computer with an internet connection. I walked over to the Radio Shack in the same plaza.

"Hi, there. Do you have something called a magicJack®?"

"Sure do."

"And I can use it to make phone calls through my computer?"

"You sure can."

"How much?"

When my older brother Will mentioned he used this device to make long-distance calls, I wrote the name down, thinking that, at some point, it could come in handy. Though part of the appeal was that calls to Canada wouldn't cost me a dime, the most important issue was that Phillip couldn't thwart my efforts to stay in touch with my friends up north, especially while they searched for Chubby.

I returned home and set up the device, then emailed Jenny the new number. I opted to unpack and do a little housework before heading to the school to help serve lunches. I was about to leave for school when I rechecked my computer. I received an email from Jenny telling me to call. My hands were shaking as I tried dialing her phone number.

"Your boy is back!" she told me.

"What? Where was he?" I asked Jenny when she told me her news.

"He just strolled up to Jody's neighbor's porch. He's messy and thinner, but otherwise, he seems ok!" I was overwhelmed with joy.

When I arrived at the school, I went to the office and asked Tammy if she would let the Beans know that Chubby had been found. She agreed, and before I left the room, she asked me if I would cater a dinner for a fundraiser the following week. I told her I would without a moment's hesitation.

Chubby's return erased the horrible day the Beans had navigating their new school. We were all in good spirits.

"I think we should celebrate!" I told them. I pulled a bottle of ginger ale from the fridge and put it in two water glasses. I poured some club soda for myself, and we raised our glasses.

"Here's to Chubby!" They laughed as we clinked our glasses through happy tears.

I emailed Phillip. That was how we communicated these days.

Chubby has been found. He is at Jody's, and I am going to get him Friday, as soon as the kids get out of school. He seems to be fine, but needs grooming. Tonight, there is a meeting at Sacred Heart I would like to attend, as some of the meeting concerns the fundraiser I agreed to cater next week. If you get this email, please let me know what time you are planning to get home. If I know the kids are going to only be alone for a short time, I will leave them here. The meeting should be less than an hour.

I relished the thought of him reading this email. I'd only been in town for a few days and had already made connections. His email expressed that he was happy they had found Chubby but offered no clue about his feelings regarding the catering job.

After the meeting at school, I called Jenny through the computer to let her know I'd be heading to Canada Friday afternoon. I heard Phillip come in, so I ended my conversation.

"Who were you talking to?" he asked.

"Jenny. I told her the kids and I would fetch Chubby tomorrow. She offered to let us stay with her."

"I thought you couldn't call Canada on your cell?"

"I can, but it eats up my minutes in roaming charges. I ran out of airtime calling Jody, anyway. Besides, I wasn't using my cell. I bought a device for my computer. It's called a magicJack. It works over the Internet."

He went ballistic. Phillip's face turned red, and he left the room. I thought he'd gone to Jack's room to sulk, but moments later, he came back and screamed at me.

"Where did you get the money for that?"

"I used some change."

"What change?"

"It was just loose change I found."

"My change? You're a thief, Kasey!"

"What are you talking about? That's not stealing. I used my loose change and more that I found around the apartment. Most of it was mine, and I had every right to use it."

That wasn't exactly true. I used the change I found in the van, the closet, the mudroom, and other places. But his response indicated that he believed it all belonged to him.

"You're such a liar, Kasey. Just wait."

He stormed off and shut himself in Jack's room. The twins sat on the couch and looked at me when I passed them and pounded on the bedroom door. I wanted to scream at him, but when I saw the look on their faces, I stopped. My need to express my anger wasn't worth putting them through this.

I started dinner in a rage. With very little food in the fridge, I made pancakes for dinner. The only spice on hand was some cinnamon. I added some to the batter. The heat from the burner rose up through the skillet, and bubbles began to form within the uncooked side of the mix. I watched them as they took form, determined to focus on the task rather than Phillip's latest outburst. I flipped them when golden brown, removed them from the pan, and placed them on a cookie sheet in the oven to stay warm. I made an enormous platter so the kids would have something for breakfast, too.

"Dinner is ready," I hollered. Jack and Lucy timidly came into the kitchen and sat down to eat. I was no longer hungry, but the glances they exchanged with one another made me reluctant to leave them alone, so I took a seat at the table.

Phillip entered the kitchen, grabbed a plate, and helped himself to the pancakes, spreading butter and pancake syrup on each. He casually asked Jack and Lucy about their day. They mumbled something about hating the math teacher. I left the room so I wouldn't hit him on the head with the frying pan.

The antique Victorian bed Phillip and I once shared was in the bedroom on the second floor, and I began sleeping there instead of on the uncomfortable couch. Phillip continued to sleep in the room designated as "Jack's room." This indicated he wasn't interested in rekindling any aspects of our relationship. That relieved me, but it also convinced me even more that he was aiming for a divorce because he was having an affair.

When we set up the apartment, we put a twin bed for Lucy in the small alcove between the kitchen and back hallway. However, both kids came upstairs each night and slept in "my" room. So I placed a twin mattress on the floor for Jack, and Lucy slept with me.

Phillip complained about this, too, but didn't seem willing to change the arrangements. I should have asked him why he thought Jack would be comfortable kicking his father out of his room at bedtime? I discovered he'd even mentioned the situation to Rachel.

Per usual, he wrote her, *Kasey is doing whatever the hell she wants to. She even has the kids sleeping upstairs with her.*

He never mentioned that he camped out in Jack's room each night with the door closed. But that was how he presented it to her, and this arrangement suited me just fine.

After dinner, Lucy, Jack, and I went upstairs and began reading a book called *The Absolutely True Diary of a Part-Time Indian* by Sherman Alexie. It was absolutely what we needed to distract us from the emotional upheaval we all experienced that day. The sorrowful nature of Alexie's protagonist, Junior, and all his troubles made us forget our worries. We laughed and were entertained by this young man determined to attend *the white school* some thirty miles from the reservation where he lived. Junior wanted the same opportunities for a good education that others take for granted. He walked or hitchhiked to school daily from his home on the Spokane Indian Reservation. Despite all the trauma he experienced, the story had us in fits of laughter. It took our minds off of the world around us.

I heard a creaking noise on the stairs as I read to them. Phillip came up to join us. He made Lucy move over and sat on the bed between the Beans. I continued to read but held onto my anger over his ridiculous outburst about buying the magicJack.

He told them to get dressed for bed when it was close to their bedtime. He said he needed to "talk with Mommy."

I held my breath. "Have you started applying for a real job?" he asked me.

"Are you talking about doing some catering for the school? That is a real job," I retorted.

"No. I mean the film class you offered to teach," he responded.

"Teaching that class will help us financially because we don't have to pay tuition. If it doesn't work out, I'll let it go after a semester."

He rolled his eyes. "Why can't you apply at Walmart? I'm sure they're hiring."

That was Phillip's solution to everything. I'd make more money in one evening as a caterer than in a week at Walmart. It seemed like he wanted me to find work that paid minimum wage so I could contribute to the household income without the ability to do anything more.

"I'm doing this, Phillip. You might not understand about networking, but I do. Most of the women I'm working with have lived in this area all their lives. They'll know who is hiring and about any possible catering jobs or any other jobs that pay better than minimum wage. If I end up quitting Sacred Heart, so be it. But, for now, I'm going to teach this class." He left, saying nothing more while I continued to stew.

I checked my email before leaving for Canada the next day to pick up Chubby.

He wrote, "What is the phone number you got with the magicJack?"

Suddenly, he saw the value of the device and wanted to use it, too.

Chapter Ten

Chubby Returns

When we returned to Cobleskill with Chubby, the Beans were happier, but not by much. They didn't like the school at all, and they were having a hard time adjusting. I tried talking with their teachers to see how they were in class, and everyone said the same thing: They sat quietly and didn't take part unless the teacher called upon them.

Their unhappiness added to the dismal atmosphere at home, and the next few weeks were fraught with more tension. Phillip insisted I was using the Sacred Heart catering job as an excuse to avoid *working*. Catering was not *work* for him. Nothing I did was *work*. Teaching wasn't *work*. Running the café wasn't *work*. Had any job I'd held in our twenty-four years of marriage amounted to *work* to him?

Without a job, Phillip insisted I get his approval before spending any money. When I suggested it would make finding a job easier if we had a phone, he told me that we couldn't afford to get a phone unless I could pay for the service. I had more problems with my laptop because the port to plug in the AC adapter was getting worse. The pin was loose and rarely allowed me to charge the computer. I could only make calls or use the computer when it was charged, which became less and less frequent. I had no way of knowing where all the money was going. He must have kept the checkbook and any records with him, because I couldn't find them, regardless of where I looked.

It kept me imagining the worst. If our new monthly rent was half what he had paid for his studio, where was that extra money? He often came home, leading me to speculate even more. Did he keep the place in Albany so he could use it to have an affair? I searched for clues but couldn't find a scintilla of concrete evidence. Still, it made no sense to me that there was no money left in the budget for a telephone, when the most basic service was less than $15 a month without long-distance service.

One night when I asked again about getting a phone, he told me, "It's too expensive." Then he asked, "Why can't you use that gadget you bought with my money?"

"I've tried that, but it only works when my computer is charged. I've explained to you I'm having issues with it charging. And please don't suggest I use my Canadian cellphone because I've run out of airtime. If you want me to find work, what phone number do I put on the application, Phillip? I have to beg you for money to pay for gas, and the instrument panel on the van is still faulty, so I never know how much gas there is in the fuel tank. But, somehow, I'm supposed to get a job without a working computer, phone line, or vehicle."

"We're not getting a phone, Kasey, so forget it," he said, leaving the room.

There were times I bit my tongue so hard I thought it would bleed.

All further attempts to reason with him failed. The impact of not being able to receive calls to find work or use a computer weren't actually obstacles to him. He insisted my resistance to finding a job was the problem. Anything I countered with was an excuse.

One day, Jack stayed home from school sick. I was conflicted about going out, knowing he'd have no way to be in touch with either Phillip or me while I was gone. I carefully worded an email:

Phillip-
I would like to order phone service here today. I believe this is a basic need; it is not good to be without a landline. I cannot rely on the magicJack because of the computer problems I constantly face, and I now have to either choose between leaving Jack by himself without emergency communication, as he is not in school, or go off and do the things I had hoped to accomplish regarding work, etc.

Please respond to this as the installation will take time and I want to start the process.

~ Kasey

He responded tersely;

I am swamped with work, so I do not have time to fully address the 'logic' or what is insinuated in this email - 'I now have to either choose between leaving Jack by himself without emergency communication.'

If you are truly concerned about our children's safety, concentrate on getting a job that helps to pay for these "basic needs" and not spending time on opening another food business. Short answer...Do not order anything in my name that I will bear the responsibility for paying unless I am fully agreed to it. You purchased the magicJack with money "you found" without any input from me. Once again, I was told after the fact. Send me the information for a landline with a phone number that I can call so I can verify costs, etc. We are not generating enough money to cover our basic monthly expenses. It's no fun being poor, but that's the reality of our situation.

BTW...Have you put together your list of discussion items for our mediators yet?

As I have mentioned before, regarding your computer, call Computer Solutions using the magicJack. Tell them (using these words) 'the power input on my laptop is loose and needs to be re-soldered. It only works when I hold the plug in a certain position. Could you give me an approximate estimate as to what this costs to fix?

After reading his email, my contempt for him had reached a new level.

Not long after he moved back to the States, Phillip suggested that we might need help resolving our marital issues. He didn't mean professional help, however. He planned to present our grievances to a friend or family member so they could judge who was *at fault* for the deteriorating situation. He determined I couldn't request one of my Canadian or Blairstown friends as a mediator while he could choose whomever he wanted.

Resisting this request while I was in Canada was easy because the distance made his suggestion unworkable. But now that we were both in the States, he returned to this idea to solve the problems within our marriage.

Knowing what he wrote in emails to his sister about what I supposedly did or didn't do left me in a precarious situation. I could use this knowledge to my advantage and prove he was lying. However, being too prepared might tip my hand and raise questions about my knowledge of positions he didn't raise in his "list of grievances." For Phillip, all our problems stemmed from my not having a job, the number of pets we now had, and Jack and Lucy sleeping upstairs in my room. I'd been in Cobleskill for a little more than a week, but he told Rachel that this was to blame for all the mayhem in our relationship.

Another thing that bothered me was agreeing to a meeting with any third party. I knew I'd be terrible under pressure. Phillip knew this, too. I could not present my side of the issue calmly and coherently. No matter how well I prepared, I knew I would get defensive and blow it. I didn't know if I could hold it all together when confronted with all the pent-up anger and frustration I carried around daily.

"Jen, you know me!" I complained when she called later that day. "I'll break down in tears, yell, or act like an idiot if we discuss this with someone. He will sit there calmly and present his side of the situation with relish. Don't you think that's why he's pushed this for months?"

"Well, I don't think it's about healing the relationship. Sounds to me like he's trying to prove his points. Don't tip your hand and let him know you know he's been lying. You need to keep that information to yourself just in case you end up in court," she warned me.

I responded to Phillip's email when I got off the phone with Jenny.

Phillip-

You can read anything you want in my email. It would not matter how I put it; it is never correctly worded for you. I am concerned about getting work and feel conflicted about leaving Jack at home. But, for some reason, this statement makes you think I am making a statement about you. Well, I'm not. It's a fact. It is also very frustrating trying to find work, making phone calls when people can't hear you. YOU TRY IT.

I am concentrating on getting a job plus making the type of income that could provide enough for all of us if you are out of work again, as you have told me you might be. I will not be put in a situation where I have no prospects for meaningful employment. While I am willing to take just about anything, I will not be put in a situation where, because I make less than you do, you feel you can dictate everything to me. Once again, I am put on the defensive about everything. I am trying to find work with record unemployment, here less than two weeks and back and forth on the weekends to Canada, have no working phone, a computer that constantly craps out, but I am not trying hard enough to find a job. Once again, Phillip, it is stuff like this that makes me wonder why I bother. You get mad at me because you think I have insinuated something in an email, but I am not supposed to respond to blatant put-downs?

IF YOU ARE TRULY CONCERNED ABOUT THE CHILDREN...." HOW DARE YOU!

I used change to purchase the magicJack that I brought to the bank. This is exactly the type of situation that I cannot tolerate. I didn't have a phone for emergencies, no cell phone that works locally, and we had a lost dog in Canada that people were trying to communicate with me about. But you can't begin to comprehend the impact this has, not having a phone, because, well, it wasn't you. The difference between you and me, Phillip, is, I want you to take care of yourself and do what you think needs to be done. You are more concerned about a jar of change and the way I spent it rather than my having a basic necessity.

BTW- No. I have not put a list together for our "mediators." I would like to address issues that are important to me without being accused of insinuating things, just like you have here. I want to address the issues that matter TO ME. How do you expect me to detail things that are matters of the heart, that outline the conflicts I have with our relationship, when I can't be assured an email about getting a phone installed isn't going to be blown up? So, no, Phillip. I haven't.

I went to a computer place on Monday. They don't do this repair. They said it doesn't last, and people get angry, so they stopped doing it. Ask the kids. They were with me. They referred me to a place in New Hartford and said I was looking at about $300. If you doubt this, call yourself, and verify.

I provided him with the phone number and address of the computer store and pushed the send button. From that point on, I began to make plans to leave him. I also called Verizon and ordered a telephone.

Chapter Eleven

The Importance of Networking

My instincts about finding a network of women through Sacred Heart turned out to be a godsend. Within weeks, I discovered more about the area and what options were available regarding possible work opportunities. I even made a friend named Maryanne. She, too, helped with the school lunches each day.

Even though she was having personal difficulties, Maryanne took the time to reach out to me and helped me in ways that made my upheaval bearable. Her granddaughter Meg also attended Sacred Heart. Although she was retired, she worked hard at whatever she did. She'd owned a bed-and-breakfast in Idaho for years and, somehow, ended up living in St. Johnsville, New York, a good forty-five-minute drive from Sacred Heart. I'll never know why she took to me, but I appreciated that she did.

One day, after lunch was over and everything was clean and put away, we went out to get coffee. We both loved to cook, and food was our most immediate connection. But soon, she spilled her guts about life's difficulties, and I spilled mine. Maryanne was planning on moving down to the Cornell area of New York to live with her daughter, Mary Jane, and granddaughter instead of trying to raise Meg on her own. All the traveling to and from St. Johnsville wreaked havoc on her aging body.

The expenses of maintaining two separate households impacted her ability to make ends meet. I understood completely. Maryanne had placed her home on the market, and as soon as it sold, she and Meg would be moving to Cornell.

My new friendship with her reminded me of something I hadn't thought of in quite a while. It had to do with the first real friend I had in

Alexandria, a woman named Diane. She, too, had come to my rescue when Phillip took the job with Marco three years earlier.

Diane arrived at my doorstep one day, completely unannounced. It was the day before the Beans were to start fourth grade. I noticed Lucy had small, inflamed, red welts on her back, and she said she wasn't feeling well. I soon discovered the same red bumps on Jack; they both had low-grade fevers.

I called Phillip in a panic. "Honey, call me when you get this message! I think the kids have chickenpox!"

I didn't have a pediatrician or a family doctor to consult. I had nothing to ease their fevers or a way to relieve the itching. I didn't want to leave them alone, and they were too miserable to come with me if I went to the store. Phillip was now living five hours away. When he finally returned my call, he doubted my assessment of the situation and seemed annoyed with me.

"I'm sure that's not the case. When would they have been exposed to someone with chickenpox?" he questioned.

"Well, how do you explain the fever and the itchy, pus-filled blistering rash all over their bodies?" I asked him impatiently. "Besides, there's an incubation period of several weeks."

I got off the phone, furious with him. I realized he had just started a new job, and my call came late at night. But as tired as he was, he was never the one to deal with their colds, bumps, and bruises. Alone and frightened, I didn't know how to soothe them. I hung up the phone that night in utter misery.

Early the following day, I heard a knock on the door downstairs. I opened the door to see a tall, beautiful woman standing before me.

"Can I help you?" I asked her.

"Are you Kasey?" the woman asked in a southern drawl.

"Yeah...," I responded incredulously.

Diana explained that while speaking to someone in Alexandria, and they mentioned that "an American couple" was opening a restaurant. She was there to see if I needed any help. I might have cried; I was so relieved to see her. After explaining that the Beans had chickenpox, she went off to the pharmacy, getting Tylenol and whatever sundries were needed.

Diana was from Georgia. Before they moved to Montreal, her husband's hometown, Diana and hubby, George, were doing quite well financially. Diana worked as a professional decorator, and George as a contractor. The two took advantage of the booming real estate market in the suburbs outside of Atlanta, buying properties to flip and turning a profit, or holding onto them for rental income. When the real estate market started going downhill, they were left with properties they couldn't sell or rent. It ultimately destroyed their finances. They moved to Quebec for the same reasons Phillip and I moved: they needed to start over.

This made it complicated for their son, who was then in his senior year of high school. To graduate in the province of Quebec, he needed to be proficient in French. He didn't even have a basic knowledge of the language. To solve the issue, Diane rented a house in the province of Ontario. That way, her son could be enrolled in the local school for his senior year, where the French language requirements weren't as stringent. She barely occupied the property, having it only to comply with residency status when paperwork was to be submitted for school. Most days, she drove her son and daughter to school round trip to their actual home in Montreal, over an hour away. With nothing to do while they were in school each day, it thrilled her to learn about "another American" in town and she wanted to meet me.

From that day on, she came to the café to help with the remaining renovations and decorating. We worked with another local woman named Crystal to finalize the menu and develop food ideas that would appeal to the local clientele. With Phillip gone, I hired a friend of Crystal's to assist with completing the kitchen renovation while Diana and I put the finishing touches on the tearoom.

Initially, I hired Crystal to be in the kitchen, and Diana agreed to wait on tables. I floated between the kitchen and tearoom, covered takeout orders, and did whatever was needed. The arrangement worked for a while because Crystal was an excellent cook and a fabulous baker. But she kept forgetting who owned the business.

"I think you're going to have a hard time selling a bowl of soup for five dollars," Crystal told me.

"That's because you've never tasted my soup," I assured her.

When we finally opened in early December, I greeted our new customers while Diana waited on tables, laying on the good old-fashioned Southern charm. I knew that fantastic food was only one challenge of a successful restaurant. Crystal and I covered that, while Diana's stunning looks and charisma provided the other part. Soon, we had a waitlist for lunch each day.

A few months after we opened, I heard through Glenn from the antique shop next door that rumors were going around town about the owners of the new café. Apparently, because Phillip was never around, people assumed Diana was one of the owners, and because I referred to her as my "partner," people thought Diana and I were a couple. There happened to be another coincidence adding to the confusion. One of my customers told me that, in Gaelic, the word "beans" roughly translated into "wives." I didn't know whether it was true, but maybe the "two beans" predisposed people to think there was another meaning behind the name of the café.

When Phillip came north, he enjoyed teasing Diana about being his other wife. He even seemed to enjoy the way it made me uncomfortable. Diana was gorgeous, and I was no longer the slim, attractive woman he married. I thought my discomfort hinged on a tad of jealousy. But I realized now what made me so uncomfortable about how flirtatious Phillip was with Diane and that, years earlier, he begged me to take part in a threesome.

Like many couples, our sex life became predictable after our kids were born. When we managed to have time alone, Phillip frequently asked me to talk dirty to him, and I discovered it was a fun way to spice up our intimacy. It seemed harmless, and Phillip got extremely excited when I did, especially when I created scenarios that involved multiple partners. This worked for a while, but then Phillip suggested we take our intimate moments to another level and wanted to make his fantasy of having a threesome become a reality. "What do you say, we put an ad in the paper? Scranton's far enough away, and we don't know anyone there. We could fix up one of our empty apartments there," he asked me casually one night in bed.

"You can fantasize all you want, Phillip, but that will never happen, so drop it."

He rolled over after accusing me of leading him on. Moments later, he turned back, expressing his full anger.

"You've talked about your fantasies for years, Kasey."

"That's the whole point, Phillip. They're fantasies. Nothing more." But watching the way he looked at Diana made me terribly uncomfortable. Fear crept in, thinking he might have pursued his desire to engage in sex with multiple partners without me when he stayed by himself in Scranton.

Diana left after her son graduated, as she no longer needed to come to Alexandria. Then Crystal and I had a falling out over a blueberry pie. By the time Sharilyn and Kate came on board, the influx of personnel had stopped, and I had the ideal situation of working with two women I loved and admired. So, even though Diana was sorely missed until recently, I never thought much about that uncomfortable feeling I had back then.

Talking with Maryanne, however, brought up those memories. It reinforced my belief that Phillip was cheating on me and may have been for a long time. Maryanne suggested I should do more to uncover the truth.

I thought about what Maryanne said, and two things became apparent. I had frequently ignored any signs that Phillip could be having an affair. His reaction to Diana was uncomfortable, but I never doubted he would remain faithful back then. But for much of our marriage, he had the perfect set-up to "swing" all he wanted, since I was miles away. If he was planning to divorce me, I wanted to continue to look for evidence of his affair or affairs. If he tried to gain custody of the Beans, I figured this could be my only way to stop him.

Chapter Twelve

Moving Along

As September moved into October, Maryanne offered to help me leave Phillip by slowly removing things from our apartment that I couldn't take outright without him noticing. She had an enormous house with many spare bedrooms to store my belongings. I feared Phillip would catch on if I used too much gas, so she suggested I bring things to her at school, and she and I could transport them to her home while he was at work.

It was almost my old habit of introducing new items to our household in reverse. Gradually, I took clothing, books, photographs, and other things I might need to start a new life, one without my husband. Because we once had two households, many items we owned were duplicates. I took nothing of Phillip's, but I took things that were ours jointly. Mostly, it amounted to older equipment that was still usable despite being outdated.

I knew it would take time to get plans in place, and Maryanne's gentle prodding reminded me I shouldn't wait. I appreciated having someone in the area who cared about my well-being. But life was pulling us in different directions. She needed to take Meg out of Sacred Heart altogether, even before her house sold, since the price of gas and tuition was eating through her meager income.

We spoke over the phone almost daily after she pulled Meg from school. She would tell me about her trials over selling her house, and I would tell her what was happening with Phillip. When I told her about my growing concerns about Phillip's stress levels and the fact that he frequently made unsettling comments, she grew more concerned. One incident in particular rattled her.

It started when I told him I wanted to address the issues with the van. I'd already broken down several times. Fortunately, I was close to Sacred

Heart or home each time. But without a cell phone, I was always at risk of being stuck somewhere, with or without the kids.

"We can't afford that right now."

"If you were driving it back and forth to work, it would get fixed. A guy from school owns a repair shop, and I'm calling him to get an appointment. Don't worry. I'll pay for the expense on my own."

"Kasey, first of all, I told you 'no.' Secondly, how will you pay for it on your own?" he asked me mockingly.

"I'll borrow the money or put it on a credit card. Phillip, you may not know this, but I have every right to do this. And guess what? I will. I know you think that just because you're the only one bringing in an income right now, you have the right to dictate everything to me, but you don't. I can and will get the van fixed. And if you don't like it, go screw yourself."

I was so mad that I stormed upstairs, where the Beans were reading, and forgot to bring my laptop.

When I got up the following day, my computer wasn't where I left it. I hightailed it into the living room, where I found Phillip with my laptop apart and a soldering gun.

"What do you think you're doing?" I shouted at him.

"I'm trying to fix your computer."

"Did I ask you to do that?"

"I was trying to be nice."

"I don't believe that for one second. You've been trying to control my every move since the day I got here, and this is just another example of the despicable things you've done to me. Put it back as you found it, and don't touch it again."

"I don't care what you believe, Kasey," he screamed, turning red in the face. "You're just a bitch, like you always are, and one day, you'll see what will happen to you."

"Oh, gee, Phillip. I'm terrified," I taunted him.

Again, I stormed off in a fury. The argument woke the kids up, and they asked if I was okay when I got back upstairs. I wasn't. I was trembling. The tone of his voice frightened me. I'd never seen him so angry. His threat seemed serious, and even though I'd pretended I wasn't frightened, I knew I had crossed a line.

My strong reaction to his working on my computer came because Phillip had no idea I was still doing the school lunch program in Alexandria. Kate and I had worked out a way she and Sharilyn could continue even though I was no longer in Canada. I'd planned on working on a new menu that very morning so I could send it to the five schools I'd previously serviced. I also had payroll to submit to the accountant. Kate agreed to collect payments and deposit them in my Canadian account. Not having a reliable computer added to the difficulty of conducting business long distance.

But I was so angry I had left it downstairs, assuming it would be okay until the morning. I couldn't assume anything at this point and should have recognized this. Even though I'd added a long password to access any files, seeing Phillip working on my computer sent me into panic mode. But hearing the tone of his voice and the ambiguous threat frightened me more.

Later, I took the kids to the library to do their homework, since they didn't have a computer at home. I decided I needed to seek outside help, and while the kids were doing their assignments, I began looking through phone books to see what options might be available to me.

The rage Phillip leveled at me was new. In the past, we'd scream at one another, but I trusted that it would never cross the line physically. More and more, I wasn't so sure. For the remaining weekend, I stayed out of Phillip's way as much as possible.

When I spoke to Maryanne that day, I told her about the incident.

"He's never struck you, has he?"

"No. He's threatened me in the past but never raised a hand to me. But, Maryanne, there was something different about this argument. The look in his eyes, the sheer hatred that emanated from his entire body, is something I've never seen before. He keeps saying, 'One day, you'll be sorry.' Or sometimes he says, 'You're going to regret being such a bitch all the time.' I'm frightened that he will snap one day," I told her.

"I wish you could just come and live with me for a while," she said with a hitch in her voice.

"Me, too. Something is eating away at Phillip," I continued. "He is tense and stressed out all the time. He treats me like I am the enemy, and he won't talk to me about anything. All I know is he hates his new job. He tells me that people are being let go without warning. I get that he's had some horrible experiences with his past employers. That alone is probably causing him a lot of anxiety. But his bursts of rage are terrifying. There are times I'm convinced he will do something horrible."

After I got off the phone, I convinced myself I was getting worked up over nothing, and I began to backpedal and soften my concern. Surely, Phillip would never hurt me. Almost every night, Phillip stayed holed up in Jack's room, working on freelance projects, since he'd agreed to do some copywriting for Marco again on the side. He said it was because we needed to bring in extra income. The image of him diligently working to provide for his family erased the one of a raging maniac.

"Do you need the money? Is he telling the truth?" Maryanne asked one day.

"I don't know. I have no idea how much he is making or how the money is being spent. Whenever we need food or something, I have to email him a list, and he goes shopping because he refuses to give me access to much cash or his debit card. Whenever I need gas, I have to ask him for money. And he expects a receipt and change if there is any. I hate the amount of control he's exerting over me financially," I explained.

After I got off the phone, my conversation with Maryanne had me stewing whenever it came to mind. I couldn't help but think of the fact that I never once thought of my hefty agency paychecks as my money versus his money. When I worked in advertising and made a six-figure income, he always had access to every dime I made. Now, the lack of independent resources humiliated me.

In another conversation, I told Maryanne what he wrote to Rachel about his anger with me. He claimed that I had stolen "his" money and was the cause of all our financial difficulties. He was referring to the money spent from selling our home in Blairstown after we moved to Canada. The business didn't open for months after he moved back to the States, and I used some of those funds for business and living expenses until the café got going and I had an income. I couldn't comprehend how he expected us to live up there without spending money, or how I would turn a profit immediately after opening.

In the meantime, even though I was back in the States, I handled all the expenses in Canada on my own. Not once did Phillip ask how the bills were being paid. It was as if he'd completely forgotten about the place. He only addressed the matter in terms of selling the Alexandria property. When the property in Canada sold, I knew he would expect half or more of the proceeds, even though my work kept it afloat. I explained to Maryanne my concerns about covering utility costs and being confronted with all the tenant issues in Canada alone. As winter approached, it would be more expensive, since two of the three rental units were heated by electricity, and sometimes, the monthly cost exceeded what the tenant paid in rent. With Sharilyn and Kate's help, I still made an income in Canada with the school lunch program, and I was hoping those receipts would be enough to cover both the business and building expenses.

I kept going back and forth over what to do. I couldn't contact friends or relatives over the phone because I couldn't make long-distance calls. Emails were problematic with my faulty computer, but I also feared Phillip might have my password and was reading them. Changing them could alarm him, so I was cautious about online communication. He'd been caught twice in our marriage reading my private letters or journals. Since divorce is an adversarial situation, it wasn't outside the realm of possibility; he, too, was snooping around to find proof to support whatever claims he imagined he could make against me.

Chapter Thirteen

What the Counselor Saw

As the weeks passed, I started having second thoughts about leaving my marriage. One moment, I spoke firmly about wanting and needing to leave, and the next, doubt crept in. It wasn't so much that I wanted to stay. I just didn't know how I could afford to leave with no money or place to live. In either case, I wanted to seek the advice of a family counselor before finalizing plans because I wanted to make sure I was thinking straight. I locked myself in the bathroom at the library and used the last minutes I had on my renewed Canadian data plan to make an appointment.

I don't recall how I arrived at the name of the man I spoke to that day. It could have been a recommendation from Maryanne, but I remember he was somehow connected to a family services organization related to the Catholic Church. His services were provided for those without means. I had no means. I was still waiting on payments from my school clients in Canada so I could deposit a check from that account into the one I'd opened at the credit union. I was so paranoid about Phillip finding out I even had those funds coming in. It left me in a constant state of anxiety.

A week later, I climbed the steps of a large brick building and walked along a windowed corridor. I arrived at a small corner office and stared at the closed door. Just then, a man I assumed was the counselor peeked his head out and told me he was running late. As I sat waiting, I heard a tearful conversation. The hushed voices caused me to review my circumstances as I sat in that empty lobby. I almost left several times, but the tightness of my chest kept me locked in place.

By the time I arrived at the counselor's door, I'd been living with increasing fear of Phillip's vague but ominous threats. I could tell he wanted to punish me. Somehow, every breath I took defied him. There was a quiet rage about him, even when we weren't fighting. He seemed distracted and agitated all the time. He had been growing even more distant toward me for some time, but now, he was noticeably different with the twins. In the past, he did his best to engage them as we sat around the dinner table. Now, he ignored me and was less patient with them, too.

While waiting for the counselor, I tried to figure out how to condense the complicated history of my relationship with Phillip into the forty-five minutes allotted for the appointment. The door to the office opened, and a woman hurried out, her head bent, avoiding my gaze. The counselor ushered me inside his office. He had the confidence of someone who spent hours untangling the lives of people who couldn't navigate the choppy waters of marriage and family. I sat down, feeling like I was about to be scolded.

"Have a seat," he said, gesturing towards a chair. "What brings you here?"

I sat down as directed and crossed my arms over my body. I stalled for a minute because I didn't know where to begin.

"I'm having a hard time figuring out what to do about my marriage. I'm so unhappy; frankly, I've become frightened over what my husband has been saying. I don't know how serious I need to take his threats."

"How long have you been married?"

"Almost twenty-five years."

"Do you have children?"

"Yes, we have twelve-year-old twins."

"Boys? Girls?"

"One of each."

"Does your husband hit you?"

"Oh, no! He's not that kind of man."

"But you said you've become frightened of him. What makes you say that?"

"Well, he says things like, 'Just you wait to see what's going to happen to you.' He's said it more than once and in several emails. I have this unsettled feeling because he seems like he's in a rage all the time."

"Why do you think he is saying these things?"

"He's mad at me. He blames me for all our problems. We've had several financial setbacks, and he's always stressed about money. He wants me to find a job, but I've only been here for a short while. I have no money of my own. He only gives me enough money for gas, and I have to provide him with receipts to show him what I've spent. I don't have a reliable car—or computer, for that matter—to do a job search. I took a job teaching at Sacred Heart because they offered me free tuition for the Beans—that's what we call the twins. So I am helping, but he doesn't see it that way."

"What do you mean, you've only been here a few months? Where were you before, then?"

It sounded so convoluted when I related the circumstances of our move to Canada and my return to the States. I told the counselor about the details of my last few months.

"When we incurred an overdraft fee on our bank account, he claimed I was financially irresponsible. I don't know if he made that up because he was in the States, and all the bank records for that account go to him. But even if I did overdraft the account, he seems to have a convenient memory of the main issues surrounding our finances."

"Give me an example."

"Well, I agreed to move to Canada if he was willing to sell some rental properties we owned. He wanted to finish renovating them before putting them on the market, and I agreed with that. But he ran up our credit cards while I was in Canada. He spent so much money repairing the rental properties we had to file for bankruptcy. Even though I lived hundreds of miles away and the expenses were almost exclusively due to costs related to the repairs on those properties, somehow, he believes I'm the one who is financially irresponsible. I didn't blame him when that went down. He wasn't buying luxury items or anything. I knew he was working hard to finish the renovations. He just invested too much into them before the market fell apart. But now, every dime I spend is scrutinized. He's even told others I am at fault for all our financial problems. He's told me that even getting a phone at the house or a working computer is an unnecessary expense. I have no idea if we can afford these things because he doesn't allow me access to the bank account."

"Has this financial dynamic between you always existed? Has he always taken such a tight rein on the finances?"

"No. When I worked full-time, we had equal access to our funds. Wait a minute. Here's the thing. Phillip doesn't count what he spends on business-related items as personal expenses. So, while operating his film business, he bought whatever equipment he needed, and I had no say. The same thing applies to costs regarding the rental properties.

"It isn't just a money issue. We fight over everything. One day, I moved some furniture around the living room. He was furious with me when he came home. He said since he paid the bills, he had the right to determine the furniture arrangement. I put it back and didn't argue because he's under so much pressure. I'm afraid something will make him snap."

"Why do you think he wants to prevent you from having money?"

"I'm not sure." I stopped to think.

"I think you know why."

"No. I don't understand it. I've never withheld money from him. He seems pleased to have stripped me of my autonomy."

"If you had the financial resources to leave, would you?"

"Yes."

"That's your answer. He's controlling you. All his actions show this is the source of his anger and resentment. Abuse is about power and control."

"I told you he's never laid a hand on me."

"He doesn't need to. Abuse isn't always about violence. When a person is trying to control someone, it often takes the form of emotional abuse or financial abuse. Even gaslighting a partner is a form of abusive behavior, because those are ways someone takes control of another individual. Not all abusers strike their victims. But let me be clear. If he exerts the extent of financial control you describe, that is abuse. He's trying to prevent you from communicating with others by limiting your access to a phone and transportation. Isolating someone is another way to gain control. You pointed out that's something he's done for years."

"I think he's just really stressed about ensuring he's providing for his family, don't you think?"

"That might be an enormous part, but he's not providing for your emotional well-being. He isn't thinking about that aspect of his behavior. I'm sure much of this is also affecting your twins." The thought made me want to heave.

"Do you think he would change if I found a job?"

"No. I think your husband would find another way to control you."

"But if I found a job, he wouldn't be able to control me, right?"

He glanced up at the clock on the wall. The forty-five minutes had already evaporated.

"What do you think I need to do?" I heard my voice pleading for a resolution to the anguish I felt.

"You need to leave and protect your kids. This is not a safe situation. Would you like to make another appointment?" he asked.

I made an appointment for the following week but never went back.

On the way back to the apartment, everything should have come into focus. In forty-five minutes, the counselor figured out what was right before me, yet I refused to see it. The word *abuse* sounded ridiculous to me. It didn't apply to Phillip.

"His need for control wasn't abuse," I reasoned. It was just the way he dealt with his stress. Neither was his desire for power over me, his dismissive attitude, and his constant humiliation over the simplest things. I assured myself none of that amounted to abuse. I wasn't even sure what the counselor meant by "gaslighting." I looked it up when I got home. I convinced myself that the counselor's assessment was only based on one session, and once we'd talked more, he'd understand I wasn't abused. Phillip and I just had significant marital issues because of difficult circumstances.

My awareness of abusive behaviors was stuck in the buried memories of my next-door neighbor. When I was twelve years old, we had moved from our home in Massachusetts, so my parents could attend Bible School. It was a tumultuous time in my life. The rigid rules imposed by the school prevented us from doing many things we were accustomed to in our daily lives, like watching TV, going to school dances or the movies, or even reading certain books.

The social obstacles of moving were compounded by classmates who made fun of my siblings and me for our New England accents. In a sea of pale complexions, our tanned skin left many overtly questioning our ethnic heritage and calling us names. The upheaval caused by uncomfortable moments left us gravitating toward kids whose parents also attended Bible School and, therefore, faced the same dilemma.

A couple with five children lived on the other side of the duplex. Mr. and Mrs. White also attended school and gave my siblings and me a ready-made set of friends. While the petite Korean woman spoke little English, my mom and Mrs. White became fast friends, too.

However, our family could hear these mysterious thuds against the wall each night. At first, we all thought the boys were roughhousing. We soon learned otherwise. The deep purple bruises revealed her story without her ever telling anyone of the nightly pummeling she endured as her husband threw her against the wall. No one at the school stood up for her except my mom. My father said it was none of our business. My mother disagreed.

"It's not right!" she told him when she learned her new friend was battered repeatedly.

The hypocrisy stung. My father's image weakened dramatically in my eyes, and I had a newfound respect for my mom. Even at that age, what happened next door, in the context of these men going off daily to preach to others, turned my stomach. Maybe that became the catalyst that caused me to question the difference between my father's beliefs and his personal conduct. There was the public side, where he was a kind man, and the personal one that didn't care about the behavior of the wife-beating Mr. White because, as he repeatedly told my mother, "it didn't concern him."

But even hearing those nightly screams, I had a lack of understanding about why Mrs. White tolerated the abuse. I responded only to the injustice of Mr. White's actions and none of the practical reasons why a woman who had no independent source of income or a means to provide for her five children would tolerate his abuse. I convinced myself my situation differed from my old neighbor's and that I could handle the situation. I convinced myself that since I was more familiar with Phillip than anyone else, I needed to be more careful not to provoke him. If I had admitted the truth, even to myself, it would have been devastating to my fragile self-esteem.

I never kept that second appointment.

I thought I had to wait until I could get a job that paid enough to support myself and the Beans. I began to think I was somehow at fault. I told myself that if I could just control my emotions, Phillip wouldn't have a reason to be angry with me.

"Don't you see," I told Maryanne one day. "Maybe I'm responsible for his terrible behavior."

"If that's what you need to tell yourself, go ahead. We do what we have to do to get through it." When I hung up, I realized she was right and was thankful she had called me out on my nonsense.

In the following days, I grew even more anxious, not knowing what state of anger he would be in whenever he walked through the door. Sometimes, he was genuinely pleasant. But, more often than not, he became tense and irritable when he arrived back in Cobleskill. Sometimes, he seemed like he could snap any minute.

After weeks of trying, I admitted that being on my best behavior didn't help much. Phillip's erratic behavior fed my unease. So much so that one day, I called Phillip at work and asked him to buy a can of wasp spray on his way home. Although he didn't ask why, likely assuming I had discovered an out-of-season nest. I had no intention of using the spray to kill wasps. Instead, I hid the can upstairs next to the bed as protection in case Phillip came at the kids and me in a sudden rage.

Chapter Fourteen

Trying to Stay Safe

For weeks, I fluctuated between challenging Phillip's need for authority and keeping my mouth shut. Sometimes, my determination to avoid being treated like a doormat kept me from remaining silent. At other times, I realized I wasn't doing myself any favors by continually arguing with him. After I saw the counselor, however, I was afraid to provoke Phillip. I thought he might go off the deep end, and arguing with him made me uneasy. Maryanne suggested I could be putting myself and the Beans in danger.

Since it was almost impossible not to piss him off, I minimized our interaction with Phillip more and more by taking the kids to the library to use the computers for their homework after dinner. I also used this time to look for work and keep the lunch program going in Canada.

Staying late at the library allowed us to avoid him, so we argued less, but there was this undercurrent of hostility that kept me alarmed. I never knew what would set him off. Maryanne suggested I couldn't wait much longer to leave.

In early November, I got a call about a problem with the heat on the right side of the building in Alexandria. I arranged to travel north once again and planned to take Lucy and Jack with me as soon as they got out of school, as Phillip had no time or inclination to deal with the Beans for an entire weekend. They were delighted with the idea.

Before I picked them up, however, I wanted to make another attempt to find evidence of Phillip's possible affair. I was still convinced he was hiding something—and that something was his infidelity. Looking back on our history, I grew increasingly suspicious but still had no proof.

Nevertheless, I couldn't imagine what else could be contributing to his hostility.

Maryanne reminded me that the only way I would ever know what Phillip might be up to would be to locate irrefutable evidence. I no longer cared about his possible infidelity; I only wanted to substantiate my theories to provide leverage in a custody battle if he started divorce proceedings. So, whenever possible, I snooped.

I carefully took pictures on a digital camera we owned to make sure whenever I moved things, everything looked exactly the same prior to moving them. Then, I deleted the photos and replaced the memory SIM card with a full but benign one. I hunted through the room where he slept to see if he might have jotted something down that would reveal a clue. I came up empty-handed everywhere I searched. I assumed that if he was communicating via email, he must have a separate email account, or even a cell phone, to communicate with her, or maybe he was hiding something else altogether.

The only thing I found was another email he sent to Rachel.

"Kasey doesn't care, anyway," he emailed her. "She never even asked about the results from the tests I had for my acid reflux."

He was right. I never asked because he never told me he'd gone to the doctor or had any tests, even though I'd been the one who sent him the information over the summer about a medical practice in Albany that specialized in gastric issues. I even offered to make an appointment for him to see a doctor about his persistent problem. He responded to me that he couldn't take time off of work right then and that he would handle his health issues on his own. I had no idea when these tests took place.

Phillip wrote copy for many healthcare and pharmaceutical companies. It made him think he could identify his own medical ailments. His self-diagnosis frequently went awry. Time and again, he made assumptions about either his or my medical issues that turned out wrong. But, I let it drop because I noticed any time I brought up seeing someone about his stomach acid, there was always a reason why he couldn't, or wouldn't, be seen by his doctor.

The email reminded me of when the Beans and I visited Phillip in the Blairstown area after he moved back to work for Marco's new company. He casually mentioned that he often spit up a white, foamy liquid when he coughed.

"Well, shouldn't you see Dr. Powers?"

"I will deal with this, Kasey. I can't afford to see the doctor."

"I thought you said Marco was providing health insurance."

"He is. It's just that if something turns up, the cost of treatment could bankrupt us. We only have eighty percent coverage with my new policy."

"If you're sick, Phillip, you need to get treated. The cost is not the important issue here."

"Kasey, you're only here for a day. Let's not bicker. I want to enjoy my time with my kids."

In the same email, Phillip told Rachel he planned to push forward with mediation. He told her he would set "strict parameters" on who could be my mediator since he wanted "someone unbiased." I thought that was a joke when he told me he'd asked his sister. While I loved and respected her, I thought Rachel would hardly provide an unbiased opinion. Rachel only knew what Phillip told her in his emails, giving her a tainted point of view. I couldn't point any of this out because I didn't want to reveal I had read them. That would open yet another can of worms.

By the time I finished snooping, I realized none of it mattered anymore. I was wasting my time trying to get the goods on Phillip. I decided to stop wasting my energy on the state of our marriage and start focusing on moving forward without him. I started to shut off my laptop, but, instead, I got to work creating the next month's lunch menus to send to Kate and redoing my resumé.

The day before I left for Canada, Phillip offered to let me use the Elantra. Even though I knew it had better gas mileage than our minivan, I was skeptical of Phillip's kindness. After all, he knew the Elantra didn't have snow tires, so I questioned his motives. The possibility of snow and icy roads led to another sleepless night. I was tense and irritable in the morning but remained committed to my plans.

The trip to Alexandria unnerved me. The weather went from snow to freezing rain. My shoulders stiffened as I gripped the wheel, trying to abstain from using the myriad of curse words that came to mind each time the car slid on the ice. I must have uttered a hundred of them under my breath during the trip.

Evening approached by the time we crossed over the border. The closer we got to Alexandria, the more I longed for the warmth of Jenny's welcoming smile. But her husband was home, so the twins and I planned to stay in the old office above the café kitchen for this trip.

Even though only a few months had passed, when I unlocked the café door, everything had changed. The aroma of coffee had been replaced with a more antiseptic smell. What was once the welcoming entrance of a small business was now a place to accommodate assembling the school lunches more efficiently. It was disorienting. I was no longer a part of my previous life in Alexandria.

After settling upstairs, I came down and wandered into the tearoom. It was now filled with antiques. Glenn had rented the space for his on-again, off-again antique business. His friend Roberto minded the store. After a brief chat, I called the plumber, who agreed to come in the morning.

The constant worries about building maintenance reminded me I was ill-equipped to handle these issues. I began to realize my only recourse might be figuring out how to sell the building. The only consolation was the money would provide the funds to start over once Phillip and I divorced. With little to do, I went upstairs to grab Chubby's leash so the twins and I could take him for a quick walk and grab some groceries.

Having access to my Canadian bank account and the money from the school lunch program provided some relief. Even though I needed to watch every penny, it gave me a level of independence I didn't have when I had to beg Phillip for money. The humiliation I endured every time I handed back the change and receipts from the grocery store or gas station reminded me of how difficult it would be to leave my marriage. Since he refused to share financial information about his new job, I had no idea what child support or alimony would look like. I wrestled with countless questions about how to provide for the Beans and myself once I left. Jobs were still scarce due to the recession, and the low-wage jobs that were available wouldn't cover living expenses. I'd most likely have to rely on welfare, or I shuddered to think we'd become homeless if I dared to leave. I breathed a sigh of relief that, once again, I had even a tiny amount of funds of my own.

Being back in the room where Phillip and I had several horrendous fights brought me circling back to all the agonizing events that led up to those moments. Sleep eluded me as the past careened through my mind. A jumble of emotions led to tears soaking the thin pillow.

I chastised myself for ignoring the growing chasm between Phillip and me. We rarely saw one another before the twins were born due to our conflicting work schedules. Most weekends, we made up for time apart. On Saturdays and Sundays, we languished in bed, making love for hours. Once we got up and showered, we headed out for a late breakfast or early lunch. We scouted for antiques to furnish our house, explored new places to dine, and then headed to the movies or some other similar event.

After the Beans were born, he spent his weekends working on our rental properties, and I initially avoided the problems that began to grow and tried to get along. I told myself it was for the twins' sake, but I found it hard to deal with conflicts between us. When we moved to Canada, he visited so infrequently that I initially resented his absence. But soon, I began to realize all the troubling aspects of our relationship.

In the late spring of 2009, when Marco's new company in Morristown, New Jersey, folded, Phillip had to move north and began living with the Beans and me in Alexandria. Our relationship began to genuinely fall apart. By then, I was used to running the café and being in charge of the business and the twins' routine. That bothered Phillip, and he tried to subvert my authority, especially over the operation. He acted out to drive his point home, putting on childish displays.

Such was the case one day when Kate, Sharilyn, and I were preparing to open. Phillip showed up in the kitchen and asked, "What's for lunch?"

I offered to heat up the leftovers from our dinner the night before. Phillip, however, wasn't interested in leftovers, so I took the time to rattle off our menu.

Standing in the middle of the tiny kitchen, he said, "That's not lunch. That's a list of ingredients," and stormed out.

His actions humiliated me. Kate just looked over and said, "Well, let's not tell our customers we only have ingredients for lunch today, shall we?"

Shortly after Kate placed the 'open' sign on the door, several customers arrived, and she began seating them in the tearoom while others waited in the foyer to be escorted to their tables. Suddenly, Phillip returned to the café, carrying a bag of groceries.

He announced, "I just bought myself something to eat. I'll need the stove for a few minutes," then, he walked into the kitchen, where Sharilyn was, and asked her to open and heat up a can of soup.

Phillip knew I wouldn't say anything in front of my employees and customers. He relished inserting himself into our daily routine and showing Kate and Sharilyn that he, too, was their *boss*. He didn't care that this also made a statement about the food quality at the café. Soup was our specialty. I had customers drive all the way from Montreal, which was an hour away, to have a bowl of our soup.

When we closed that day, I told Kate and Sharilyn I would finish up because, by then, I was seething. I climbed the stairs and let Phillip have it.

"What do you think you were doing with your little stunt this morning? It's not enough that you refuse to help me, but now you want to sabotage my business?"

"That's just it, Kasey. This is your business. It's always about you and what you want."

"What do I want? Do you think this is about what I want? You were the one who wanted to move here. Did you think I would just step aside because you're here now?

"I wanted some lunch. Was that too much to ask? Are you saying I can't even use the kitchen for a few minutes?"

"Did it ever occur to you that we have a kitchen in our apartment? This had nothing to do with you wanting lunch, Phillip. You wanted to show who is in charge." I left him, slamming the office door shut, and, as usual, we didn't talk for days. After that, he spent even more of his time in the office.

For a short time, I thought things might be turning around, and we'd finally found a way to work together. The situation that led to this began the previous summer when a woman came into the café and asked if I would be interested in buying a property about a mile outside town. While I already knew we could not consider purchasing the property, I told her Phillip and I might be interested in renting it and that I would talk to him about it.

I loved the idea because I'd become nervous about living above the café. Not only had my minivan been vandalized, but someone kept ringing our doorbell after midnight. Phillip still lived in the States, and I frequently told him I thought it might be a disgruntled customer I kicked out of the café one day. Regardless, the man insisted on coming into the café even though I refused to serve him. The property the woman spoke of was about a mile out of town. Since the man I suspected of harassing me didn't own a car, I thought I would be safer living a short distance away.

I was convinced when she mentioned the property included a "music barn" where Andrea Rabe, a concert pianist from Montreal, had performed for decades. She and her husband Saul owned five acres of land and had a stage constructed in the Barn, surrounded by hardwood floors. They held free concerts in the rustic setting until they moved to another venue, and the farmhouse and music barn had been vacant for years.

It seemed to make sense, since I could rent out the apartment above the café for a bit less than the house's rent. Phillip agreed initially, because the kids would have an enormous yard to play in, and we would all have a place to relax away from the business on weekends. The only drawback was that Chubby would remain alone all day.

We enjoyed our first summer there, but when winter arrived, I realized why no one had lived there for years. Despite what I had been told, I learned the house wasn't insulated, and the pipes froze constantly, making it miserable to come home to during winter. The kids and I had moved back into our apartment above the café, and the farmhouse sat idle. Phillip was furious that we were paying rent for the house and not using the place. It became another source of friction between us because he said he never agreed to rent the home, even though I had emails that contradicted this claim.

In early spring, Shaun and Marie Gagney, a couple involved in the local entertainment scene, entered the café. Shaun had a band while Marie ran a small business out of their home. They'd assumed that Phillip and I owned the farmhouse and were interested in doing a co-production of some kind in the music barn.

While Phillip now lived with us, he wasn't there for whatever reason. I suggested the three of us meet with him when he returned. About a week later, we all sat around a table in the tearoom and agreed to work together to produce an event we called *The Glengarry Music Festival.* Marie would book the talent, Phillip would produce the events and build the website, I would cater meals to accompany the show, and Shaun would use his connections to fill seats. Everyone agreed with my suggestion to call the venue *2Beans in the Barn.*

Because Phillip could take on a more active role in the business, some of the friction between us got buried for a while. He designed an elegant website to advertise the festival, and Marie had booked a stellar lineup of talent for our series. Shaun provided his band for the opening act, and I developed a themed menu to match the musical events being featured. For a while, everything seemed on track.

We sold out for every performance we had booked when things fell apart. Shortly after the first several concerts, Phillip began complaining constantly about Marie. He hated working with her. Instead of approaching her with the problems he had with what she was doing, he complained to me and said he thought she deliberately did things to piss him off. In reality, I believe Marie's assertiveness threatened him. Everything she did was wrong, according to him. Yet, Phillip acted shocked when the Gagneys pulled out of the festival.

Even though my responsibilities only extended to catering for the performances, Phillip blamed me for the failure, and claimed I talked him into doing the festival in the first place. He conveniently forgot about sitting down, discussing the idea with the Gagneys, and agreeing to the co-production. When I reminded him of that, he said he "just went along" to appease me.

Without the festival to distract him, Phillip once again took aim at how I operated the business and wanted to make changes that he assured me would make the restaurant more profitable. I constantly defended myself against his allegations that everything I'd tried to do to make the business successful was a failure and he needed to take over.

Phillip had zero culinary skills, and the entirety of his restaurant exposure was based on a two-week stint at Friendly's Ice Cream shop, a job that he quit because he didn't like the work. However, he told me his years of working in advertising and promoting companies related to the food service industry made him an expert in all aspects of operating the café. In his opinion, the school lunch program, my catering work, the hours of operation, and all matters pertaining to the café's operation were wrong. According to Phillip, the school lunch program needed to go because I couldn't do it without the cost of my employees, Kate and Sharilyn. He believed I should open for dinner and do more take-out because I was "free labor." I would be tasked with all the work involved with accomplishing this expansion since he was unwilling to assist by waiting tables or doing any of the prep work.

Whenever I asked how I was supposed to wait tables and cook the meals simultaneously, he told me I had to purchase meals already prepared by food service companies that could be microwaved or quickly reheated. Phillip insisted the time and effort of preparing quality food was a waste of money. When I pointed out that we were incurring bigger losses because the rent we were collecting for the two other apartments didn't cover ongoing maintenance and utility costs, he accused me of making excuses.

This led to even more tension between us, and it grew to the point where he stayed in the room above the café more than he stayed in the apartment with the Beans or helping me run the restaurant. He completely took over the office above the café, which I had used for years. When I complained about him putting the business records I had on the desk in the closet, he claimed he needed the space for his computer to look online for work, dismissing my needs. Every time I went up there, I entered Phillip's private domain.

Things came to a head one day after the kids started school again. The aromatic smell of biscotti in the oven alerted me to the limited time I had to return to the kitchen before they burned. My feet ached from running back and forth, trying to bake desserts for the next day while helping the twins with their homework as they sat at a table in the tearoom. I was frantic as I hustled myself up the stairs to the office.

Even with the door closed, the noise from the TV could be heard as I climbed. I entered the room without knocking. Phillip looked up from a small, portable television with a built-in VCR and grimaced. He turned back and intently studied the screen of his computer.

"Busted," I thought before confronting him. "Phillip, the twins have some math homework tonight. Would you see if you can help them? I've got some desserts in the oven, and I'm afraid I'll burn them if I keep going back and forth from the kitchen to the tearoom."

"Sure, I'll come down in a while. My show is over soon."

"Can't you watch that later? You've seen it a million times."

He turned to look at me as though I were asking him to leave a patient in the middle of surgery.

"I told you. I'll go when it's over. They can wait a while."

"But I asked them to do their homework now so they'll have time after dinner for other things. It wouldn't kill you to spend some time with them."

His body stiffened. "I will go to help them when I'm ready."

"Well, they need help now, not later."

"I'm getting my resumé together."

"Oh, and you're consulting with Captain Picard?"

"I can have the TV on and work, Kasey. I'm trying to find a job and love that you can't even allow me a bit of peace and quiet while I update my resumé," he snarled. "Spending time with the twins is a luxury for me."

"That takes the cake."

"What's that supposed to mean?"

"It means the only time you spend with them is watching TV shows they hate. It means that you spend more time away from them and offer excuse after excuse about why you'd rather stay here in this stupid office than be with your own kids. It means you were the one who left your wife and kids behind when you took the job with Marco," I screamed.

"I had no choice," he yelled back.

"Don't rewrite history, Phillip. You took the job with Marco back then and never even discussed it with me. And you were the one who wanted those damn rental properties."

"So, now being away from my kids is all my fault? Is that what you're telling me?"

"I didn't say that, Phillip. Stop putting words into my mouth."

"Someone has to provide for our family, and that someone is always me."

"Really? Did you once stop to think about how much that decision cost us? It took me months longer to open the business, and I had to hire people to do things you weren't here to do. And while we're on the subject, did you even once add up all the expenses you incurred living down in New Jersey? Those costs and additional expenses gave us a net gain of practically zero. You never even stopped to think if it was worth living apart!"

"You loved being without me. You only want me here to help you and run errands for you."

"Help me? Please! Is that what you call it when you refuse to do anything except shop for groceries?"

"And what have you ever done for me? The fact is, Kasey, I will have to support you and the twins for the rest of my life."

"Oh? Are you forgetting that I worked full-time for years while you got to freelance or work to build your company? And how about the three years you stayed home, working on the house after your business partner emptied your joint bank account? Except for that small job you got from my employer, you didn't work because you said you were too busy working on our house. But somehow, during that time, you magically wrote a play."

"Well, at least my play was worth producing."

"Of course, it was because I was out there, working every day, to support you, pal!"

"You've never worked at anything more than an admin job."

I walked over to the office closet where my café records were stored. While trying to locate something earlier in the week, I found a box of old invoices from my time at one of the ad agencies where I worked before the babies were born. I pulled it out of the closet and threw the papers at Phillip. The bi-weekly invoices were for $5,550.00 each.

"They don't pay a person this much for an admin job, even in Manhattan, Phillip. You can lie to yourself, but I have the physical proof here."

He wouldn't look at them. It was all right there in black and white, yet he denied it. I left the room, disgusted, and shouted over my shoulder,

"You left us in Canada, just like you plan to do again. If you want to blame someone for not having time with your kids, look in the mirror."

With that, I rushed downstairs, hoping the biscotti hadn't burned. I stayed in the kitchen to see if he'd leave the office or ignore me. He chose to ignore me. From that point on, I could tell that Phillip hated being there. He resented everything about living in Alexandria because I'd made friends and carved out a life that didn't center around him. He kept to himself and even slept and ate his meals, except for dinner, in the office upstairs. The only time Phillip came over to our apartment was to watch videotapes with Jack and Lucy.

I knew how unhappy he was, but by then, my resentment had grown to the point where I felt a sense of relief when he told me not only was he applying for jobs in Canada, but he was also looking online for work back in the U.S. Looking back at the night years earlier, I realize that was probably when he decided to divorce me.

Chapter Fifteen

A Bitter November

The curtains that had once hung on the windows of the old office had been taken down, and without them, the bright lights from the pizzeria next door created shadows throughout the room. This didn't seem to disturb the Beans, who slept peacefully, one on each side of me. As much as I loved the warmth of the small bodies, I could barely move. I pulled the covers over me and burrowed under them to coax myself into slumber, but I couldn't force myself to relax enough to drift off to sleep. Instead, I delved into memories of the past, rekindling all the hurt that led me to careen toward the emotional abyss. For whatever reason, I needed to recount the justifications I had for leaving Phillip.

At the top of my list was something that happened that previous November, and my anger turned to sorrow when I thought about the time my brother Ray called to tell me my father had passed away. Phillip was up in the office. I trudged upstairs and delivered the news, ignoring the glow of the TV monitor. I told Phillip my dad had passed.

"That's too bad," he said, returning to watching one of his favorite sci-fi shows.

The callousness of his comment left me unable to move. He never cared for my father, and I understood he had reasons. The moment shouldn't have been about how he felt about my father but about the loss I was experiencing. What he said reminded me of how often this scene had played out in small ways throughout my marriage. Whenever I showed even the slightest emotion or feeling, he invalidated it. I couldn't possibly be hungry if he wasn't hungry. I couldn't possibly be in pain if he wasn't in pain. He shut me down as if anything I experienced wasn't real because it wasn't happening to him. The magnitude of my father's death finally made me see Phillip's actions and reactions for what they were. He did try to control, dominate, and degrade me. He distorted my reality because nothing anyone experienced was real if it wasn't about him. I turned and rushed downstairs without further comment. He came down moments later and found me in the kitchen crying.

"Should we send flowers?" he asked.

I turned to him, exasperated. "Who would you send flowers to? My brother Ray?" I asked.

"I don't know. I'm trying to help," Phillip said sharply.

"I'm calling Sharilyn and Kate to let them know I need to close the café tomorrow," I said, then headed upstairs to use the phone in our apartment.

"You can't do that! We can't risk losing that business," he yelled as I crossed the room.

"We," I thought bitterly. There was never a 'we' in running the café.

I crossed the tearoom and opened the door connected to the foyer to make my way upstairs to our tiny apartment above. Phillip followed me. When I reached the bottom of the staircase, he grabbed the back of my arm and stopped me before I climbed it. I threw his hand off my arm and faced him.

"This is what it means to have a business," he ranted. "You don't get to close up shop because something happens." It was as if I said I was closing to have my nails done or spending the day at the spa. In the three-plus years we owned the place, I rarely took time off, missing many holidays or special occasions with family and friends. He even threw a tantrum when I wanted to attend Jenny's sixtieth birthday celebration, so I didn't go.

"I'm going to call them to cover for me or close for the day," I said bitterly.

"We can't afford it," he replied to my back as I walked up the stairs.

I turned back to look at him. "Of course not. It doesn't matter, because it's my family. If this were your father, you would have been heading home within minutes of getting the call." I continued into the apartment and locked the door behind me. I couldn't fathom what had just happened.

The Beans came out of their room when they heard me sobbing and asked me what happened. I told them of my dad's passing. We all sat on the couch, embracing. I held them as tightly as they held me, and we all cried together.

As I thought about that night, I finally understood why that event had been so painful. It wasn't just the night I lost my dad. That night, I could no longer deny that my marriage was over.

My father was 93 years old when he passed away. Despite his age, it was still inconceivable. His influence on my life was immeasurable. I idolized him as a child, and my goal back then was to please him.

As a little girl, my dad favored me because I was the youngest. Whenever my older siblings wanted something, they asked me to ask him, knowing he was more inclined to say 'yes' to me. As I grew older, I memorized Bible verses and tried to "save" all the neighborhood kids, seeking to convert them to his brand of Christianity. I knew what he wanted from me, and I happily obliged. I adored my dad and knew he loved me. I spent hours sitting in the background when his friends gathered at our house to sing and play their guitars. I listened with rapt attention to my dad's beautiful tenor voice and learned to sing harmony to all the hymns so I could be a part of his world.

He had that effect on others, as well. He captivated the neighborhood children by giving them rides on his motorcycles. He performed small magic tricks to entertain them. He worked with the youth groups at church, and they adored my dad, a charming and funny, all-around lovable guy.

He was generous with his money, and my mother admonished him for donating too much of his income to our local church. And yet, while he generously gave to local charities, his children wore ill-fitting hand-me-downs, and my mother counted pennies and shopped at thrift stores.

He never offered even one of his seven children rides on his motorcycle, and he cultivated relationships with teens from the church before taking time out of his busy schedule to spend with my older siblings. He relished the adoration of so many people, but his children and wife saw a very different side of him.

To say we had a contentious relationship as I got older would be an understatement. When I hit puberty, my father seemed to abandon me. My new interest in boys angered him, and nothing I did seemed to please him anymore. My good grades and obedient behavior were no longer enough to satisfy him. As I became a woman, he acted as if by growing up, I had betrayed him.

When I was around eleven, my dad convinced my mother that he should give up his job as a welder at a General Motors plant in Framingham so they could attend Bible school in western New York. My mom didn't want to go since she had been diagnosed with rheumatoid arthritis and had other health issues. Regardless, he insisted we sell our house in the small town where I grew up. First, we moved into a trailer, then into a duplex that belonged to the school they were attending.

The entire family hated the change, but no one more than my mother. She, too, had to attend school, and she resented my father for it. She had been ripped away from her family and friends and the life we had back home in Massachusetts. Now, more restrictions were placed on her already restricted life. There were rules against just about everything. My father loved the spartan way the Bible school required us to live and the authority he gained as the man of the house. But my mom hated giving up her pleasures, like television, cigarettes, and red wine.

My parents seemed to argue more, and the topic frequently revolved around our neighbors, Mr. and Mrs. White, the couple who lived on the other side of the duplex. I recall being told they had met while he was stationed in Korea during the war. On the rare occasion we saw him in the yard, Mr. White gave us a cheerless smile and would quickly disappear.

While it took time to get to know her, Mrs. White was warm and welcoming whenever we gathered at their apartment to play. My mom became fast friends with the quiet woman.

When my mother found out her new friend's husband beat her nightly, she was outraged. She confronted my father, who told her it was none of our business. My mother disagreed.

"We should do something!" she told him.

Once I learned the truth, the purple welts I saw on Mrs. White's arms and face sickened me. But at twelve years old, I didn't understand the whole dynamic of the situation and simply wondered why Mrs. White chose to stay with her husband, since I believed she could just take her five children and leave.

I soon began to question what I thought were absolute truths based on my upbringing. In many of the sermons I listened to on Sunday mornings, the pastor brought up the sanctity of marriage. While I don't recall the specific words used, I thought the union between a husband and wife was sacred, and assumed most couples loved one another the way my parents seemed to love each other. While my father was very domineering, he acted lovingly toward my mother and expressed a deep affection for her.

I began to notice the two different sides of my father. His sincerely held religious beliefs seemed to conflict with being willfully tolerant of the violence next door because, as he claimed, "it didn't concern him." Soon, I saw my parents differently. My father's image weakened dramatically in my eyes, and I had a newfound respect for my mom. I began appreciating the hard work of raising seven children and keeping our household running. Things I had taken for granted about her sacrifices had me reevaluating her. Looking through family photos, the beautiful outfits she made us for special occasions and the meals she prepared for large family gatherings stood out. I had never appreciated the graceful way she made daily contributions to my life that had gone unnoticed.

The situation between the Whites also seemed to impact my parent's marriage. My mother became more outspoken and expressed frustration with my father and his unwillingness to defend Mrs. White. While she never said the words, I believed my mom thought it wasn't fair that my father got to make all the decisions. Despite his faults, he showed his love and support in ways that made it more acceptable for her to tolerate their relationship's uneven power dynamic. I believe the longer they were married, the more they understood one another, and I eventually appreciated how attentive he became to her needs.

When Bible school was over, we lived in the town where it was located for another year before we moved to the Catskills. By then, I was a junior in high school, and my siblings were all out of the house. The move resulted from my dad's new job with a missionary organization in Brooklyn, New York. Their goal was to convert Jews to Christianity. I was appalled at this, mainly because most of the boys I dated in high school were Jewish and I feared he might try to convert them.

As my dad became more and more devoted to his religious convictions, he tried to exert more influence over my decisions. I constantly had to battle him to exert myself and what I desired for my own life. I didn't rebel by doing drugs or drinking. Instead, I started exhibiting physical signs of severe stress. At seventeen, I developed uncontrollable diarrhea.

Because of my mom's deteriorating health, my dad assumed most of the parental oversight during those years, including taking me to appointments. He was the one who accompanied me when the situation got so bad I had a hard time attending school. My mother finally convinced him to take me to the doctor to determine the cause.

At the appointment, the doctor began asking me questions.

"How frequently does this happen?"

"Well, I..."

My father cut me off. "Sometimes, I've noticed she has to get up from the dinner table. Maybe it's something she's eating?" he asked.

The doctor acknowledged him with a nod. "Do you notice that certain foods affect you?" the doctor asked.

"Well, I..."

My father cut me off. "Didn't you tell me mustard upsets your stomach?" he asked me before consulting the doctor. "Could she have an ulcer?"

The doctor ignored him and nodded for me to respond.

"It seems like..."

My father cut me off again, but after answering for me a third time, the doctor had had it with him.

"Mr. Rogers, I am not asking you. I am asking your daughter, and I want you to let her answer for herself. Have I made myself clear?" he admonished.

My dad sheepishly nodded, but I could tell he was mad. He was used to being in control of even the words I uttered, and he didn't like that the doctor advocated on my behalf.

I spent my eighteenth birthday in the hospital, and after a week of tests, they diagnosed me with what they called spastic colitis. The doctor determined the primary cause of the spastic colitis to be stress. As my high school graduation approached, I became anxious to leave home and be on my own.

I applied to colleges recommended by the school guidance counselor. My father told me he wanted me to attend Bible school so I could become a missionary like he was. Whenever discussing my future, he told me he knew what was best for me. While I wanted to attend music school and had received a full scholarship, he prevented me from going by refusing to cooperate when I needed to complete administrative tasks the college required. With the help of my counselor, I ended up applying to and attending a college closer to home just to escape my father's parental authority. After leaving home, he never approved of the path I navigated on my own. It was just one of the many reasons for the friction that grew between us.

I only returned home briefly after dropping out of school, so I rarely saw him afterward unless my parents were up from Florida, where they'd moved. For years, I called home once weekly to check on my mom. By then, she was mainly bedridden, and hearing from her children brought her a great deal of joy. But other than a brief greeting, I avoided talking with my dad because he often said cruel and hurtful things. My mom tried to buffer our relationship by reminding me he loved me despite his harsh words. She understood how difficult her husband could be.

While I rarely spent much time talking over the phone with him, he kept trying to reach out by sending me heartfelt letters that I read with a hardened heart. But I found that I couldn't throw them away and often opened the shoebox where I kept them to remind me he was at least trying to make amends.

Then, he would sabotage all his attempts at reconciliation with his thoughtless comments, as he did once when I called home. On that occasion, he told me my mother was very ill and was in the hospital. She was so sick, he said, even if I called her, she wouldn't be able to talk on the phone.

"I hope she'll be okay!" I said through tears. "Please tell her I love her, and I'll pray for her."

"God doesn't hear your prayers," he told me. After that, I refused to speak with him altogether.

My mom's health continued to decline, and nine months after the Beans were born, Phillip suggested we go to see her. This surprised me.

"It's probably the last chance you'll get to see her," he told me one day.

"I know, but seeing her means seeing my dad. Are you ready for that?"

"He doesn't bother me as much as he bothers you, and you're going to regret not visiting her once she's gone. She wants to meet her grandkids, and I think we should plan a trip."

I wrapped my arms around him and was so grateful, especially when he offered to make the travel arrangements. Phillip booked tickets on the Auto Train, and we traveled with the Beans to Florida.

A month after we returned, my mother passed away. Phillip's insistence that we go see my mom did more than allow me to visit with her one last time. The trip healed the fractured relationship between my dad and me. Not because my father changed or did anything special, but because I realized, after seeing him gush over these two little beings that I loved dearly, that I wanted him in their lives, even if it meant I would need to tackle the difficulties in our relationship.

I consoled myself, knowing I wasn't the only one in the family he had alienated. He had a contentious relationship with almost all my siblings, leaving me to believe I was not the problem. This allowed me to tolerate some of his behavior, but it didn't mean I couldn't speak up. I chose not to argue or fight with him over our disagreements. But I would state clearly that I disagreed. Somehow, as the years passed, we managed to have a more loving relationship. As the kids grew, he visited every year, making the trip with my older brother Ray, who had been caring for him.

When I received the news that he had died, I was heartbroken. My dad, the man who taught me how to sing harmony, the father who loved me with all his heart, if not his words, was gone. Losing a parent is one of those times when we all become children again. It doesn't matter how old we are or how old they are when they pass. The anguish is different and changes our world forever. I felt abandoned and lonely and longed for the comfort of his loving arms. The fact that I would never see him again erased any remaining anger. That night, I loved him in the ways I loved him as a child. I saw his good side, the humor he exhibited, his enjoyment of life, his intelligence and spunk. When he was eighty-four years old, he still rode his motorcycle. I admired his gumption and began to work through the anger I held onto for years.

Thoughts of that cold November night left me careening toward an emotional abyss. The tension between Phillip and me robbed me of the time I needed to grieve, so I shut down and couldn't process my sense of loss. Instead, I stuffed those feelings deep inside and carried on as expected. But a year later, my two worlds collided, and all the grief I'd suppressed overwhelmed me because my dad was gone, and now, so was Phillip.

Chapter Sixteen

The Plan

Two days later, the plumber had fixed the heating issue on the right side of the building. The Beans and I left Canada, and we made the lengthy drive back to Cobbleskill. The long drive allowed me to talk with the twins alone. They told me how miserable they were at school. I already realized it wasn't the right place for either of them. Their grades were slipping, and they had regressed socially.

We arrived late at night, exhausted and unkempt. I sent Tammy at Sacred Heart an email outlining the situation, explaining why the twins would miss yet another day of classes. There was no way I could send them to school without getting some more rest and showering. They were already feeling ostracized, and I didn't need to give them any more anxiety about attending school.

It didn't matter what I did; I couldn't find the right balance between the kids' needs, my needs, and Phillip's. But after that weekend in November, I knew I had to get a plan in place.

Later that day, I called Maryanne to tell her about my trip. During our conversation, I expressed how I found it strange that when I thought of Alexandria and the café, it had changed from my sanctuary, to the place where my relationship with my husband had gone off the rails. I told her I'd finally decided to let go of our property in Canada.

I tried to figure out how to leave safely without Phillip gaining knowledge of my plans. I wanted to avoid incurring his wrath so the Beans would be spared the ugliness of yet more fighting. We would need a place to stay until I found work, so I reached out to my brother Jake and was very candid about the state of my marriage and my plans to leave Phillip. He discussed it with Meredith, and they agreed to let us come.

Because one of the tenants in Alexandria emailed me about a problem with her water heater, I told Phillip that was the main reason for a trip north. That was partially true. I informed him that once the plumber resolved the issue, I planned to head to Vermont to spend time with my brother on the first anniversary of my father's death. That was also partly true. Phillip questioned nothing.

The Veteran's Day holiday fell on a Thursday and the kids had no school. I calculated that if we left on Wednesday after school, I'd have Thursday to handle the plumbing issue and purchase the supplies needed for the lunch program. Afterward, I would head to my brother's house. Once there, I could evaluate my options and determine if Jack, Lucy, and I could live there until we could find a better arrangement.

Since Jake had said we could stay for a while, I hoped I would have time to work out the rest. Admittedly, it wasn't a brilliant plan, but until I could sell the property and split the proceeds of the sale with Phillip, I couldn't think of any other way that would allow us to begin a new life.

There was a lot to remedy on both fronts; however, anything was better than our current circumstances. I reasoned that Phillip had been perfectly happy seeing our children every other weekend, on and off, while the Beans and I were in Canada and he had the apartment in New Jersey. For that matter, he seemed content with a weekend arrangement when we were in Blairstown, and he spent much of his time in Scranton. I kept reminding myself that he rarely chose to hang out with them, even when he lived under the same roof.

Knowing I was ending my marriage before he did it for me allowed me to be kinder to Phillip. I knew he loved our kids and would be hurt when we left. Even when he wasn't always there with them, I had no doubt he cared for them deeply. I tried to understand and believe it didn't mean he loved them less than I did. He just loved them differently.

I recognized that the pain of ending our relationship would affect both of us emotionally. I cared about his well-being. I even admitted to myself that, to a great extent, I still loved him very much. Leaving him wasn't about love. It wasn't about getting even or seeking revenge, either. I honestly had no desire to hurt him or cause any needless suffering. The heartache of knowing how little he thought of me weighed heavily into my decision. He never seemed to appreciate my contributions to his life and our marriage. I couldn't understand how he was able to dismiss all of the years I supported him for a version of our lives where he single-handedly played the role of sole provider. Instead, he tried to convince me these were figments of my imagination. There were days I sought out physical reminders of the truth because he got into my head in a way that caused me to doubt myself again.

His inability to recognize I wasn't the only one contributing to the problems in the marriage made me concerned about something else. I spent hours leading up to our trip on Wednesday trying to untangle the events of the past, wondering if Phillip genuinely believed what he said. He said scores of hurtful things about my character. It wasn't just my character, though. My family, my tastes, my whole being, somehow were a target of his insults. Everything about me was wrong. The music I liked, the way I fixed my coffee, and how I laughed too loud and too often were things he criticized. It all amounted to me being unacceptable because I wasn't Phillip.

I knew that so much of what Phillip said was more about his insecurities and inability to achieve his goals, but they still left me emotionally wounded. I imagine what bothered him was that an *uneducated* woman eclipsed his success. He often brought up my lack of a college degree when disparaging me.

While still working in Boston, Phillip had established himself as a talented filmmaker. Yet he seemed to have lost his way once we moved to New York. He was clearly jealous that I'd managed to navigate a career in commercial films while he never achieved the same degree of success he had in Boston.

Phillip frequently expressed his feelings of being overshadowed by his sister's accomplishments and told me, when we first met, that he was the black sheep of his family. He wasn't. That very perception skewed the truth and allowed him to ignore reality. When he discussed his childhood, he described himself as constantly feeling inferior. What we believe about ourselves often drives our behaviors, and the ghosts of his past colored every aspect of his life. The unfortunate part was that all this gripped his head and heart because, in reality, he was one of the most brilliant, charming, and talented people I've ever met.

Much of his insecurity appeared connected with the idea that he competed with Rachel for his parents' love. He seemed to think he could earn their love and respect by accomplishing more than Rachel, a very high achiever. He told me that because he moved away and worked in a less stable industry, his parents weren't as proud of him as his sister. I explained to him that Rachel and her husband, Dennis, had a different relationship with Phillip's parents because they lived closer, and therefore, they all spent more time together.

Whenever we visited, Phillip insisted he try to make up for his life choices. Instead of enjoying their company, he found ways to make himself useful and valued in their eyes. He did this by offering to fix anything that needed to be repaired whenever we visited. This wasn't limited to his parents either. He often busied himself addressing minor maintenance issues for Rachel and Dennis, too.

A pattern emerged after each visit to his folks. Phillip would comment about his perception of our visits in terms of successes or failures, as though his family measured their love of him by what he'd accomplished. And while perception is a truly powerful thing, it is not, in fact, a reality. Phillip's view of what happened or didn't happen never matched my own. He somehow always managed to feel slighted and expressed resentment that regardless of how much he did for them, he could never measure up to the expectations he perceived they had for him. I'd begun to realize Phillip seemed to have his own reality—it just wasn't true.

This was the same in our marriage as well. By telling himself I created all our problems, Phillip could absolve himself of his self-loathing. Somehow, by invalidating me, he could validate himself. I figured he could not love me because, essentially, he didn't love himself.

I thought about this endlessly. It helped me understand how we got to where we were and why I needed to empathize with him, even if I didn't accept Phillip's actions or reasoning. However, the lengths to which I strived to comprehend what lay at the heart of his actions wasn't altruism on my part. They were acts of survival so I could be at peace with my decision to leave.

Once I concluded I had no choice but to leave, it became easier to accept what I planned to do. I had no reason to believe anything would change now that we were living back in the States, and I had no desire to continue going along the same path, repeatedly fighting over the same issues. In the days leading up to my departure, this understanding allowed me to be more civil and less defensive with him. He seemed to think I was relinquishing control to him. The irony wasn't lost on me.

Because he still had so many gastric issues, I cooked several meals so Phillip wouldn't have to contend with preparing dinner for himself over the long weekend. I made a few of his favorite dinners, put things in the freezer, and baked some chocolate chip oatmeal cookies and a loaf of banana bread before leaving to fetch the Beans from school. I emailed him to let him know what I did. He responded with a "thank you" and offered to give me some cash for our trip. I was dumbstruck. It made me pause. But only for a minute.

When I stopped by his office in Albany to pick up the money, I started to feel like a villain. Phillip had no idea I was not only going to Jake and Meredith's to honor my father. This time, when I left, I didn't plan on coming back.

The Beans and I were staying with Jenny on this trip to Alexandria. When we arrived, her gentle hug and knowing smile restored my faith that, somehow, life would go on. Her friendship provided the antidote I needed from my gloomy outlook after days of being immersed in the complexities of my marriage. Jack and Lucy went downstairs to play on their Game Boys while Jenny and I talked. It helped to hear her perceptions of the events that led up to this moment because she genuinely liked Phillip. She reminded me that while he could be "a nice guy," it didn't mean that he couldn't be a controlling asshole, too. Being married was far more intimate than being a friend. It wasn't okay for him to treat me like he had for much of our relationship.

Something she said helped me to realize that losing my father had been completely overshadowed by the pain inflicted by Phillip's reaction to his death the year before. The physical distance between my family and me allowed me to bury my feelings and ignore my sorrow. Instead of taking time off to feel my sadness the day after my father died, I simply carried on and suppressed my anguish.

While Jenny chatted with the kids, I went downstairs to her guest room and composed an email to Phillip. After reporting on the progress of the maintenance issues, I wrote:

"If I stayed here tomorrow and left for Vermont from here, would you be able to come on Saturday?

I have been struggling with dealing with the loss of my father. I had a difficult relationship with him, as you know, and letting go of him has been much different than letting go of my mother. But I think part of why it has made me so very sad is that, in many ways, I feel I lost you, too, at the same time.

Things simply cannot stay as they have been between us. We are all suffering from the dysfunction in our relationship, and we have to talk about that. We have tried talking before, and things always end up in a screaming match or worse. I think you're right that talking away from the stresses of our lives with two people who love us and want the best for everyone concerned is the way to go.

We have been talking about trying to mediate some of the issues between us, with Jake and Rachel helping us, so this weekend, I believe, is a good opportunity. I have given Jake Rachel's phone number and he is going to contact her to see if she is available. (This may already have taken place; I am not certain.)

I am hoping we can put our anger aside and work toward a relationship that serves the best interest of the kids and allows us to heal some of the pain we have both been suffering.

I will let you know where things stand as far as a plumber is concerned. I just called the guy who worked on Tracy's basement. I am hoping that connection will get him to call back. ~ Kasey"

I never heard from him that evening. I started to worry. The two or three glasses of wine I had with dinner made me sleepy, and even though I wanted to head to bed, I was uneasy. I kept going to check to see if Phillip responded to my email.

I knew Phillip wanted to push forward with the idea of mediation. He presented it to me as a way to resolve our many problems, but I considered it a power play. He knew my weaknesses, and this orchestrated event would expose what he thought to be all my flaws. I believed he was rehearsing his side of a custody argument since he often said, "You'd never win in court." Perhaps he got legal advice that he should start practicing that day.

Years earlier, we pursued counseling; however, it ended in a disaster because the counselor asked me to speak first. My candid response was met with Phillip's condemnation when we left the office.

"You're unbelievable, you know that?" he told me. "You sat there for fifteen straight minutes telling this guy what an asshole I am, and not once did you mention the shit you put me through daily."

"What did you want me to say, Phillip? Did you want me to go in there and say everything is just ducky? Isn't this the whole point of seeing someone? Aren't we supposed to tell them what bothers us about the marriage so we can address the problems? You didn't hold back. You painted a pretty clear picture of the issues as you saw them. The only difference is, I told him about my problem with the way you treat me. You told him all the ways you wanted me to change into someone I'm not." Until he came up with the idea of mediation, he'd never agreed to attend counseling again. Perhaps the scrutiny was too much.

Since he had already asked his sister to be his mediator, I asked Jake to be mine. While Phillip wasn't aware of my plans to leave, I wanted to at least go through the motions of solving our marital problems. Allowing him to voice his opinions would give me insight into how he planned to present his side of our marriage. Even though I knew it would be brutal, at this point, I just hoped I could control my emotions and temper so I could clearly state my beliefs regarding what I saw as the core of our problems.

I still cared about his well-being, and worried when I didn't hear from him. I thought about calling him, but I couldn't face hearing his voice. I lay in bed, trying to fall asleep, but my fears of an uncertain future kept me awake.

I didn't want to start over again, but I couldn't continue living with someone who thought so little of me. I didn't want to hurt Phillip. I just wanted to stop hurting myself.

Chapter Seventeen

False Start

In the morning, I found his response to my email.

Kasey-
I don't know if you have been trying to reach me thru the home phone, but I just discovered a little while ago that it had been unplugged.

Thought it was too late to call. So please call me tomorrow to let me know what is going on.
~ Phillip

I still had to address a few more building repairs that cropped up that morning before the Beans and I left Canada to head toward Vermont. I called Jake to alert him of the delay. In our conversation, I told him I was reasonably sure my marriage was over, and I planned to leave Phillip.

Soon after my call, Jake reached out to Phillip's sister, Rachel, about coordinating our get-together on the weekend. It felt odd, after all these years of trying to keep our two families apart so the secret of our marriage wasn't revealed, that our siblings were speaking to one another. I dropped the phone when Jake told me that he accidentally told Rachel of my plans to leave Phillip in their conversation. Picking it up, I listened while he revealed that she planned to alert Phillip. I hung up in a complete panic.

It could change everything if Phillip knew I was planning to leave him. The element of surprise was one of the few things I had on my side. Pacing the floor of the café kitchen, my mind spun out of control. As I waited for the plumber, all my despair turned into fear that I was doing something wrong and would get caught. I imagined Phillip telling the authorities I had kidnapped the Beans, and they were coming for me. Roberto came into Glenn's shop and stopped to chat. I was too distracted to converse and bolted upstairs to go online.

Using the internet, I tried to figure out the laws and if Phillip could have me arrested. Nothing I read about described my situation, but I was desperate to leave Canada and get back over the border. I was initially relieved when the plumber arrived, but waiting for him to finish was torture. What was taking so long?

When the plumber completed the repairs, I paid him and ran out the cafe door. Returning to Jenny's, I briefly explained what happened and instructed Jack and Lucy to get Chubby and get into the car. I barely breathed until I got to Vermont.

When I arrived at Jake's late that night, I checked my email, and sure enough, Phillip now knew my plans.

Kasey,

I've been up all night thinking about all of this. I don't how we got to this point, but I don't want our marriage to end, nor do I want our family to break up.

So I would like to resolve things today. You don't have to come up with a list as we had discussed. We can either have Jake and Rachel discuss things, or we can talk directly.

Regardless of how and where this anger between us has come from, I want it over. I heard our new neighbor and her husband (boyfriend?) laughing with their children tonight and they seemed so happy to be together. Here they were, moving into a crummy little apartment and they were so full of joy to just be together. I broke down and cried for a long time.

I want my wife and I want my kids. Nothing else is more important to me. Let me know how you want this to proceed.

I do love you. I always have and always will.

~ Phillip

I could imagine him sitting alone in the apartment in Cobleskill, wondering how things went awry. But I couldn't understand how he was so blind to the disintegration of our marriage. Was I the only one that was so unhappy? How could he think the issues between us would magically be resolved over the course of a day? While his remorseful tone touched me, I wasn't convinced that anything had changed just because it finally occurred to him it might be over. I composed an email response, trying not to further damage the relationship but firmly stating what I believed to be true about his email.

Phillip-

I honestly am very, very baffled at your statement, 'I don't know how we got to this point.'

I do not want to be cruel and level any more anger at you, as I feel you are beyond your capacity to deal with any more pain in your life. But you had to have known, on some level, that you could not simply say some of the horrid and hurtful things you have said to me without my taking them to heart. You have to have known you could not simply level all your anger and frustrations about things and have me just absorb them without them having an impact.

My decision to come here was not one made overnight. I tried for weeks and weeks to see some sign that things were going to change between us. Things did not get better, they got worse. I was never certain of what was on your mind, especially when you would say things like, 'You just wait until you see what is going to happen to you,' like you did the morning we fought over my laptop. The level of uncertainty I have been living with became unbearable. I could not remain there.

I came here because I needed to be with my family, specifically my brother who is kind and level-headed and who I know loves me with all his heart. I needed the protection of his arms and the guidance he could offer because I am overwhelmed by the pain of this situation and could not be certain of anything other than the need to put an end to the suffering I have been feeling. Most importantly, however, I needed to remove the kids from the level of stress they were absorbing from both of us.

I knew this would hurt you and am truly sorry you are suffering. But you are always telling me that everything's my fault, we are where we are because of me, that I am responsible for your frustration and anger, and I have made every decision in our marriage, you simply have just gone along because I am so very persuasive.

My question to you is: if you feel this way, why in God's name do you want me to stay? Why do you want to remain married to me when you have expressed to me you have nothing left but disdain? You are now telling me you love me. Is this regardless of how flawed you think I am? I cannot process this emotionally or mentally with the vast majority of recent emotions and experiences in our marriage that have told me otherwise. I left because I had no other choice. I left because I could not survive the pain and destruction that I identify with our relationship.

Jake told me he feels I need to simply step back and not be reactionary. By letting some time pass, it will let me deal with things rationally. I feel this is sound advice because I always feel I am on the defense in our relationship. I think it would be good for both of us to reflect on things before moving forward.

You want things that have built up for years to be resolved in one day. That simply cannot happen. I would like you to consider coming here next weekend to talk. Jake is genuinely concerned about you and I know he will in all ways try to be as

helpful as possible. I believe this would be the same for Rachel,
who, if willing and able, should be here too.
I will await your response.
~ Kasey

We arranged a meeting between the four of us on Saturday. To keep things neutral, we met in a conference room at a church about halfway between Marblehead and my brother's home in Vermont. From my perspective, the entire meeting was a complete fiasco. The genuinely concerned husband who wrote an impassioned email imploring me to set aside our differences did not attend the meeting. The Phillip I had been battling for months, however, was there.

My journal of that day is blank because I had removed all those items from the apartment in Cobleskill, and everything was still at Maryanne's. My recollection of events is that it was an unmistakable disaster with mudslinging on both sides. All the recriminations from years of dysfunction were on display. Phillip returned to his sister's that night, and I returned to Jake's house. Now, I was more determined than ever to divorce him.

Phillip called me from Rachel's the next day and asked to visit the kids before returning to Cobleskill. I never wanted to prevent him from seeing his children, so I agreed. Jake and Meredith were also deeply concerned about Phillip's well-being, so no one had a problem with his visit.

The reunion was awkward because the kids knew what might happen. They loved Phillip, but the years of constant separation had shaped their relationship as much as it had shaped his and mine. After a brief and loving visit, the twins became antsy, trying to avoid any unpleasant conversation. They kept looking at me with questions in their eyes. I signaled my assurances that they were behaving appropriately, but it became uncomfortable when they both became silent.

Phillip turned to me and asked me if we could talk. I reluctantly agreed. I figured nothing could be any worse than the day before, so we went out in the car to sit and talk. He couldn't stop crying; he sobbed for what seemed like hours. I tried not to be frustrated. Any time I cried, Phillip would admonish me, telling me my tears were manipulative. I tried not to let the past color the moment, so I comforted him. It was hard, however, not to feel played.

He apologized for his behavior during the meeting, and his regret seemed sincere. He said it frightened him to think of life without the Beans and me. He acknowledged his unfairness in placing all the blame on me for our problems. I told him I, too, was sorry for acting like a madwoman at times.

While he expressed his love and commitment to change, I held out little hope that things would ever be different. I desperately wanted to believe him, but my doubts were well-founded. We had resolved nothing. There was no new understanding of one another. We weren't beyond all the triggers that led to our unhappiness. He didn't take any responsibility for all the hurtful things he'd said for decades or for distorting the facts of my contributions to our finances. Not once did he even pretend to understand why it hurt so much when he told me in a thousand ways I was unacceptable. Why couldn't he see the enormous difference between calling someone out for bad behavior and attacking their personality for their individual preferences? I couldn't see how we could pull through this horrible experience when we couldn't even be in the same room without spewing animosity toward one another.

"Why, Phillip? Why do you even want me to come back? I get that you miss the kids, but name one reason you want me back?"

"I just do. I miss you."

"That's not enough. You miss the relationship, but you don't miss me."

"That's not true. I love and miss you, too."

My mind raced, waiting for his answer. It didn't come. He couldn't even name one reason he loved me. Why? I loved his crooked smile. I loved his sense of humor. I loved how smart he was and how he made me want to be more accomplished. I loved learning about the things that interested him, even if I didn't find them interesting myself. I loved his creative nature and how he excelled at just about anything he tried. I loved how he kissed me and the way he grabbed me from behind to hold me. I loved the way he walked with the oddest gait. I loved it when he woke me up in the middle of the night to make love. I loved his dedication to his parents, sister, and friends. I loved the fact he cherished his family's heritage. I tried, for years, to show him just how much I loved him. I wanted him to love me back.

I understood he missed the kids and me. He was used to being in a relationship. But that wasn't the same as loving someone. When you love someone, you want as much, or more, for them as you want for yourself. I wanted the world for him, yet he didn't share those feelings. I wanted to ask him to explain how I could change everything about myself and still be the person I was. Why did it matter that I never finished college? Why did he complain about the way I drank my coffee? How could the music I liked be stupid? He seemed to understand a desire for friendships outside of marriage wasn't abnormal or harmful to him. Why was my desire to have friends such a problem? The list went on and on. How could he utter the words "I love you" when he didn't like anything about me anymore? Maybe he loved the attention and support our relationship once offered, but was that love? I wanted more for Phillip. I knew, without asking, that he wanted so much less for me.

At that moment, I wished I could see into his heart. I wanted to believe he truly loved me, but I didn't. I wanted him to accept me, warts and all. The love he gave me was conditional, and in his eyes, I constantly failed to meet those conditions.

"Kasey, I don't want things to end."

"What's ending, Phillip? We barely speak anymore without it ending in an argument. How am I supposed to react to your contempt? Do you even realize that, a year ago, you refused to even let me take time off to grieve for my father?"

He hung his head, and I saw tears spilling onto his jeans. He asked me if I would consider returning to New York. I told him I would think about it. He left to return to Cobleskill so he could return to work the next day. I went in to talk with the twins about the hard decision we needed to make.

Part 3

A Revised Approach

"Your strength doesn't come from winning.
It comes from struggles and hardship.
Everything that you go through prepares
you for the next level."

~ Germany Kent

Chapter Eighteen

Returning to Cobleskill

The Beans and I had a long talk that night. They missed their dad and their cats. We agreed to give it one last try, and I promised to look into changing schools. The next day, I called Phillip to tell him.

"Hi."

"Hi."

"The kids and I talked about it, and we're willing to try again. But things have got to change, Phillip. I mean it. I'm not going to come back to the same bullshit that forced me to leave in the first place."

"It will. It will change. I promise."

I hung up the phone and told the Beans we needed to pack.

Over the next few months, I noticed a significant change in Phillip's behavior. I was cautious, however, because this had happened before. I wanted to believe him, but I couldn't. I'd been through these reprieves too often to trust it would last. I welcomed the calm, but continued to expect the storm. During this time, I found myself still in defensive mode. I tried to pull back, but part of this was because Phillip remained adamant about having me report every penny I spent. Even if he wasn't combative about it, I found it humiliating.

His habit of closing himself off in Jack's room each night didn't change. He was still very private about conversations that I imagined were about something he wanted to keep from me. So even though he tried harder than ever to temper his frustrations when he spoke to the twins and me, I wasn't convinced that anything had changed. I just couldn't do anything about it without money. Phillip still exerted control over all our finances. He still kept his salary and income a secret. But since he wasn't ranting or threatening, I focused more on getting a job since that was the only way I could ever regain my independence if things got ugly again.

It wasn't easy putting a resumé together because my work experience was all over the place. Since I left the advertising industry, I have built websites, got my realtor's license, and taught school. I also worked as a mobile notary, did graphic design, and owned and operated the café. Finding a well-paying job after I'd been out of the regular workforce for years would be challenging. I was also middle-aged and looking for work in a recovering economy. I briefly explored the idea of opening another café or catering business before realizing it couldn't happen without money, and I had none.

My other focus was trying to get the kids the help they needed. Both kids were very smart, and seeing them struggle in school broke my heart. Redirecting my attention kept my frustrations about my marriage in check.

I made an appointment to meet with an adjustment counselor from the public school system who I learned could help me navigate a transfer of the Beans to public school. I worked with the teachers at Sacred Heart to make the transition smoother than if we just yanked them out without considering all the aspects of their emotional and educational needs. There were things to consider, and we decided it would be best to wait until after the Christmas holidays.

In early December, I finally landed a small, part-time job, cold-calling potential clients for an insurance agent. It wasn't the best job in the world, but having even a tiny income helped me relax, because I didn't always have to ask Phillip for money.

The holidays had a calming effect. We both tried to refrain from past feelings of anger and resentment. I told myself not to let Phillip off the hook for what had happened in the past, but I couldn't allow myself to punish him when he seemed to genuinely try to be pleasant.

I blasted off an email to my friends in Canada right before Christmas.

Happy Holidays, My Dear Friends,

I hope this email finds you well and knowing that I miss you all. Life has certainly taken some unexpected turns in recent months, and I am in the States, basically doing whatever I need to do to survive, play nice, and keep whatever sanity I left Canada with intact. Kate and Sharilyn are still running the Healthy School Lunch Program out of the café, and the tearoom is being used by Glenn for his business.

I am trying to remain philosophical about the changes in my life and do things time didn't permit when I was running the café! I have started to write again (which keeps me sane), and I am teaching a film course at the school Lucy and Jack are attending.

We all miss our adopted home more than I can express. It is very hard to say what our future holds, as the economy is holding us captive. But I am forever an optimist and hope my future brings me north once again. We spend as much time in Alexandria as possible, but time is always so short. Please know that while I may not always be in touch, I think of you all, and you remain in my heart and mind.

Love,

~ Kasey, and the 2Beans!

In my mind, it was still the twins and me. While Phillip and I weren't fighting, we weren't behaving like a couple, either. We didn't sleep together, and we treated one another like two roommates rather than two people who would be celebrating our twenty-fifth in less than a year. The upcoming event highlighted the dysfunction in our marriage because we couldn't celebrate it openly. Many people still thought we were married three and a half years after we actually had been. The secret still loomed over us, but I didn't know if a celebration was in order, anyway.

We spent our holidays with Phillip's family. It felt awkward at first because I didn't know what had been said to Phillip's parents. Thankfully, there was no indication of a rift between us, and his parents were as kind as always. Being around other people helped keep the acrimony at bay, since the season brought back memories of wonderful times.

I went to Alexandria shortly after the holidays to deal with more tenant issues. Every month, I was chasing rent or dealing with a significant maintenance issue. Phillip appeared utterly uninterested in our property in Canada. As soon as the lunch program ended for the current school year, I knew I should cut ties with the business side of the building. The school lunch program barely paid the mortgage and all the other expenses. I was falling behind.

While I was up there I spoke with Kate and Sharilyn and Kate said she might be interested in renting the kitchen and continuing the program. I was thrilled because, by now, I knew that I wouldn't be able to go back there. Things had already changed. The hole I'd left in the community had already been filled in, and life there was going on without me.

In late January, Phillip got word that his Uncle Joe had died. He was very close to his father's identical twin brother.

"I'm sorry, honey. I know how much you loved him. I wasn't aware he was that sick," I said when he called from the office to tell me the news.

"My dad is really upset. He didn't get a chance to say goodbye."

I planned to prepare lasagna for dinner that night. I hadn't made one for a while since the various cheeses cost a small fortune, and Phillip insisted on shopping for groceries. When I saw that Ricotta cheese and fresh mozzarella were on sale, I asked him to get some on his way home. I already had some ground beef and pork, so I made two lasagnas and froze one for another meal. I had all the ingredients out when Phillip came in and asked what was for dinner.

"I'm making one of your favorites, lasagna! That's why I needed the groceries. Did you pick them up?"

"You know I can't eat that!"

"Since when?"

"The tomato sauce will kill my stomach."

Phillip put down the sack of groceries and then left the room in a huff. It was the first time he'd lashed out at me in weeks, leaving me confused. Why didn't I know he was struggling with eating foods like lasagna? I had been cooking a lot of comfort foods because they were cheap, and Phillip and the kids enjoyed them. But when had things progressed to where he struggled to eat? I knew he told Rachel months ago about some tests, but I couldn't reveal that without him knowing I read his email. He was on the couch, and I sat beside him, trying to casually approach him about my concern.

"Did you ever call that gastro doctor?" I said this with as little reproach as possible, but my question still made him angry.

"When am I supposed to schedule an appointment? Barry laid off Debbie a few weeks ago, and she had no notice at all. For all I know, I could be next. I can't afford to take time off, Kasey."

I knew better than to press the issue. It was a flashpoint, and we were avoiding those. I went to put the cheese and other ingredients away. I wasn't in the mood to cook anymore, so I made a quick frittata, and when it was done, I called everyone to dinner. I watched Phillip from the corner of my eye, again questioning what I was missing.

Chapter Nineteen

Happy Birthday to Me

At the end of January, Phillip went to his uncle's funeral for the weekend. The kids and I stayed behind because attending would have meant missing more school.

I was in an excellent mood because I didn't have to try hard to be on my best behavior. Jack read a book while Lucy watched something on TV in the living room. I sat at the kitchen table, creating invoices to bill the schools in Canada for the school lunches. I stopped typing and called to the Beans, "You guys want some hot chocolate?"

"Sure," they shouted in unison.

I put on some music, pulled a saucepan out of the cabinet, and gathered all the ingredients needed to make the hot chocolate. I searched for some marshmallows and then recalled that I'd begged Phillip to buy a can of whipped cream and knew we had some left. I grabbed that and placed it on the counter as well.

Pouring the milk into the pan, I watched as the steam rose, careful not to scald it. As I stirred, I added the dark, rich cocoa powder, sugar, and a pinch of salt. The motions caused the chocolate to form swirls before blending into the warm liquid. The aroma tempted my taste buds, and I looked for something to indulge in myself. Before pouring it into mugs, I did a little digging in the cabinets above the sink to see if I could find us a snack. I found some microwave popcorn, a few bottles of red wine, and a bottle of Glenlivet, Phillip's favorite scotch. Everything was unopened and had gathered dust. It made me realize it had been quite a while since I had seen Phillip partake in a glass of wine or a few fingers of scotch neat when he came home. When had that stopped? I put the booze away but left out the popcorn to give the Beans a snack with their hot chocolate.

I thought about what had happened the night before, with the lasagna incident. It stunned me that Phillip was having bad enough problems with his stomach that he couldn't eat one of his favorite foods. Since he refused to acknowledge he'd had some tests done months earlier, I thought he must be all right since tests would have revealed any problems by now.

These moments alone caused me to think about feelings I'd managed to shove aside for a while. Phillip's absence began to resurrect my resentment. When my father died, I was discouraged from taking time off to grieve. Yet he left for an entire weekend to attend his uncle's funeral. The matter underscored the continued hierarchy in our relationship. I didn't resent him for going to his uncle's funeral. I resented that Phillip felt he had the right to determine if I could go to my father's. I began to think again about our marriage. I realized the only difference between now and November was that we acted more civil toward one another. I avoided wondering where it would all lead so I could enjoy my time with the Beans.

The following weekend, things were "back to normal," whatever that was. As I washed the dinner dishes, Phillip entered the kitchen and leaned against the counter, watching me for a minute before asking, "What do you want for your birthday this year?" The casualness of his question caught me off guard. I wasn't prepared to answer him. I had no funds of my own to buy him anything for his birthday and had put thoughts of celebrating our birthdays out of my mind.

In recent years, birthdays have seemed more obligatory than celebratory. We usually traveled to Phillip's parents' home because his mother's birthday fell between Phillip's and mine. Since we weren't going back to see his folks this year, I assumed we'd be staying in. I wasn't thinking of doing anything more than maybe having an enormous glass of wine while I made something special for dinner. I had spent time looking through grocery store circulars trying to find crabmeat on sale so I could make him Maryland-style crab cakes or seafood stuffed scallops. I thought we'd both enjoy it and hoped it wouldn't upset his stomach.

When I heard Phillip's question about what I wanted for my birthday, even I was surprised at what flew out of my mouth.

"I want you to see a doctor." I spun around to face him. "I want you to take whatever is happening with this whole swallowing thing more seriously than you have. That's what I want for my birthday," I said sincerely.

"Don't go there," he warned me. "I'll go to the doctor when I damn well please, and in case you haven't noticed, I barely have time to take a shit these days because I'm working non-stop to keep this family afloat. I know how to treat this, so mind your business." He stormed out of the room.

"Well, I guess I'll just have to make do with a big ole glass of wine for my birthday," I said under my breath.

As I washed the dishes, my mind raced, wondering what he meant by, "I know how to treat this." I knew better than to bring it up again. Not only was he working a full-time job, but he had also taken on freelance writing projects for Marco. Phillip always focused on his work assignments to the exclusion of everything else. Whether it was his regular job or a freelance assignment, he always worked over and above the call of duty, hoping to stay employed. I emptied the sink and watched the water go down the drain, hoping my concerns were unfounded.

As weeks passed, I tried to believe that if something were wrong, Phillip would have sought the advice of a trained professional. However, a nagging feeling bothered me. The more I thought about it, the more I became troubled. A war waged inside me. We'd lived apart for years, and part of me insisted Phillip had ample opportunity to address his health issues on his own. However, the other part saw him struggling to eat, and my instinct to love and protect him took over.

Finally, I decided since I didn't know if he had done anything about his health, I would. I called and made an appointment to see our new family doctor. Since he was booked for weeks, I agreed to see his nurse practitioner.

A few days later, I sat there doing a Sudoku puzzle in the waiting area, rehearsing what I planned to say so she couldn't refuse to answer my questions. Once in her office, I told her why I'd come to see her.

"I know that you can't discuss my husband's health with me without his permission. I know that," I said bluntly. "What I'm asking you is what advice would you give me if I came to you with these symptoms," and I began reciting what I'd observed in Phillip without giving her a chance to cut me off. "I've had acid reflux for many years now and am taking omeprazole. But I'm having a difficult time swallowing, and sometimes I regurgitate into my mouth unexpectedly and sometimes spit up a kind of white foamy liquid. It doesn't seem to affect my energy level, but I still have persistent heartburn, even with the medications. What could cause these things?" I asked her and started to tear up.

She looked at me with great compassion and gently leaned toward me.

"He needs to seek treatment now," she warned me. "As soon as he can." She drew a breath, reached out, and took my hands.

Then she said, "Look, I don't want to scare you. Without seeing him and running tests, there is no way to know what's causing the dysphagia, but this could be very serious. One of my favorite professors had similar symptoms when I was in school. It turned out he had cancer, and he died within six months." Again, she assured me she couldn't accurately diagnose Phillip's condition without testing but the concern in her voice terrified me.

My heart was heavy as I drove back to Cobleskill that day. I knew if I told him about going to the appointment, I risked alienating him further since it still pissed him off that I asked him to see a doctor. But I knew not telling him would be irresponsible. Regardless of his anger, I knew I had to have a tough conversation with him when he got home that night.

When I got home, I still had hours before the kids got out of school, so I researched the internet. I'd written the word "dysphagia" on a piece of paper since I was unfamiliar with the term. None of what I read about dysphagia eased my mind.

"See your doctor if you regularly have difficulty swallowing or if weight loss, regurgitation, or vomiting accompanies your dysphagia," warned the Mayo Clinic.

Holy shit! The weight loss! These were all symptoms he was experiencing! I'd assumed he'd dropped a few pounds because he'd started jogging again, or worse, he was trying to be more attractive to a secret lover. He'd really trimmed down. Except for being unable to swallow sometimes, he looked healthier than he had for years.

I studied a picture I had of him in my wallet. He was holding our Beans as toddlers, cradling them, one in each arm, sitting in an oversized chair in their nursery in Blairstown. His radiant smile beamed from the past, capturing the emotion he felt as I snapped their picture. These little beings were his pride and joy, and he loved them.

Hot tears streamed down my face as I confronted my fears and emotions. There were times I resented him. No, I hated him. Our relationship had fallen apart, and it was still extremely fragile. Sometimes, I still suspected he had planned to file for divorce and could have been having an affair. Perhaps my threat to leave him made him decide against divorcing after all. I still thought he stayed in our marriage out of habit and wanted to maintain the status quo. But he was trying. He was trying harder to get along with me than he ever had before, which counted for something. I needed to tell him what I did and report what the nurse practitioner said.

He was angrier than I'd seen him in months when I told him. He didn't speak to me for days. He never spoke of the incident, but he sent me an email from work a few weeks later.

Can you call and make an appointment with the doctor you saw?

After that appointment, they scheduled some tests. Phillip wouldn't share the results. I suspected he told Rachel and considered checking his emails to see if he'd said anything to her. But I decided not to do that again.

I was satisfied that, even though he was angry with me, for once, I got what I wanted for my birthday.

Chapter Twenty

Sigh of Relief

The Beans' birthday was at the end of March. Tammy from Sacred Heart had asked me to cater a murder mystery dinner theatre event on the day of their birthday. Despite my reluctance to interfere with this family celebration, I took the job, hoping it would bring in more paying events so I could finally start making a decent income.

Phillip and I agreed to celebrate the following weekend. We took them into Albany for the afternoon, visiting the bustling Museum of Science and Technology, or *CMOST*, which offered a range of activities we all enjoyed. It was a tremendous hit, and we allowed each twin to get a small gift at the gift shop. They even enjoyed seeing *Hop*, a movie they were initially reluctant to visit, complaining it would be too childish for their thirteen-year-old sensibilities. We topped the celebration off by going out for dinner, something we rarely did on our tight budget, and concluded the day with a homemade cake, ice cream, and the opening of their presents. That day was the first time in years that it felt like we were a real family. Phillip uncharacteristically held my hand as we walked and seemed full of tenderness as we ushered the kids through the city.

Shortly after we returned to the apartment, Phillip entered Jack's room and closed the door. I tiptoed closer to the door and heard him leaving a voicemail for his sister.

"Just an update... I have a gastro and GP consult tomorrow. I have a surgery consult on Thursday. Still don't know when they will actually do the biopsy. According to my doctor, they were supposed to do it this week. I don't think I should tell Mom and Dad till next weekend when I know more. Call me later. Love you." I heard him hang up the phone.

I quickly went into the kitchen so he wouldn't know I was eavesdropping. I knew he needed the support he received from Rachel. Usually, I would have been upset that he wasn't telling me this news but that no longer mattered. I was happy that he had seen a doctor and would soon feel better.

Some of my relief also came from knowing that I'd made it through the worst of the winter months with the property in Canada. Soon, the chaos of maintaining the property long-distance would be behind me. Once the lunch program was over, I planned to list the property.

The following day, I took Chubby for a walk. The clean, dry air and cloudless cerulean skies welcomed me and my furry companion into the backyard. I noticed that a bright yellow and purple crocus poked through the last mounds of dingy gray snow in the winter-fatigued backyard. This harbinger of spring raised my spirits. I started to think perhaps everything has finally changed for the better and wondered if maybe my marriage wasn't headed for a divorce after all.

When Chub and I returned, I went into the kitchen and called to the kids in the living room watching TV.

"Hey, do you guys want scones for breakfast?"

They responded with a resounding "Yes!"

Because there were few foods Jack and Lucy both liked, I decided to make chocolate chip scones because chocolate chip anything was the exception to their divergent food preferences. I began assembling all the dry ingredients onto the counter.

Grating the frozen butter into a bowl, I worked quickly, careful not to scrape my knuckles on the rough edges. Soon, I floated in and out of thoughts about the world I'd left behind seven months earlier. Cooking of any kind triggered thoughts about all the hours I had spent in the kitchen of my beloved café. It wasn't just cooking that brought back memories of the café. The dishes I used to serve my family were the same ones I'd once placed in front of my customers. All the happiness that came to mind made it hard to let go of the past.

With the oven warmed and the scones ready to go in, I placed them on the middle shelf and closed the oven door, setting the timer for twenty minutes—plenty of time to shower and get dressed.

I hollered to the Beans, "Last call if you need the bathroom," but I hurried in before anyone could respond.

As the water covered my body, I lathered my hair with shampoo. I tried to break away from my earlier thoughts. Even though I'd done a few catering jobs for the kids' school, there were more challenges to carving out a niche for myself as a caterer in Cobleskill. Many well-established businesses had their own kitchens.

I'd looked into the possibility of opening a small shop, but there were too many obstacles. Then I considered joining forces with another woman I'd met who also had thoughts of operating a café. We even looked at a small shop available to rent. But all that took more money than I could come up with, so I finally acknowledged that opening a new business wasn't a reality.

As I showered, I questioned if I wanted that anyway. While I loved owning the café, it was never my dream. I loved to cook simply because it allowed me to express myself. I'd done that by writing, painting, acting, and singing. Cooking was another outlet for my creative expression.

As I toweled off, I glanced in the mirror. I barely recognized the woman looking back. My obligations over the past few years had consumed me. No, I didn't want to start another business where I would be required to work fourteen hours a day just to make ends meet. I wasn't sure what I would do, but I knew more than anything, I was driven to write again. The script and music for my play languished in bankers boxes packed and stored deep within closets. They hadn't seen the light of day for years. It seemed silly to even think about reviving that project. But I knew someday I'd get back to writing. I just had no idea when that would happen.

I had a job interview scheduled for the next day as a sous chef at a restaurant in Albany, but I saw an ad in a local newspaper for a similar position at a resort closer to our apartment. I emailed Phillip and let him know I would apply for both jobs. He replied, asking me to check on the details for the two tests being performed on Wednesday. I quickly obliged and reported that, according to the doctor's office, the procedure would take less than two hours, and he would most likely feel well enough to return to work.

I went to the library to print out my resumé. I wasn't exactly excited about landing a job at either one of the restaurants, but I thought of it as a step toward rebuilding my life and regaining the financial independence I once had. Both jobs paid better than the other positions I'd looked at, and I hoped I'd get the one closer to home. It was a start.

Meanwhile, in Alexandria, Kate and Jenny helped create a list of personal and business possessions that still remained there. Jenny helped price them for sale. I was reluctant to sell some items we had purchased for our former home in Blairstown, but I knew I had to let them go. I needed the money with Hydro One in Canada breathing down my neck for back utility payments.

I still had to retrieve the things I'd left with my friend Maryanne in St. Johnsville. I didn't see her often since her granddaughter no longer attended Sacred Heart. We exchanged calls and emails occasionally, but that became less frequent because she had sold her house and had to organize her move. Trying to make arrangements for me to retrieve the belongings allowed us to catch up, and I shared my news about Phillip's health issues.

When I'd packed those things and stashed them at Maryanne's house, I never dreamed I'd leave them there for four months. November now seemed like ages ago. I could barely recall what I had brought there. I feared that if Phillip found out I'd removed items from our apartment, it could open old wounds. I was determined not to let that happen.

Chapter Twenty-One

The Anguish of April

April 8, 2011

Phillip's tests were scheduled for the morning. The facility was about an hour from home. We had to take the kids with us because they would have no one to get them to and from school.

After we arrived at the testing facility and Phillip was checked in, I took Jack and Lucy for breakfast at a nearby diner. The nursing staff assured me that Phillip wouldn't be ready to go home for hours. I alerted one of the nurses that I'd be carrying Phillip's cell phone, asking them to call if, for any reason, I needed to come back.

I tried to appear nonchalant at the diner because I didn't want my deep concerns to register with Jack and Lucy. After we ordered our meals, they read books they had brought along while I did a puzzle from a newspaper that someone left behind. Our meals had just been delivered when I got a call from a nurse telling me to return immediately. As I paid for the food, my heart was in my throat, arguing with the waitress I didn't want the food to go.

All the way back to the facility, I feared the worst. I assumed they found something horrible during one of the procedures. By the time I arrived back, I couldn't hide my anxiety as I rushed into the testing facility lobby. I waited for the kids to catch up. At the desk, I was told, "We can release your husband once he wakes up from the sedation. When the results of his tests are in, they will be sent to his doctor." I pushed my anger aside, thinking they had alarmed me over nothing.

The Beans and I sat in the waiting area until Phillip could be released. I sat there looking at the twins, playing and talking quietly. Maybe the anxiety of not knowing the test results drove my thoughts to dark places. But now that Phillip's tests were done, the situation seemed far more serious. I kept trying to shove aside all the reasons for concern and convinced myself that the doctor would suggest some minor procedure and Phillip would mend in no time. I told myself Phillip would never have let things get too far without addressing his health issues.

Before heading back home, Phillip wanted to get something to eat. The Beans were hungry, too, so we headed for a Subway in a nearby strip mall. We sat opposite one another, avoiding eye contact, as he ate a turkey sub methodically. I busied myself by fidgeting with the placemat that listed all the local businesses. By the time we left, I couldn't recall even one.

I convinced Phillip to take the rest of the day off work as he didn't look well enough to focus on writing copy for his clients. He agreed with me for once and called in sick once we got home.

He sat on the couch, dozing on and off. I called Jenny to kill time. She and Roberto had recently agreed to occupy the old tearoom since Glenn had abandoned it shortly after renting it. They wanted to use the space for a joint venture selling antiques. Having them there to keep a watchful eye on the place gave me a sense of relief. They also agreed to sell some things that belonged to Phillip and me to help us financially.

Jenny reminded me that even without test results, it was great that Phillip was following through on getting answers regarding his medical issues. Maybe after his health issues were addressed, he would be more like himself, she told me. Her positive spin was the antidote to the malaise that hovered over my heart that day. By the time we hung up, I was convinced I had been letting my imagination get the best of me.

Later that evening, I heard Phillip telling Rachel over the phone that all the way back in February, he had developed a small but persistent and progressive nodule in the area of the neck just above his collarbone. *Were the tests he'd had that morning related to this issue?* Hearing him tell Rachel about his concerns once again raised my anxiety over the uncertainty of his condition. It didn't ease as the following days passed without any news regarding the tests that were performed.

April 11

The following Monday morning, we still had no results from Phillip's tests. I tried to remind myself it was unlikely they'd process tests over the weekend, and I was being impatient. But when the phone rang, I nearly jumped since I was sure the doctor's office was calling. I was wrong.

The call was from the human resources department at the resort I'd applied to, offering me a position as a sous chef in one of their many kitchens. We discussed some dates for training. I related that I could confirm my availability once I had a chance to discuss my proposed training schedule with Phillip.

It was hard to contain my excitement. By now, I'd become used to asking Phillip to purchase food. But when I needed him to pick up personal hygiene products, it wasn't just uncomfortable; I was embarrassed. Explaining why I still needed sanitary pads or what kind of deodorant I preferred degraded me. When he shopped, he bought any item on sale and claimed I was ungrateful if I made the slightest complaint. Sometimes, he couldn't find time to go to the store, and I had to beg him for money so I could go on my own. He usually resisted and told me I could wait, but if he relented, I was still expected to provide receipts and return the change. This job was a huge step in having a sense of security and confidence I could provide for myself and the Beans. I beamed as I returned to the living room to return the portable phone to the charger.

I almost knocked on the door to Jack's room to tell Phillip, but let him sleep instead because I knew he wasn't feeling well. However, a part of me simply wanted to relish my good news alone.

After I cleared the dishes off the table, I took a long shower. It was still my go-to thing to relax and have time for myself. I closed my eyes and let the water drench my head and face, smiling as I imagined his reaction to my getting a job. I wondered how he'd react? He clearly wanted me to contribute to the household income. But did he realize it also meant I would finally have some real money and the choices that would give me? Phillip's ability to call all the shots would end.

Knowing I'd have options allowed me to relax a bit. I still wasn't sure if I wanted to remain in my marriage. But if I stayed, it was because I chose that for myself. I wasn't just doing it because I was stuck in a financial quagmire. And if the marriage was over, I would have the resources to extricate myself and the Beans after the property in Alexandria sold.

I had just finished rinsing my hair when I suddenly heard Lucy banging on the bathroom door.

"Daddy needs help," she shouted over the sound of the running water.

I've been saying that for years, I thought sarcastically as she interrupted my moment of solitude.

"Tell Daddy I'll be right there, honey." I wanted to stay in my wet cocoon, but I shut off the water and toweled off.

When I went into the bedroom and saw Phillip's face, I felt guilty for making light of the situation. "Honey, what's wrong?" He looked pale and clammy. "Do you want me to call an ambulance?"

"No. It's my neck. I'm in so much pain," he said through tears. "I might have pulled a muscle, but it feels worse than that. Can you take me to that walk-in clinic?" he pleaded.

"Of course!" I told him. I instructed the kids to get their Game Boys for the car, and we left a few minutes later.

Instead of going to the closer walk-in clinic, I convinced Phillip it made more sense to return to the medical center where he had the tests. While the forty-five minute trip there was a bit further away, his new doctor had an office in the same complex, and there was an urgent care unit right on campus. He couldn't nod, so I made the decision before he could disagree and got on the highway instead of heading toward the route for the walk-in clinic.

I wish I could say I was a model of compassion and grace on the drive there. I was not. I wish I could say I focused solely on my husband's well-being. I did not. No matter how many times I wished I'd risen above the negative impulses that sometimes consumed me, as we traveled to the medical facility, I stewed. The words that came out of my mouth directly conflicted with my thoughts.

"It will be okay," I assured Phillip. "Once we get there, they'll give you something for the pain, and you'll be all right." What I kept thinking, however, was, *This is so typical. If it were me, he'd accuse me of faking it or tell me to take a few Motrin.*

The resentment built up during our marriage was always right below the surface. I tried to learn that the vicious cycle we'd created was counterproductive. But in that moment, I couldn't move beyond one of the major obstacles in our relationship, our invisible scorecard. I began to justify my thoughts with the recollections of the countless times I was hurt, ill, or emotionally bereft, and Phillip would not offer me an ounce of compassion or sympathy. Even if I'd just spent days nursing him back to health, if I came down with the same cold or flu, anything Phillip did to help me was done begrudgingly.

Almost more annoying was his need for one-upmanship whenever one of us was sick. If I had a headache, he had a migraine. If I had a cold, he had the flu. When I was diagnosed with carpal tunnel and needed surgery, he began wearing a wrist and hand brace, too. Even after the diagnosis and surgery were performed to remove the tumors on my parathyroid glands, he continued to insinuate my claims of exhaustion were just an excuse for tasks left undone and said I was just lazy. It was as if the surgery corrected the problem, and I automatically recovered the following day. The concept of healing seemed to be beyond his grasp.

However, this wasn't just in moments of illness. When I needed a "favor" from him, Phillip would ask, "What will you give me for it?" While his words were always framed as a joke, he was serious. He only seemed willing to do something for me if he would benefit from whatever I asked him to do or if I offered something in return.

As I drove, these memories left me keeping score instead of sincerely being there for him. I convinced myself what was happening that day was purely Phillip. I thought he probably slept with his head in an awful position. Not once did I connect the dots to the tests he'd had that past Friday.

Once we arrived, we sat in the waiting area for more than an hour, waiting for his turn to be seen. Because I was convinced it was a minor problem, I was initially more concerned about how much time it took to be seen rather than being concerned about my husband's well-being. The Beans sat quietly in the corner, playing, while I sat close to Phillip, trying to contain my frustration.

However, after a while, it was difficult to watch him struggling to cope with the pain while they took others in to see a physician. Finally, I told him I'd be back in a minute and approached the nurse's station.

"Excuse me," I said to a petite young woman behind the desk. Her name tag read "Liz," but I called her "Miss," almost hissing the word. "I brought my husband in over an hour ago, and it seems like people who just came in recently are being seen ahead of him. He's in a lot of pain. Can you tell me what's going on?" She looked over her shoulder at another nurse standing a few feet away with a clipboard.

"His doctor is aware that he is here, and we're consulting with him," she told me.

"What the bloody hell?" I said to myself as I returned to the waiting area. I wondered if that was the standard procedure. That didn't seem right, but I didn't know how to express my concerns.

Ten minutes later, I returned to the nurse's station. "Is there anything you can give him, at least?" I inquired.

"That's why we called his doctor," she said politely and walked away.

A while later, they sent him home, loaded up on painkillers.

Phillip slept in the chair when we got home, so I checked my email. Jenny had issues identifying keys for the building, and I updated her on Phillip's condition. I told her I assumed the agony was caused by a pulled muscle or the awkward positions he slept in to deal with the persistent stomach acid. She encouraged me not to worry too much. By the time I got off the phone, I convinced myself Phillip would be fine.

April 12

Despite the heavy painkillers, Phillip's pain was worse the following day. He agreed we should go back to the urgent care facility. I had no idea how long we would be gone so we'd have to take the kids with us even though they would miss part or an entire school day again. I was at a loss for what else to do.

We piled into the car and returned to the same facility we visited the previous day. This time, however, the nurse I had spoken to the day before came to us immediately and informed us Phillip's doctor, the one who had ordered the testing, wanted to see us. As we were escorted through a series of corridors connected to the medical offices in another complex area, my fears began to mount.

Once we arrived at the doctor's office, Jack and Lucy comfortably sat in the nearly empty waiting room. They huddled close together for support, looking at me nervously. I tried my best to assure them everything would be okay, even though the pit of my stomach was doing flip-flops.

Phillip held his neck stiffly as he sat down. While clearly in pain, his demeanor was almost relaxed. I stood, unable to remain calm enough to take a seat, and braced myself for what the doctor was about to say.

"I have some unpleasant news," he began. Phillip and I exchanged a look. "I'm sorry it took so long to get back to you, but we needed to ensure the results. In reviewing the images, we found hundreds of small white masses. The needle biopsy is consistent with adenocarcinoma, which is a type of cancerous tumor. The endoscopy revealed lesions that extend down to your gastric body. A large mass could be the cause of the pain you're experiencing. We found that it is dangerously close to your spinal cord. The only way to know, with absolute certainty, what we're dealing with is to do further testing. At this point, I would advise you to check into the hospital immediately so they can conduct more tests. I've contacted an oncologist on your behalf, and he will order additional tests. I am so sorry to be telling you this," he said, handing me some paperwork.

Phillip remained composed, while I couldn't say anything for fear of falling apart. "Is there any chance that it's something other than cancer?" Phillip asked him.

"I wouldn't count on it," the doctor replied, shaking his head.

We left his office in a daze.

I drove to the hospital in silence. I couldn't trust myself to speak. I was bombarded with the widest array of emotions I'd ever experienced. The magnitude of this diagnosis was devastating. And yet, I was so angry at Phillip. Why had he waited to get treatment? Now, he was gravely ill. The guilt of my private thoughts earlier haunted me. I realized it was time to put away the scorecard. I relegated those thoughts to the back of my mind and had the good sense to know that whatever I was dealing with regarding our fractured relationship meant nothing at this point.

Chapter Twenty-Two

St. Joe's

As we headed west to the hospital, I couldn't imagine life moving forward. It was as if everything had come to a grinding halt, and we were caught in some sort of time warp to allow us entry into a hidden dimension. When we arrived, the sound of the receptionist's voice was muffled and distorted. The lights were too bright, and I wanted to squint. I moved my arms and legs, eyes and mouth, but they did not feel like they were a part of me. Then Lucy reached out and grabbed my hand as we rode the elevator to the floors above, and I was once again grounded in the moment. The Beans needed me, and I had to be strong for them.

When we arrived on the floor, a nurse escorted Phillip to some unknown destination. I could feel the urgency now. I wanted to go with him but didn't want to leave the kids behind. I wasn't even sure if they would have let me accompany him. Instead, I allowed myself to be led to the hospital room they'd assigned to him.

The Beans and I walked into a sea of blue: light blue walls, blue vinyl floor, striped blue curtains, navy blue visitor's chair. There was a laminated oak bedside table and a TV mounted high on the wall. I looked for the remote so I could turn on the TV, hoping to take our minds off of what was happening.

The curtain was drawn, dividing the room. I heard snoring on the other side. I didn't know what to say or how to act. I kept thinking, *"What am I going to tell Phillip's parents and sister?"*

I flipped through the channels, looking for anything the kids might like to watch. I settled on the Animal Planet channel, airing reruns of *The Crocodile Hunter*. They shared the navy blue visitor's chair and watched the episode with rapt attention.

When the nurses wheeled Phillip into the room, it hit me. This was real. He wasn't coming home with us tonight. I waited while the nurses helped him settle in, then retreated into the bathroom to wipe away tears I couldn't contain. We stayed all day, eating dinner in the cafeteria, playing cards, and watching too much TV. The news programs were never so interesting.

We were told they planned to conduct more tests later in the evening, followed by another battery of tests the following day. However, based on what they knew from the earlier tests, Phillip had esophageal cancer. A CT scan of his neck showed a large, calcified mass. An MRI revealed multiple enlarged lymph nodes, and there was a pathological compression fracture of his C7 vertebra with an approximate 30% compression. They started him on steroids and morphine immediately.

I could barely keep up with the medical jargon. Phillip wrote copy for pharmaceutical clients for years. He needed to explain most of what they said. It seemed cruel to make Phillip go into depth about how this disease had infiltrated his body and was consuming his life. But, I wanted to know as much as possible about his condition because, later on, I would have to tell others about the gravity of his illness. I took notes, hoping it would help me keep things straight as if, somehow, getting the information right would improve his chances of survival.

In the morning, they would do more ultrasounds and X-rays, an esophagram, an EGD, and some other tests I didn't have time to write down. Until they were done, we didn't know the exact extent of his illness—we knew it was cancer but not the prognosis.

I needed to get back to Cobleskill at some point. Chubby had been home all day and hadn't been walked. I also wanted to bring Phillip his belongings because he only had the clothes he had been wearing. The only thing he had with him at the hospital was his work laptop since he'd brought it with him for some reason when we left home.

"I guess I should let Barry know and try to wrap up my work," he said as I was about to leave.

I leaned over and kissed his cheek, trying to avoid breaking down. This was purely Phillip, I thought. He's facing a major health crisis, and he's still worried about his job.

Phillip asked me to call his sister when the twins and I got back to Cobleskill. Knowing all the negative things he'd been telling her about me made it difficult to imagine how she would receive the news coming from me. From this point on, I knew I just had to suck it up because it wasn't the time to focus on our marital problems. We were all officially trying to save a life.

Chubby greeted us at the door when we arrived back in Cobleskill. I'm sure he would have been crossing his legs if he could have. "Hey, guys. Can you walk Chub and then feed him and the cats? Just take him over to the bushes. I'm going to go upstairs so I can call Auntie Rachel."

I sat on the bed, staring at the small notepad where I had scribbled all the notes I had taken earlier. None of it made sense. I put it on the nightstand, grabbed the portable phone, and then got a long-distance phone card I kept in my wallet. I opted to use it because my laptop's power cord was worse and barely held a charge. I couldn't see through my tears. My hands shook as I tried to enter the long list of numbers but kept entering them wrong.

"Damn it!" When I finally entered all the numbers in the correct sequence, Rachel and Dennis' phone rang a few times then their answering machine picked up.

"Hi. It's Kasey. I just got back from the hospital. Phillip has cancer. It's bad. Call me when you get this message," I blurted out.

I hung up the phone as if an electric shock had passed through the lines. *What did I just do?* I screamed in my head. *How could I have left such a message on her answering machine? What a dope!* I sulked into the living room, where Jack and Lucy sat on the couch with Chubby and collapsed in tears. They both snuggled close and hugged me. Chubby climbed onto my lap. I let the tears flow because there was no reason to stop them.

When I finally calmed down, I made everyone a snack. I tried to think of something we could do other than just watch more television, so I grabbed a book I'd given the twins for their birthday. The title of the book was *Kasey to the Rescue*. A handsome young man with a blazing smile graced the cover. A small Capuchin monkey hovered on his shoulder. When I looked closer at the book in the store, I realized that the author, Ellen Rogers, and I had the same last name. Ellen wrote the book, a memoir, about her quest to get help for her 22-year-old son Ned after a devastating car accident in June of 2005. Lucy, Jack, and I needed to hear about miracles, and Ellen's story was about all the obstacles she overcame to get Ned back East for treatment. Their story was the inspiration we needed. I had no idea then how much of a role this book would play in our lives in a few short months.

Regardless of the fact they were both excellent readers, we often snuggled on the couch, and Phillip or I would read out loud to them. When they were little, we went from *The Trumpet of the Swan* to *Watership Down* and, later, to *Harry Potter and the Sorcerer's Stone*. One of my fondest memories from their childhood began when we journeyed from chapter book to chapter book, one evening after another. I loved reading *The Pokey Little Puppy* or *Good Night Moon*; however, when we still lived in New Jersey, it was the longer pieces that kept us snuggled in the oversized chair in their room for hours, and we savored each moment.

I had just started to read when the phone rang. I heard Rachel's voice. Given my abrupt voicemail, she was much more gracious than I would have been as I related what we'd learned at the hospital regarding Phillip's test results. Rachel would have me pause every so often to convey the information to Dennis as he listened in the background. They were both willing to do whatever they could to help. When I got off the phone, I felt a bit of hope.

Shortly after I hung up with Rachel, the phone rang again. This time, it was a doctor whom Barry, Phillip's boss, had contacted on Phillip's behalf. He guided me through the various questions I needed to ask tomorrow regarding Phillip's treatment plan. Since Phillip couldn't advocate for himself, I needed to be there to speak for him.

The kids were back on their Game Boys by the time I hung up with the doctor. I suggested they get into their PJs, and we could continue reading upstairs. I offered to prepare some hot chocolate while they got dressed. We continued our reading on my bed, and before I knew it, they'd both fallen asleep. I put the book down and closed my eyes, too.

I heard Chubby scratching at the door downstairs and got out of bed to take him out. I walked down the steps to the first floor as quietly as possible to avoid waking the twins. I slipped on my jacket and went outside with Chubby.

The night air was warm but refreshing. Chub peed and used his back legs to lift the dirt, scattering his scent behind him. He looked up at me. His wagging tail signaled he had completed his mission, so we returned to the apartment.

He made himself comfortable under the table while I fixed a cup of tea. I was too awake to go back to bed. I needed to immerse myself in something that would take my mind off the events of the day. As was my habit, I started to bake.

I searched through the kitchen and saw I had everything I needed to make some banana bread. I knew the recipe by heart, so I assembled the ingredients and placed them on the counter.

Cooking and baking were my go-to things whenever life got too complicated. It eased my mind to have a sense of purpose. Rolling out dough for a pie or watching the butter brown when I made a roux calmed me, allowing me to focus on a task that was within reach rather than trying to fix something beyond my control.

Phillip never seemed to understand my love for cooking and baking. This led to many petty arguments after we married. Our upbringings were so different. I grew up with seven siblings and learned to cook at my mother's knees. There were always big family meals or relatives or friends gatherings around the table or the backyard fire-pit. My dad and his buddies would play their guitars and sing. The kids would play tag or hide-and-seek. It happened at least once or twice a week during the summer.

While there were many family events in Phillip's family, he never connected my love of preparing food with my family's traditions. Phillip thought (and often expressed verbally) that taking the time to make food from scratch was pointless when you could save time by purchasing it already made or partially prepared.

Phillip tried to eat well, but more often than not, he settled for convenience. His hectic work schedule left him eating at drive-through windows and pizza joints. For years, his thrifty nature had him opting for canned or frozen meals over freshly prepared foods. When the Beans were born, and Phillip began working full time, he set a food budget of a hundred dollars a week for four. It wasn't until I broke down the cost of items and showed him our regular grocery bill that he loosened the purse strings so I could buy most of what I usually fed our small family. Since moving to Cobleskill, he controlled all the money, which included buying groceries. Fresh foods and produce were often ignored in favor of cheaper processed foods.

Phillip had a different perception of the value of food and nutrition. Despite his complaints, however, he always seemed to enjoy the end results of my cooking or baking. It finally occurred to me that he resented the time and energy it took, something he liked to control.

I put the loaf pan in the oven. It would take an hour to bake. I couldn't just sit there thinking, so I got out some yeast to check the expiration date, and since it was still good, I made some bread dough. I got out my large mixing bowl and measured the ingredients, thinking about all the times a loaf of fresh bread had come out of my oven. I didn't get back to sleep until about 5 a.m.

When my alarm went off at seven, I emailed Tammy at Sacred Heart about the kids being absent from school again and explained what was happening with Phillip. Typing the words made it more real.

I needed more sleep but knew it would be impossible, so I got up instead. I woke the Beans and told them to shower and get ready to go. I packed some drinks and snacks, and put some plastic wrap around the banana bread to bring to the hospital in case Phillip could eat some. I hoped the small loaf would express my love.

Chapter Twenty-Three

Erasing the Tally Lines

The Beans and I arrived at the hospital mid-morning. Phillip wasn't in his room when we arrived. While we waited for him, I tried reading Phillip's medical report. Even with my limited understanding of medical terminology, I knew the news was grim.

The report read, "The gastric tumor showed a glandular pattern, with a locally cribriforming pattern, and other areas of an irregular, invasive glandular pattern. The tumor cells show a moderate degree of atypia and some areas of abnormal mitosis. In the esophageal tumor biopsies, there appears to be a relatively greater volume of the tumor, with this adenocarcinoma undermining intact benign squamous epithelium in some areas. One fragment showed the tumor cells' mucin production, with individual "signet-ring" tumor cells invading through the stroma. This is indicative of a high-grade adenocarcinoma. The tumor may have started in the esophagus, given the greater volume of tumor noted in this location."

As I read, a nurse wheeled Phillip back to the room. After he was settled in, I asked him for a translation so I could relate the information to his family as accurately as possible. I tried to write everything down. As difficult as it was to keep up, it was more painful to know that these terms would explain the depth of his sickness.

He then asked me to send emails to his freelance clients. I powered up his work laptop, and as I looked over at him, he gave me his email passwords. As I typed, I tried not to focus on the irony of it all. He then dictated a brief note, letting them know the situation.

Hi guys,

My biopsy came back this morning as being cancerous, so my life just got more complicated. They found another mass in the esophagus and stomach. That said, until I know more, I will be unavailable for any more freelance work. The docs are presenting options tomorrow, etc. I am in the hospital so Kasey is going to be handling any loose ends. (EG, I have invoices that I still need to send your way, etc.). Please keep good thoughts and prayers coming my way. Many thanks again for all your previous good thoughts, prayers, and the card. I will try to keep you posted when I can.

Once I emailed everyone, I put down the laptop and made an excuse to leave the room so Phillip wouldn't see me cry.

The results of some of the testing didn't come back until late afternoon. The expression on the doctor's face when he came into the room indicated he would be delivering more dreadful news.

"The cancer isn't your only problem, I'm afraid. The fragility of your neck is quite serious. Further tests have revealed the extent of the damage. An MRI of the cervical spine showed a destructive lesion involving the C7 vertebral body extending into the epidural faccia. While there is no evidence of spinal compression, the bone scan we performed demonstrates abnormal activity near the left thoracic inlet that probably involves the rib.

What I'm trying to tell you, Phillip, is that you've been walking around with a broken neck."

As he continued to speak, I wanted to throw up. He explained that a sneeze, a fall, or a sudden movement could sever Phillip's spinal cord, leaving him unable to breathe. While I sat listening to the doctor tell us this, I could only think about recently when Phillip had been out jogging.

We also learned that his team of doctors thought Phillip's neck was so fragile that they couldn't release him. This presented a huge conundrum. St. Joe's specialized in cardiac care. They only had one part-time oncologist on staff, who told us Phillip should be moved to a hospital specializing in cancer treatment. However, the question was, how would we get him there? Consulting with his colleagues, they believed it would be best for Phillip to be seen by a doctor at Massachusetts General Hospital in Boston. But, for the moment, they wouldn't release him until something could be done to stabilize his neck.

After I contacted Rachel with the latest news, she graciously offered to let us move into her finished basement in her home in Marblehead, Massachusetts, about an hour north of Boston. I contacted one of the highly recommended doctors and waited to hear if she would consider taking Phillip's case.

Phillip's parents and sister still lived in the same town where he grew up. It was the place we visited for holidays and other family events. I didn't want to move yet again, but our options were limited. Phillip's doctor made a couple of phone calls on our behalf. Once we were given the green light for him to be released from the hospital, we planned on traveling to Marblehead, hoping the proximity to Boston would offer more treatment opinions.

While there were benefits to moving back to Massachusetts, there were problems, as well. On the plus side, the Beans weren't adjusting to Cobleskill and Sacred Heart. As lovely as the people were there, the twins felt alienated. The plan to have them transferred to the Cobleskill public school system was on hold. At least Marblehead would be familiar to them. They had a cousin their age, so Phillip and I thought it might make for an easier transition. In the past, Lucy in particular seemed to have difficulties transitioning to new situations. This was one reason we'd always kept the kids in smaller schools like Sacred Heart. However, Jack seemed to be struggling too. I hoped that if they attended a public school for eighth grade, they would get more help.

My sister-in-law had been the principal at an elementary school in Marblehead. She promised to help us navigate the system and help them catch up on all the work they'd missed. She loved the kids, and they loved their fun, Auntie Rachel. Undoubtedly, it would be much easier for them to be surrounded by family.

I considered the reality that moving into my sister-in-law's home would be an enormous adjustment. It would be the first time I would be living under the same roof with other adults since I left my parent's home decades ago. Phillip and I had always lived far from his parents and sister in our twenty-five years together. He liked the independence that distance brought him.

But at the heart of my concern, Phillip made me feel like an outsider when we visited his family in Marblehead. Phillip's attitude shifted during and after our visits. He often became highly critical of either the twins or me. He not only implied that the twins and I didn't measure up to whatever ideal he had of a family unit, but he told me without reservation that his parents and sister should be the models for the family he and I had created.

Recalling these instances, I struggled to figure out how to preserve my renewed sense of self while doing what I believed was right for the sake of the man I had married. I knew the challenge would be balancing our mutual best interests without allowing Phillip to exploit my insecurities. Despite my fears, I agreed to move to Marblehead once the transfer could be completed because, in the end, it was the right thing to do.

Chapter Twenty-Four

More Bad News

The next day, they gave us even more dire news when his doctor told us Phillip's cancer had progressed to the state where he might only have a few weeks to live.

"The cancer has spread too far for treatment options, and given the complication of Phillip's neck injury, there is little we can do," Phillip's doctor explained. "Since I know you've contacted a physician at Mass General, I've consulted with a neurosurgeon specialist about how to deal with transporting Phillip, considering the severity of his neck injury. The only way to prevent further injury is to provide him with a specially constructed device called an Aspen® Collar before they can release him from the hospital."

I nodded my head when he finished, holding my emotions in check. I asked all the questions I'd written about the treatment options the night before. "The bottom line is, none of those options are viable considering the extent of Phillip's cancer and the fragility of his neck," his doctor responded. "Your best option is to wait for the Aspen Collar and see about having him transported to Boston by ambulance."

He walked over to Phillip, who was listening intently, and rubbed his arm. As he started to leave the room, he turned to us briefly.

"I wish you both the best of luck." I wondered if he wanted to add, "You're going to need it."

While we waited for the specially constructed device to arrive, the kids and I traveled to the hospital to visit Phillip over the next few days. It made no sense to have them in school, anxiously wondering if he would be alive when they got out. For the first time in years, the Beans spent almost entire days with Phillip. Watching them huddled together by his bedside helped me set aside all the troubling issues we had in our marriage. It didn't erase them. It didn't change what had happened. It just allowed me to put everything into perspective. The three things that mattered most were right in front of me.

While Phillip had additional tests, I scoured the Internet for information about his disease. When he returned, he wanted to reach out to his best friend, Kevin. Phillip knew Kevin from their high school days. Kevin was a very gentle man with a quiet grace, a quick wit, and an easygoing demeanor. His intelligence was apparent to anyone who spoke with him, and yet, he never seemed snobbish or overbearing. Over the years, the two friends stayed in touch and swapped stories of all their teenage years' mischief. I'd always liked Kevin, and especially enjoyed his wife, Stephanie.

Unable to move his neck, Phillip asked me to send an email that he dictated.

Hello, my friend,
As has been the course of my life for the past few years, I have some more bad news.

I have been diagnosed with esophageal cancer and, unfortunately, it has spread to the point where I'm told it's incurable. I don't know how much time I have left. I haven't asked, and don't want to know just yet. I've always been a very deadline-oriented individual (now there's a pun) but this is one date that I'd rather not rush toward.

I'm currently at St Joseph's Hospital in Albany, but I am being transferred to Mass General. The staff here at St. Joe's are great, but their specialty isn't oncology. Kasey and my family think there's hope for a miracle at Mass Gen. Also, there is little to no support system here in Albany. The many perils of constantly moving for work is not making many solid emotional connections. Most of our family and friends are back in Massachusetts so, like a salmon, I'm coming back home.

As I am quickly realizing, dying is not an experience shared by those around you. I had a nice chat with a Franciscan nun here about the topic of hope, which is shared by all those involved in stories like this. You know I'm a born pessimist, so you know how long a stretch this is for me. While my docs here agree that Boston is better for treatment, they believe there's no missing the final "deadline." My brother-in-law Dennis has connections that lead to the Head of Oncology so they are hoping to grease the skids, getting me in there ASAP. I might be transported by ambulance later today. (Contingent upon my insurance company's decision.) One of my cancer complications is that there is a tumor near my upper spine that is touching the spinal cord. The fear is that a bad road bump or fender bender could also leave me paralyzed from the neck down, so immobilizing me till I can get the tumor shrunk, or cut out, should save me from that threat.

I'd like to see you when I'm back. I will have a lot of check-in protocols and other procedures when I first arrive so I don't know what my "schedule" will be like over the next few days. The spinal issue and nutrition issue (some sort of feeding tube) have to be addressed immediately, so I may not be available much. But, hopefully, beyond that, I have some quality time. Either I or Kasey will be in touch.

Love you, man.

~ Phillip

I typed the words he dictated. Later, while Phillip dozed beside me, I vowed to reconcile the past and present. I knew one day I would have to look back at these moments; I needed to know that I had risen above all the dysfunction of our fractured relationship. I knew I wasn't always easy to live with, and I'd contributed to some of the problems I faced. But there were two separate issues here, and I had to be mindful of that to get through our ordeal.

All marriages must work through a set of dynamics to create a successful partnership. I'd read book after book early on, trying to master the essential elements of a good marriage. Things like communicating, trusting, respecting boundaries, etc., were fundamental. For a short period after I'd left him, he appeared willing to confront his part of our problems. I wanted to believe he would continue to be respectful. But knowing our past, I tried to be vigilant about making sure that I didn't allow his illness to become an excuse for his mistreatment.

Guilt is for the guilty. I was not responsible for Phillip's cancer, and I couldn't allow my sympathy for him to pardon his poor conduct. I acknowledged that I had to work to get past the grief I still carried over losing myself and not allow self-doubt to creep into my soul. I needed to care for myself the same way I cared for others. I promised myself not to want less for me than I wanted for him. What I wanted was for him to know I loved him. But I needed to love myself, too.

I started by mentally listing all the positive things about Phillip and highlighted those things instead of focusing on the past. I recalled some of our favorite times together. Our trip to Tombstone, Arizona; our passion for scary movies; the way we both laughed at *Calvin and Hobbes*; silly things that defined us. Phillip and Kasey. Kasey and Phillip. What made us a couple? I looked over at the Beans, who were now reading. It wasn't hard to find.

I spent every moment of those horrible days trying to find ways to help him through this horrendous experience. The only reason I left at all was to walk Chubby and feed him and the cats. Each time I left the hospital, I could barely breathe. I tried to learn as much as I could about his disease because knowing what we were facing helped. I bought used books about ways to boost the immune system, grasping for any hope offered.

As we stared into the abyss that first week after the diagnosis, I was full of bitterness over a system that seemed to work against us when every moment mattered. The doctors' answers about transporting Phillip to Boston seemed to be in the context of the cost to either the hospital or the insurance company. Even after the Aspen Collar arrived and Phillip was using it, the hospital hesitated to release him.

My rage grew, and I directed it at the people who prevented us from getting the help Phillip so desperately needed. I told the nurse at the desk I'd arranged for an oncologist to see Phillip at Mass General, one that specialized in the very type of cancer Phillip had. They told me that Phillip could only be released after the hospital got the insurance company's approval. I wanted to shout, "This is his life, you ass-wads!" Instead, I threatened to call the press if they didn't let him go.

"You realize no one can come up here on this ward without passing security?" she scoffed, calling my bluff.

The next day, I was determined to resolve this situation somehow. Shortly after I arrived, I told Phillip and the kids I would be at the nurse's station until I received news regarding his discharge.

"I understand you're both eager to leave, but your insurance company has instructed us that we have to get approval from his provider to pay for the ambulance to transport him," the first nurse I spoke to told me impatiently.

"I get it," I told her. "His insurance company doesn't want to pay for it. They're happy to take his premium payments each month, but, hey, let's not go wild and cover the cost of an ambulance for a guy with a broken neck," I vented.

She looked at me with a withering smile.

"I'll let you know as soon as we hear back."

"I'm not leaving this desk until I get an answer. I know you're just doing your job, but my husband has so little time, and I'm not wasting the only chance he has while some penny-pinching bureaucrat keeps us waiting. I'll sit right here and wait, thank you."

She turned her back and continued speaking with whoever was on the other end of the phone. I wanted to scream, but I was afraid I'd never stop.

While I sat there, I tried to calm myself. I knew that getting worked up wasn't helping. Finally, the nurse gently told me she'd have an answer by noon and would come and tell me when she heard back. I needed to use the bathroom, so I agreed and practically ran down the hall.

When I got back to his room, I offered everyone some goodies I'd baked, and even Phillip enjoyed some. The Beans and I sat side-by-side next to his bed, and we took turns telling them stories about our funny adventures before they were born. They often asked Phillip to tell them about our cat, Squirt. It was one of their favorite stories.

"Mommy and I rented an apartment in Blairstown before we bought our old house. It was in the same neighborhood, just a few blocks over. One day, when Mommy was taking a walk, she found a little gray kitten. He was about twelve weeks old. We already had Boo Boo Kitty, our Maine coon cat, so we didn't want another," he explained. "Your mom and I put up flyers, trying to find his owner, but no one called us so, finally, we placed an ad for a "free kitten" in the paper. Someone came and got him, but they brought him back later that day because their son thought he was too old. So we kept him," Phillip told them. As often as they had heard the story, they leaned forward to hear more.

"Mommy worked in the City and didn't come home until late at night, so Squirt became my pal. He used to sit on my keyboard, and every time the phone rang, he jumped at it. At night, he'd bite my toes, and sometimes, I'd find pencils from my desk on the floor next to my bed. And whenever I went out, Mommy said Squirt would somehow find one of my socks and drag it from one end of the hallway to the other, meowing." Their favorite part was still to come. "Sometimes, I'd tease Squirt by blowing into a bottle. He hated the noise," Phillip continued. "After I did this, Squirt would wait for me at the far end of the upstairs hallway banister, and when I'd walk up the stairs, Squirt would hit me in the head and run away!"

No matter how often he told the Beans about Squirt, they always laughed, imagining our silly cat's antics. Hearing him regale the twins with Squirt stories, I had to leave the room. Memories of our sweet, funny cat were filled with both joy and sadness. While I was pregnant with the twins, we discovered a lump on his back. The vet diagnosed him with cancer. For months, we took him to Manhattan for treatment at the finest veterinary clinic in New York City, but he ultimately succumbed. I wondered if Phillip was thinking about that, too.

Finally, a little after noon, the case manager came to his room to deliver the news. The hospital agreed he could leave. However, the insurance company refused to spring for an ambulance.

"You're free to leave," she told us, "as long as you agree to sign the papers releasing the insurance company of any liability should anything happen because of his neck injury." The stack of papers must have been half an inch thick. There would be no ambulance. Instead, after we returned to Cobleskill, I would have to drive him to his sister's home in Marblehead since the doctor at Mass General wouldn't see him for days.

By three that afternoon, I had my family in the car, and we headed back home for the evening. I could feel my heart in my throat each mile I drove. The forty-five-minute drive to our apartment seemed to last forever. I wasn't sure how the hell I would make it, driving him, the kids, our dog, and three cats all the way to Marblehead, let alone getting him into Boston. But I knew I had to try.

Chapter Twenty-Five

Back to Massachusetts

Phillip's appointment with the oncologist at Mass General was on the morning of April 18th. Upon arrival, I pulled into the Fruit Street garage, one of the hospital's many parking structures. Phillip and I exited the building at street level.

We could see the Massachusetts General Hospital building directly in front of us, clearly identified with large metal lettering. It was framed by two other buildings—the steel and glass Lunder Building on the left and the red brick Wang Building on the right.

An expanse of concrete between the three structures could easily be navigated by foot if one walked straight ahead. The horseshoe-shaped area was large enough for several cars or ambulances. A sign pointing to the emergency room entrance and patient drop-off area was visible from where we stood.

Even with Phillip's slowed gait, we could have walked approximately two hundred yards to the revolving entrance door within a few minutes. However, after reviewing the medical records forwarded by the hospital in Albany, Phillip's oncologist, Dr. Allison, was deeply concerned for her new patient's safety and instructed us to call her office when we arrived. After calling, we were told to wait where we stood by the garage and that Phillip would be escorted to the emergency room.

Soon, an ambulance pulled up. A three-person EMT crew unloaded a stretcher and approached Phillip and me. He explained to them he could not lie down on a gurney. Apparently, no one told them before they arrived what they were dealing with regarding the fragility of Phillip's neck. They were at a loss for what to do. They moved out of earshot to discuss options while Phillip and I stood there waiting.

They wanted to use a type of gurney that would allow Phillip to sit up and planned to carry him to the hospital. After further discussion, however, they determined it would jostle him too much. We still stood there waiting.

One of the three attendants called a manager, expressing concern about their liability if something tragic happened while they transported Phillip. They assured us that a return call from someone higher in management was expected any time now while we stood there waiting. Almost an hour passed. After numerous phone calls were exchanged and after much deliberation, they ended up surrounding Phillip on all sides and walked him into the emergency room. Our introduction to Mass General gave me an uneasy feeling.

Dr. Allison was right to be concerned. The fracture of Phillip's neck made his care more complicated. She wanted the emergency department to evaluate the fracture further. We weren't there long before they whisked him away to review the situation while I waited.

After Phillip was seen, they admitted him. We already knew that the severity of his condition warranted being hospitalized. We were also aware that the extent of his cancer meant they would not offer him surgery or a procedure called kyphoplasty, which would stabilize the bone. They offered him a feeding tube, but Phillip opted not to have it implanted since he still had some ability to swallow and wanted to enjoy the simple pleasure of eating. Phillip had begun his journey as a 52-year-old male with metastatic gastroesophageal carcinoma.

I traveled from Marblehead to Boston daily. When I arrived, Phillip eagerly reported everything that had happened during my absence. These interactions made me believe we were moving past some of our marital conflicts, and I listened patiently to everything he recounted about what he experienced.

As I sat on a chair next to Phillip's bed, he began describing an incident that had occurred after I had left the day before, relating the details of being seen by a herd of physicians with various specialties.

"You missed all the drama after you left yesterday," he said.

"Why? What happened?"

"There was some confusion when they conducted the procedure," he told me.

"Honey, which procedure are you talking about? You've had so many of them," I didn't know how to respond. I nodded to show I shared his concern about all that was happening to him, even though much of it was over my head. As Phillip continued to relate the situation to me, I felt like I was underwater and knew someone was talking but couldn't make out what was being said.

"They were supposed to put in a port, but they put in a PICC line instead."

"What's the difference again?" I asked, keeping my voice in check.

"PICC's an acronym for a "peripherally inserted central catheter." It's different from a port, which is a small medical device placed beneath the skin. They wanted me to have a port before I get chemo, but, somehow, they initially put in a PICC."

"So, how did this get messed up?"

"I'm not really sure, but you should have seen all the doctors here consulting with my primary team of physicians. They decided to go ahead and put in the port anyway, but then they put it in the wrong place," Phillip explained. "I heard them talking to Dr. Allison, and they said that a chest X-ray showed that the line terminated in the right atrium. One of the doctors they consulted with recommended that they 'pull it back' to make it end at the Cavo atrial junction, but someone else advised her that was too risky."

I silently seethed as Phillip concluded by telling me of a potential risk of arrhythmia or infection if they tried to adjust the port or replace it. Deep inside, it irritated me that the medical terms rolled off his tongue. That informed me he was cognizant of so much about his medical condition, yet he had waited so long to seek treatment. I shoved these thoughts aside and continued to listen.

"I had them leave it in place. The vascular interventional radiologist assured my primary care team that the PICC was okay to use, so they'll just use that for the chemo instead," he finished.

"Well, I'm glad they could resolve things," I told him, hoping I'd struck the right tone. I held his hand and tried to quell the dueling emotions raging inside me. When he remained silent, I checked to make sure he hadn't fallen asleep, then began telling him about the Beans to change the topic.

Within days of being admitted to Mass General, Phillip developed a deep cough. This alarmed me because the abrupt motion could further injure his neck. They gave him a drug called Levaquin to relieve the irritation that caused his modulated voice to become thick and hoarse. The medication gave him nausea and diarrhea, which left him unable to eat. He grew weak. Like dominos, one bodily function after the next was falling apart due to the side effects of each medication.

Life beyond Mass General had to go on. The world does not grind to a halt over these types of diagnoses, and a great deal is expected of both the patient and their families. Beyond Phillip, my most immediate concerns were getting the kids into school and traveling back to Cobleskill, mainly because we'd left the cats behind with multiple bowls of food and water and extra litter boxes.

My Aunt Lil had agreed to take our two older cats while the kitten would be coming to Marblehead with us. The anxiety of leaving Phillip during this time was almost too much to bear. I didn't want to be that far away but had no choice as there were loose ends in Cobleskill and Alexandria.

Phillip's palliative care social worker called me while I was in New York. I was overjoyed to have someone to help me traverse the insurance and healthcare systems. I was learning first-hand that navigating any type of catastrophic illness or injury was like picking through the wreckage of a house after a tornado. There are bits and pieces of a life previously lived that you're trying to salvage, but you can't find all the fragments.

I told the social worker I didn't know how we would survive financially, as Phillip would get his last paycheck at the end of April. Our financial realities were bleak, since we canceled our life insurance policies when Phillip lost his job in 2005. He balked at taking out new policies when things got more financially stable.

"I don't want you profiting from my death," he joked.

I didn't find it funny back then, and I certainly resented that decision now. But there was no way I could go back and change things, so I had to live with the knowledge that I was facing some real financial difficulties even if I sold the building in Canada. The social worker told me he could connect me with someone knowledgeable about my questions. He also informed me that Phillip would be eligible for social security disability, which I wasn't unaware of.

During the two days I was gone, Rachel and his best friend Kevin visited. Having access to his family and friends seemed to make a tremendous difference. When I returned to see him, I saw that he was in an excellent mood and his outlook had improved.

When Phillip discussed his health issues, it seemed more about his irritation than his overall condition.

"My biggest concern is I'm having trouble sleeping," he told me. "My mind is always racing. It makes it hard to get enough sleep. I wish they would let me take off this damn thing," he said, trying to scratch under his Aspen collar. "My doctor is only letting them take it off when I'm being bathed, but that only gives me a few minutes of relief each day," he moaned.

I got out of the chair and stood behind him. Using my nails, I scratched his neck under the collar as gently as I could.

"I feel imprisoned by this fucking device," he groused as I scratched.

While the brace kept his neck isolated, I knew it must be terribly uncomfortable. I kissed the top of his head and reached further down his back to scratch, hoping to ease his discomfort the only way I knew how.

Chapter Twenty-Six

Hope for the Hopeless

During my next visit, Phillip discussed his condition and treatment options with his oncologist. I heard him tell her what he had written to Kevin in the email he dictated to me: "I don't want to deal with specific time frames regarding the prognosis of my condition. I'm used to working with deadlines," he joked again. "This is one deadline I don't mind missing."

Someone coming in to check his vital signs interrupted their conversation, so I asked his doctor if I could speak with her in the solarium, a short distance from his room.

"I know Phillip doesn't want to be told if the chemo and radiation will improve his chances, but I do," I blurted out.

She looked at me through thick glasses and, in a calm and slightly condescending manner, told me, "There is less than a 5% chance it will be effective. He is a Stage 4B cancer patient. There is only the slightest hope it will help. He has months, not years, to live. But we have to do as he requests. If he chooses to have the chemo and radiation, we'll honor his wishes."

I didn't know what to say. I believed Phillip needed to spend time with his family and his friends. I wanted to tell her that every moment he had remaining should be filled with joy and doing things that reminded him of how much we love him. I wanted to ask how much money the hospital would make treating a man who was a "Stage 4B cancer patient," using air quotes and getting right up in her face. I wanted to support him, even if I disagreed with his decision. I nodded, unable to say what I was thinking.

That same day, I met with Phillip's social worker in person. He came to visit Phillip when someone from the brace department arrived to see about making some adjustments to Phillip's Aspen collar. While Phillip spoke with this technician, I asked the social worker if we could talk privately in the solarium.

He was as warm in person as he had been on the phone. He made me feel heard and didn't talk down to me, like some of the other healthcare workers I had to deal with, regarding Phillip's treatment. While we spoke, he looked at me unflinchingly. I felt I could trust him to level with me about what to expect. I told him what the oncologist had said earlier, that Phillip most likely had months, not years, to live. I questioned the wisdom of not telling him. He agreed with Phillip's doctor that it was best not to tell Phillip if he really didn't want to know. The social worker's compassionate attitude helped me understand this honestly must be about Phillip's wishes. I was very grateful for his insight and the way he addressed me with kindness. His approach to alleviating the anxiety I faced was beyond helpful.

When I returned from speaking with the social worker, they had taken Phillip out of the room for his first radiation treatment. They hoped to stabilize Phillip's C7 vertebra by calcifying the tumor, thereby strengthening his neck. I wasn't sure how any of this would help, but this was my understanding of why the radiation treatment was suggested. An ongoing course of chemo would follow this, along with a chemotherapy regimen referred to as FOLFOX.

He saw nutritionists and dietitians for his continued weight loss, and psychiatric doctors to assess his mental health and emotional well-being, on top of seeing his oncologist. He was getting the care he needed despite the screw-up with the PICC line. I was very grateful.

The following week, the Beans came with me to visit Phillip at Mass General. It amazed me how fortuitous it was that we had read the book *Kasey to the Rescue*. Ned, the young man and central figure in the book, had become a quadriplegic after a car accident. He, too, had received treatment at Mass General. Most important to the kids, however, we discovered while reading the book that Ned's family brought their dog to visit him in the hospital. It would never have occurred to me that we could bring Chubby with us into Boston.

His presence certainly made the outing more pleasant. The twins beamed with pride, walking their charming pup down the hall to visit their dad that day. They held his leash tight and led him through the hallway from the elevator to Phillip's room with a bit of swagger. The nurses and other patients commented on our sweet pooch, and Jack and Lucy were over the moon.

Having Chubby with us made it easier for everyone during this visit. They didn't know what to say to their father under these circumstances. When the small talk evaporated, uncomfortable silences remained. With Chubby as the focus of their collective attention, Phillip and the twins could pass the time enjoyably instead of enduring an awkward visit.

While I knew Phillip wanted to see the twins, his rapid weight loss left him weak. Concerned he was overexerting himself, I suggested we leave. Phillip smiled and blew them kisses as we left his room, not knowing how long it would be before he'd see them again.

On the ride home, I promised the Beans I would send Ellen Rogers, the author of *Kasey to the Rescue*, an email about this experience and thank her for writing a book that helped ease my children's challenging encounter with a large hospital. (She replied with an invitation to visit her, Ned, and, of course, Kasey, their trained Capuchin monkey that was Ned's service animal, when things calmed down. The twins were stoked!)

At the end of April, they finally discharged Phillip from Mass General. In less than two weeks, our lives had changed completely. By that time, I wasn't sure how anyone coped when a loved one was diagnosed with cancer unless they were fortunate enough to have the kind of support our families and friends gave us. I tried to stay hopeful that his life could somehow be extended, and whatever time he had remaining would be absent of our marital dysfunction. Phillip's oncologist's words regarding his prognosis loomed large in my mind, but I promised myself that, regardless of what lay ahead, I would try to have more patience.

I knew that would be challenging, but as harsh as it was to hear, what she said moved me to change my relationship with Phillip. More than anything, I just wanted to give him my better self, a more honest, compassionate, and loving self—without being a doormat. I wanted to be there when he needed me most. I kept thinking about a quote I'd read once from Erich Fromm in his book, *The Art of Loving*: "To be loved because of one's merit, because one deserves it, always leaves doubt. Maybe I did not please the person whom I wanted to love me, maybe this, or that—there is always a fear that love could disappear.'

For much of my marriage, I strove to believe that Phillip truly loved me. I tried to prove I was worthy of his love from the day we married. I began to understand that my entire self-worth had been based on this faulty notion. This shift in perspective gave me more control over my own happiness. I knew if my self-esteem was no longer in the hands of another human being, I could let go of so much of the insecurity that kept me chained to the repeated negative messages I received from him. I was determined to learn that I didn't need to prove myself worthy of his love. In the end, that is truly what saved me.

Chapter Twenty-Seven

Looking for Miracles

After Phillip was released from the hospital, I refused to face reality and became skeptical of anyone who suggested otherwise. Despite the midnight trips to the emergency room because Phillip vomited blood or experienced unexplained pains, I remained convinced that a miracle would happen if I just stayed positive. I wanted to believe he could beat this.

I resented anyone who painted a grim picture of his prognosis because he seemed so much healthier and looked terrific. I convinced myself they would never have released him if he wasn't getting better. Even when one of my closest friends tried to reason with me, advising that I should prepare myself for the worst, I scoffed. I told myself there were cures; I just had to find them. I started looking for signs that a miracle could occur. I truly believed that Phillip would end up in medical books as having been the most severe cancer case to have survived.

It didn't take long to figure out that my thoughts and beliefs weren't grounded in reality. I knew I was in denial. Those who are suddenly faced with the type of diagnosis Phillip received frequently experience similar notions. A part of me truly believed he would somehow get better. There was another part of me that knew it was hopeless. I vacillated between these two conflicting thoughts hourly.

In the back of my mind, I kept looking for a place to hang my hope. I reminded myself of how disheartened I was when we first moved to Canada, and Phillip left the Beans and me behind. I started feeling better in those early days in Alexandria because I believed someone was looking out for me from above and protecting me in those weary first months.

It started with minor things. For instance, I would notice each morning that the odd item I needed for the café's lunch special was on sale when I went to the grocery store, like when I wanted to use some roast beef for sandwiches as a lunch special. I looked for horseradish sauce to use on the side. Usually, the price would have prohibited me from buying it. The sale price had me putting it in my shopping cart. Initially, I wasn't convinced it was more than a coincidence, but this happened so frequently that it was uncanny.

Then, a series of events that should have or could have ended in a tragedy didn't end badly at all. For example, shortly after we had opened for business, I got a call from Solange, who managed a thrift store a few doors down from the café. She would alert me when something that I might need for the café became available. That day, it was a refrigerator. I had no idea how, or if, she knew that our fridge was on the fritz, but I welcomed her call. She said the men who moved furniture and appliances for her could deliver a new fridge that afternoon. They would even remove the old fridge and pick up a check after the café closed. We sealed the deal.

After the men left, I realized the fridge door swung from the left, not the right. It frustrated me because the counter we used to assemble food was to the fridge's right in our galley-style kitchen. Having it swing open from the left meant I would have to open and close the door more frequently to remove needed items. One of my employees assured me it could be switched to swing the other way, so I relaxed, knowing Phillip could do that the next time he came to Canada.

I made the kids nachos for dinner that night and prepared them in a Pyrex dish I'd used a hundred times. The Beans were seated at a small table outside the kitchen entrance. I took the nachos out of the oven and placed them on the top of the stove. Then, I crossed to the fridge for the various condiments. I opened the door and ducked down to grab some things off the bottom shelf when the Pyrex dish exploded. There were shards of glass all over the kitchen. Some even reached the ceiling. We dug enormous pieces out of crevices for days after this happened. I remained unharmed because the fridge door shielded me entirely.

There were other things, as well. In the spring of 2008, I rented the farmhouse we eventually used for the music festival. Shortly before I was ready to move into the place, I talked with Yves, who owned the coffee roasting company where I purchased my beans. I asked him why he called his business Justin Café. I thought it was an odd name for a coffee-roasting company. He explained that the name came from a café he and his wife had owned years ago north of Alexandria. When I asked why they closed, he told me he and his wife were off to their baby shower one day before their son's birth. On the way out, he heard an odd crackling sound. They were in a rush, so he didn't check to see what was causing the noise. When they returned later, their place had burned to the ground. The crackling noise had been an electrical fire in the walls of their old building. His story gave me the chills.

A week later, I moved into the farmhouse and planned to hand over the keys to our apartment above my business to the new tenant. I had a catering job the night before, so early the following day, I went to finish cleaning before the tenant arrived.

I left at about seven am and brought Chubby with me because he hadn't been walked earlier. I opened the outside door to the foyer area that led to the apartment and climbed up the stairs. I was about to put the key in the apartment's lock when I noticed Chubby in the corner of the landing. His head was cocked to the side. I tried coaxing him into the apartment, but he just stood there and refused to come in. Then I heard it. I heard a crackling noise—the conversation I'd had with Yves only a week before came to mind. I called the fire department, two doors away from the café. They were there in minutes and put out an electrical fire that had started in the wall. Somehow, I believed I had angels watching over me.

Moving to Rachel's home in Marblehead happened so rapidly that we still hadn't moved out of the apartment in Cobleskill. We couldn't afford to continue paying for an apartment we weren't using, so I developed a plan to move out before the end of May.

With the help of my brother Jake on one trip, and my niece Ronnie on another, I could return the keys to the landlord by Memorial Day weekend, with Rachel tending to Phillip's needs while I traveled back and forth.

As the rental truck got full, I realized there were many things I couldn't take with me, so I offered them to Greg and Patrice, the lovely young couple who had purchased the house next door. It thrilled me that they could use things and even helped Ronnie and me load the rental truck and empty the rest of the apartment.

While we loaded the truck, Greg told me he worked on antique cars. I said I'd keep that in mind, since Phillip still had a 1966 Mustang in a garage back in New Jersey. Weeks later, when Phillip and I were trying to figure out what to do with the Mustang, I thought about Greg. I couldn't recall his last name, so I put our old address into the Google search engine to locate a phone number. I was appalled to learn that Greg had recently been released from prison, where he had spent time for raping his six-year-old niece. I shook, thinking about my young daughter playing in the backyard at our apartment, the one that connected to theirs. We may have miraculously escaped some horrible event by moving away when we did.

I knew deep inside none of these things proved miracles happen. But I had to have hope. It was the only way I could avoid being overwhelmed. At that moment, I needed to hang on to something. I'm glad I didn't have a crystal ball because sometimes an illusion of hope is better than no hope at all.

Another thing that kept me going during that time was the communications I regularly received from my friends up north. While I still needed to address selling the property in Canada, our accountant (who was also our attorney) advised me not to sell the building yet. He told me that the influx of income might disqualify us from some financial help we were getting for Phillip's medical expenses. He suggested letting go of the building's contents instead, which would also help drive down the cost of moving things once the building sold.

I notified my friends and those on the café's email list, telling them of my plans. They met my email with warm responses that once again illustrated why I desperately missed my life there. I truly appreciated all the support and outreach that came via calls and emails.

Hi Everyone-
I have decided to sell many of the belongings I used to furnish the 2Beans Café and Tea Room and some of the other things that I can't hang on to any longer. Yes, even the granite tables are available! Jenny has lots of larger pieces. Roberto has items for sale in the Café's tearoom. As silly as it sounds, knowing that these things that brought me much pleasure while owning my little business are in the hands of people I know and love is more comforting!
Thanks bunches,
~ Kasey

Days after I sent out the email, I heard from Sondra, one of my favorite customers. She had a thick Scotch-Canadian accent and a wry smile. She often wandered into the café to join me for a cup of coffee late in the afternoon as she shuttled from one project to another.

She wrote,

You are learning one of the most difficult lessons life teaches...'
letting go'...No one in this world goes through life without ever

having learned, in some way, this lesson's meaning...We fill our lives with so many unimportant nothings, just to avoid learning this most difficult lesson of all. Your life will take on new meaning and in the process, so will the lives of your children...This is how the world functions...You are doing the best a person can do, Kasey, by responding to what life requires from you at this time. Go with the present and always remember, 'all is exactly as it should be at this time'...Thanks for your kind offerings...I have already mentioned it to a few of your 2 Beans Café patrons...Bye for now...Sondra.

Her kind words and sage advice boosted my spirits and encouraged me when I needed it desperately. It occurred to me that angels protected me— just not as I first imagined. As painful as it was to let go, it was what needed to be done. I read and reread this email repeatedly to remind me that life was exactly as it should be.

Part 4

Letting Go

"Life is a series of natural and spontaneous changes.
Don't resist them; that only creates sorrow.
Let reality be reality. Let things flow naturally
forward in whatever way they like."

~ Lao Tzu

Chapter Twenty-Eight

Same Ole, Same Ole

As much as I wanted to believe Phillip and I had managed to put aside our problems, they reemerged after he was released from the hospital. It didn't happen all at once, but cracks appeared, especially when I returned from being away for a few days.

At first, what he said and did wasn't bad enough for me to call him out on his behavior. But his actions were hurtful and reminded me of our past conflicts. However, by the middle of June, something happened that made me realize nothing had changed. It was only glossed over because of our circumstances.

That night, I heard him call out to me well after midnight.

"Honey, what's wrong?" I said, rushing into his room.

"I don't know. I have a sharp pain in my lower back that's coming in waves. I can't stand it. I need you to take me to the ER."

By now, I'd become accustomed to the sudden trips to the hospital, and we traveled into Boston so frequently that it was almost routine. But that night, the intensity of his pain forced us to opt for a hospital in Beverly, a small city that was much closer.

The doctor came into the cubicle where Phillip waited to be seen. He reviewed his charts from a previous visit.

"Hello, I'm Doctor Misri. Can you tell me what you're experiencing? Where is the pain?"

While Phillip described his pain, I ducked out quickly to use the restroom. When I came back, the doctor was still reviewing Phillip's chart. Noting the situation, he asked Phillip if he wanted to be resuscitated if he were to go into cardiac arrest.

"Yes."

"Have you designated a healthcare proxy? We need to make sure everything is in order," the doctor told him. Phillip nodded.

Moments later, a nurse entered the room with papers for Phillip to sign. He read them, filled out the appropriate information, and signed them as routinely as he signed dozens of other documents.

While waiting for the doctor to return, he said, "Just so you know, I've made Rachel my healthcare proxy. The last thing I want is to have you be in charge of pulling the plug," he told me matter-of-factly.

I turned and looked at him, my mouth agape. I couldn't respond. I felt a chill, even though it was the middle of June. I clutched my purse closer to me, then glanced at the floor, determined not to cry. When I finally composed myself, I told him, "Whatever you want is fine." And it was.

They whisked him off for some tests and determined he had a kidney stone, and it had passed. I didn't see him again until they were ready to discharge him.

A palpable silence existed on the ride back to his sister's. After arriving home in Marblehead, we both went to bed without saying goodnight. I climbed into the bed I shared with Lucy, trying not to wake her. Sleep eluded me for much of the night. I couldn't understand how Phillip could be so callous. Then I realized that, in many ways, he had done me a huge favor. By choosing Rachel as his healthcare proxy, Phillip let me know where I stood in our relationship.

Phillip's love was conditional and always had been. When he needed me, I was of value to him. When he didn't require my help, I didn't matter. When Phillip signed that paper earlier, it revealed something I had long suspected but couldn't admit to myself about my role in his life. It wasn't flattering.

The words, "The last thing I want is to have you be in charge of pulling the plug," echoed in my brain. At first, I blamed it on the impact of leaving Phillip eight months earlier. However, looking back, I realized he had made equally damning statements before that when he said things like, "I don't want you profiting from my death." Whatever his reasons were, his concern about my receiving money as a beneficiary of his life insurance obscured his concern to provide for his wife and children. Those were things he said long before I left him.

That night, I tried to reconcile that, for whatever reason, Phillip believed I was unworthy of his trust, protection, loyalty, or commitment to our marriage. I knew I should have realized long ago when he refused to tell his parents we got married. However, that night, I finally understood that his words and actions were more of a statement about his character than mine. I may have loved him imperfectly, but I loved him.

I lay there, wondering if maybe he floated in and out of being in love with me all those years. Loving someone and being in love with them were separate matters. I thought about the years I'd given him enormous chunks of me. I'd sacrificed for the concept of us. I convinced myself we were a team, but for whatever reason, Phillip treated me as though I was a bit player.

Phillip's attempts to control me and change me weren't acts of love. When you love someone, you want as much, or more, for them as you want for yourself. Whatever he felt for me, it wasn't love. What I started to feel for him was pity. He could have experienced a deep and committed relationship, but he opted to marginalize me whenever possible. It made me sad instead of angry.

It wasn't possible to go back and change the course of our marriage. There wasn't enough time to alter what had been etched in the past. What I could do was feel compassion for him. It was unfortunate that he only appreciated me or was grateful when it suited him.

Still, I didn't want to become a scorekeeper again. I had erased all the tally lines, but it wasn't the only thing that needed to change. I tried to stop replaying his voice in my head. I knew the narrative had to change if I wanted to honor the vows I made to him and, more so, those I made to myself. I could be that better self if I could find forgiveness for the self-doubt that started when I allowed him to define me. I had to take responsibility for my flaws but knew they didn't make me unworthy of his love. They made me human.

I kept thinking about everything my friend Sondra from Alexandria had said. I'd read her email a bazillion times. "Go with the present and always remember, 'all is exactly as it should be at this time."

When morning broke, I was still awake. As I finally drifted off, I realized I would have to stop myself from wallowing in self-pity and attempt to grow and learn from this horrible experience. It would not be easy to push aside the anguish of this recent revelation. But in the end, if I could acknowledge the pain and move past it, I would come out of it a better human being.

Toward the end of June, I had to return to Canada to clean out the apartment of a former tenant once again. I needed to get another renter into the apartment immediately because I needed the income desperately.

I would be leaving the day before our wedding anniversary—the one his parents knew about. In reality, we should have celebrated our twenty-fifth wedding anniversary in January. Still, because of the awkwardness of the second ceremony, Phillip's family wasn't aware we'd been married that long. I wasn't sure what to do about acknowledging the occasion. The special day seemed to blend into the background. I took it in stride because, with so many other things going on, it was hard to celebrate, anyway. But I kept thinking this would most likely be the last anniversary Phillip and I would ever have. The marriage that, nine months earlier, I had desperately wanted to be over was coming to an end in the most unexpected way.

I went to the store and bought Phillip a card. Pangs of guilt washed over me because I knew he wouldn't be able to do the same unless he asked someone to take him. It was a no-win situation all the way around.

I wondered if he even thought about this milestone, considering the fragility of our relationship. A sense of grief crept over me. I grieved for what I thought we once had together. I grieved because I knew his days were numbered, and there wasn't anything I could do that would ultimately prolong his life. I grieved because he couldn't understand that I had a right to grieve.

"You're not the one who has cancer," he told me again and again.

We were downstairs in Rachel and Dennis's basement when he spoke those words. I had entered the room where Jack and Lucy were sitting with him, reading. I asked if they would walk Chubby, and they readily agreed. When they left, I turned to Phillip.

"I'm leaving for Alexandria early in the morning. Amelia emailed and said she has no hot water again, so, on top of cleaning out the rear apartment, I'll have to get a hold of the plumber." When he said nothing, I tried to fill in the awkwardness. "I wish I didn't have to go north."

"Well, I can't go," he said with a tone of sheer contempt.

"Phillip, I'm not suggesting you can. Don't be like that, please."

"Be like what, Kasey? You don't understand what this is like because you don't have cancer. You're going to be seeing your friends while you're up there. Don't lie."

I was tired of holding my tongue. I realized Phillip was suffering, but I was compelled to say something.

"Does your mother and father or Rachel have cancer?"

"What are you talking about?"

"You constantly tell me I can't possibly be suffering because I don't have cancer. And yet, you understand they're suffering because of your illness. How is it that you think I've escaped the pain of this?"

He looked at me with disdain. I wasn't arguing or emotional. I presented him with a valid statement. He pursed his lips and seemed about to object, but then he refused to comment.

"Just because I don't have cancer, Phillip, doesn't mean it doesn't affect me. It affects me in ways you refuse to recognize. You recognize their pain and suffering, but somehow, you think I'm immune. That's sad." With that, I left him alone and went upstairs.

The kids came back from walking Chubby. Their grandmother had given me money to buy them ice cream. "Hey, you guys. Memere gave me some money to buy you a treat."

We all piled into the van, and I took them to their favorite ice cream place. When we returned to the house, I asked the Beans to take Phillip a Chocolate Frappé we had ordered, but I stayed upstairs until I thought he was in bed. When I could safely go down, I made my way to the basement. The door to his room closed. I casually asked the Beans where he was, and they confirmed he'd gone to bed. Before I left in the morning, I put the anniversary card on his nightstand. He never acknowledged receiving it.

Chapter Twenty-Nine

A Girl Named Ellie

Phillip and I were making weekly runs into Boston for one reason or another: chemo treatments, check-ups, and sudden trips to the emergency room became routine. In each department we visited, the various personnel became almost like friends. Emma, one of Dr. Allison's nurse practitioners, told us funny stories. Denise, an RN in the infusion unit, made us comfortable and showed extraordinary kindness each time Phillip went in for the chemotherapy. They made the day brighter because of their overwhelming compassion toward those they cared for each day.

Not only were his various caregivers considerate, but there were other patients on similar schedules that we chatted with regularly. While it wasn't exactly a social event, smiles were exchanged, and familiar faces were acknowledged.

A young girl named Ellie became Phillip's chemo buddy. She had a wisp of bright red hair that peeked out of the colorful bandanas she wrapped around her balding head. Her beautiful smile was so engaging, it made it impossible not to smile back at this young woman who battled brain cancer. She beamed at Phillip in a way that made me think the fight they shared was one I could never truly understand. To my knowledge, they never spoke, but Phillip always liked it when we were escorted to an infusion chair where he could see her and exchange a thumbs-up.

One day in mid-July, we noticed Ellie wasn't there when he went in for his infusion. He asked the nurse if she'd come in earlier because their schedules didn't always mesh. We learned she'd had a stroke or something of that nature and didn't make it. Phillip left the hospital that day in a somber mood and went to lie down as soon as we got back to Marblehead.

Sometimes, incidents like that caught up with me, and I finally accepted the inevitable. But other days, I found myself searching for ways to fight the cancer that insisted on killing him. Maybe I couldn't save him, but I could help preserve his strength.

I noticed a local Borders Bookstore was closing days later, so I ventured in. I found and purchased a book called *Anticancer, a New Way of Life* by Dr. David Servan-Schreiber. The book told about a doctor who, as a medical student, discovered quite accidentally that he had a brain tumor. He beat cancer once but, eventually, it came back. The second time, on top of treatment, he changed his diet and lifestyle radically. He lived with his condition for another fifteen years. Sadly, I learned he died a week after I finished reading the book.

I also learned from my best friend, Leigh, that her sister-in-law had battled a very advanced case of breast cancer and had survived. We swapped book titles to further our understanding of how to help our loved ones. When I got off the phone, I was determined once again to support Phillip in any way I could to fight this horrible disease.

One of the most notable things about the book *Anticancer, a New Way of Life*, was that Dr. Servan-Schreiber suggested avoiding sugar. When I reached page 61, I read, "The German biologist Otto Heinrich Warburg won the Nobel Prize in medicine for his discovery that the metabolism of malignant tumors is largely dependent on glucose consumption. (Glucose is the form of digested sugar in the body.) In fact, the PET scan commonly used to detect cancer simply measures the areas in the body that consume the most glucose. If a particular area stands out because it consumes too much sugar, cancer is very likely the cause."

I learned from other things I'd read that there was a growing body of information about the connection between cancer and sugar. All the statistical information regarding the increased risk of cancer because of lifestyle diseases like obesity was alarming. I was dealing with a man with cancer while increasing my risks by not addressing my growing weight issues that stemmed from diabetes.

Back in 1997, a routine test at my obstetrician's office led to the discovery I had gestational diabetes. I took insulin during the rest of my pregnancy and was a borderline diabetic for years before my bad habits caught up to me, and I developed Type-2 diabetes. I hadn't been to a doctor to check on my own health in many months, and I began chastising myself for being so careless. I wanted to present a better example of self-care to my kids, which meant eating healthier. But without a source of income, we had slipped into poverty that summer and were struggling just to stay afloat. Trips to the grocery store were a constant source of anxiety because our budget and eating healthy were frequently at odds.

We were receiving SNAP benefits, but much of that money went to purchasing specialty food items that were easy for Phillip to consume. I will never forget the look of disdain the cashier gave me when I bought ice cream for him using this food program. I wanted to smack the self-righteous look off her face with the back of my hand. He could not swallow much, and if he needed or wanted ice cream, he would get it.

When we consulted with a nutritionist at Mass General about what Phillip should eat, she gave us coupons for Ensure and a print-out of a diet, but that was about the extent of her input on nutritional advice.

Unfortunately, the products she recommended, like Ensure and Benecalorie, were not just expensive; they made him vomit because they were too thick. With her help, I learned how to change the consistency so he could tolerate them. I grew concerned that the amount of sugar in these drinks might help advance his cancer growth. One day, I decided to approach Phillip about the subject.

"I've been reading a lot about the connection between sugar and cancer, and they load those frozen drinks with it. Maybe we should see if something else is available?"

"What do you want me to do, starve to death?" he complained.

"Of course not. Don't be angry, Phillip. I'm trying to help you. Can't you see that?"

"You can help by letting me decide what I can and can't eat. You don't understand what it's like to even think about giving up the few remaining things I enjoy."

"Okay, fine," I told him.

Phillip agreed to ask his doctor about the link between his diet and his cancer. Dr. Allison came into the room for a moment before the nurse saw him, but he remained silent. After exchanging pleasantries, I piped up and took the opportunity to ask my lingering question.

"Dr. Allison, I have a question. I've been reading about the link between cancer and sugar. Do you think changing Phillip's diet will help at all?" I asked her.

"If he wants to eat cake, let him eat it," she told me.

"It's just that—"

"Let's get your vitals, shall we? I'll have the nurse come in," she said, beaming at Phillip as she left the room.

When I turned to face him, he had a victorious grin on his face. I knew there would be no support for changing his diet to eliminate sugar. I wondered if Dr. Allison was telling me this because Phillip's cancer was at such an advanced stage she believed he should be able to enjoy whatever foods pleased him, or had it bothered her that I was boldly raising the question? If I pressed the issue, I would be opening old wounds. I let the subject drop.

Instead, I began trying to re-evaluate what I was cooking. I made soft, starchy foods for most meals because they were easy and cheap for Phillip to eat. I never thought too much that these foods contributed to my difficulties in maintaining healthy blood sugar levels. Learning about the glycemic index and how it measures whether a particular carbohydrate-containing food increases blood glucose levels stunned me. All the foods I thought were healthy because they were low in fat or weren't sweet weren't doing much for us.

I sat on the couch in Rachel and Dennis's living room, reading the book's last chapters. I knew I should be addressing my own needs, but I struggled since Phillip's needs were the priority. It wasn't something that just happened because he had cancer, either. It reminded me that, as a child, I watched my mother always put her family's needs, especially my father's, before her own. That expectation was cemented long ago. As a woman, I, too, sacrificed my own needs for my family.

I looked over at the Beans, watching a movie as I read. It seemed like an impossible situation. Here, I'd just finished reading a book about self-empowerment. Servan-Schreiber observed that lifestyle changes can fight cancer. Yet, the needs of others drove my lifestyle. Servan-Schreiber's book outlined some fundamental reasons that nutrition, exercise, psychology, and meditation were essential to a person's well-being. However, I was constantly stressed, ate poorly, didn't exercise, or do anything else he recommended in the book. Regardless of what was going on in my life, I had to do better. I finally understood that taking care of myself was taking care of my family.

Chapter Thirty

More than the Lack of a Cellphone

Each day that summer seemed to bring either a fresh challenge or a revision of an old one. The medical moments had us coordinating and working together to provide Phillip with everything he needed to fight the cancer inside him. But the everyday moments, the ones between the frequent medical crises and routine treatments, forced us to confront the problems in our relationship. Those days that we should have been cherishing were instead filled with conflict.

My impulse was to argue or defend myself or the Beans, especially when Phillip made comments that stung. I sometimes thought my tongue would bleed; I bit it so frequently to avoid retaliation for his thoughtless criticisms. I sometimes suspected Phillip's hurtful remarks were a bit of payback. After all, I had almost left him less than a year ago. That worked occasionally, but often, I wanted to stay right there and level the same anger at him that he leveled at me, and avoiding it led to a building level of frustration. He tapped into my emotions and knew exactly what to say to drive me over the edge. When a quarrel began brewing, I tried to refocus his attention or ignore him by changing the subject or finding an excuse to leave the room. I knew when I appeared less salty with him, he lost steam and left me alone, but oftentimes, I wanted the satisfaction of winning an argument with him until I realized neither one of us ever really won anything.

At the doctor's office one day, another pattern emerged. When we were in the company of others, Phillip always presented me as a saint.

"You wouldn't believe what an excellent cook she is!" he told Emma, his nurse, at one visit. "The other night, she made me a delicious soup. I loved it so much, I had three bowls," he continued. "When we owned our restaurant, customers came all the way from Montreal for her cooking," he bragged.

"I didn't know you guys had a restaurant," Emma responded.

"Oh, yes," Phillip told her. "For years. We owned a small café, but we did a lot of catering and other things on the side. We even rented an old barn and hosted a music festival." As Phillip chatted with Emma and described the café and our time in Canada in such glowing terms, I simmered because it occurred to me how often he did this. To others, he offered a totally different view of circumstances than he had presented to me. I wasn't sure which portrayal was the more accurate one. Was he proud of the café and the music festival, or were they the massive failures he told me they were?

On the ride back to Marblehead, I thought about this and understood the significance of his conflicting presentation of situations. He didn't want to portray me negatively in front of others because, to Phillip, that would reflect poorly on him. By praising me, he actually praised himself.

Realizing that Phillip kept his admonishments out of the earshot of others offered me a way to circumvent his callous words. I began avoiding being alone with him whenever possible. I would leave the room, or take the dog for a walk, or just pretend I wanted to use the bathroom. I used this excuse so often that I thought he might begin to think I had a bladder infection.

My plan didn't work out all the time. At the end of July, my brother-in-law Dennis told me that I had racked up their cell phone bill with roaming charges the previous time I'd traveled to Canada. I had no idea that could happen, and I apologized and told him I would compensate him for the expense. Despite this, Phillip ambushed me when I went downstairs to grab Chubby's leash.

"We need to talk right now," he told me from his room.

"What's up?" I asked him, trying to sound casual.

"When you go to Canada this week, you have to leave the cell phone in Marblehead, Kasey. I spoke to Dennis and promised him I'd have you give it back to me. He said he couldn't believe how irresponsible you are sometimes."

"Did he?"

"Yeah, he did."

"I've already apologized to Dennis. I didn't realize that I'd get roaming charges when I was in Canada. So, yes, I racked up a hefty bill. But I promised to give him money to cover the additional expense."

"Whatever your excuse, I want it back," Phillip insisted.

"So, you're telling me I shouldn't bring it while I'm traveling?" I asked him incredulously.

"It's not yours. Dennis gave it to me. Why you ended up with it is a mystery to me."

"Mystery? I took it initially because you handed it to me and asked me to hold on to it. I kept it on me because we don't have a cell phone of our own."

"This is so typical of you. You ran up an enormous bill, and now you're offering excuses."

"Oh, it's an excuse to want to have a cellphone on me while I'm the one who travels all over the place in a van that shouldn't even be on the road?"

"Don't tell me all those calls were made because of your traveling. That's a load of shit. You use it to call your friends, too."

"Yes, I call my friends. I call my family, too. But you're making it sound like I intentionally ran up the bill. You're the one that's blowing this up."

"I'm always the bad guy for pointing out how irresponsible you are. This is what you do to me. You make me out to be the villain. You have to go there despite everything I'm going through."

I left the room and grabbed Dennis's cell phone from my purse.

"Here. I won't use it anymore. I'm sorry I used it in the first place. I'm even sorrier that you have so little concern for my safety." I grabbed Chubby's leash, stormed upstairs, and took him out for a walk.

A pathway behind Rachel and Dennis's house led to the woods. A lush array of dense greenery stretched around a marshy area that led to a pond. With their long, wispy needles, Eastern White pines overshadowed smaller Red or Pitch Pine conifers. Ferns grew in clumps at their edges, covering the brown leaves that blanketed the forest floor. As Chubby and I walked by, the trunk of a decaying white birch tree with peeling bark provided a chipmunk with a place to hide. The sound of beating wings and sudden motion caused me to look toward the small body of water. The rapid retreat of the ducks who had gathered at one end of the pond told me we'd frightened them.

While Chubby sniffed at whatever scent he discovered, I looked for flowers or birds as we meandered along the path. Over the summer, it had become a refuge I sought frequently. Whenever we headed there, it usually meant something had just happened with Phillip. This time, I tried to focus on the moment instead of going over what Phillip said about the cellphone situation, but I couldn't let go of our argument. Instead, I berated myself because the whole situation made me feel inept again. But, as I walked Chubby, I had a sudden insight into a pattern of our behaviors. Phillip had no control over how I felt. I was the one who subjected myself to those feelings, and I had every right to use that cell phone! I agreed to pay Dennis for the overage and apologized. I took responsibility for my mistake. I tried to justify my behavior every time Phillip accused me of wrongdoing. I wasn't asking to use the cell phone just for pleasure. I also needed it to make calls to his doctors, or while I traveled, in case I broke down. Once again, I had allowed Phillip to get into my head.

When I sought his validation, I asked for his approval. In doing so, I handed over my well-being by allowing him to define my actions as excuses. I finally avoided sabotaging myself again by accepting my responsibility for my emotions. There was nothing wrong with my need for my friends and family's love and support. No amount of arguing would change how Phillip saw me. I'd been down that road too many times and knew where it ended.

As I walked along, I knew I had to stop buying into his version of me. None of that was true. His lack of self-esteem manifested in his need to boost his ego by deflating my accomplishments and assaulting my character. Phillip's outbursts weren't a statement about me. They were about his own internal conflict. Showing others he was better than they were made him feel superior. When I stopped letting him define me, I reacted less defensively and took the power out of his hands to manipulate my emotions.

We never spoke about the cellphone issue again, even when I was about to leave for Canada a few days later. He had either forgotten about it or just didn't care that I would have no way to get help if anything happened. But before I left the next day, I went to the store and purchased a cheap cell phone so I would have one before heading north to return to Alexandria.

Chapter Thirty-One

Trying to Survive

By mid-July, Dr. Allison advised Phillip that continuing the chemotherapy was inadvisable. Tests showed that it was ineffective, and Phillip's cancer had spread to other organs. Regardless of her advice, he declined to stop treatment. I understood that, for Phillip, stopping chemo meant giving up and acknowledging that time was growing short and the treatment was what kept him going.

What kept me going, though, were all the little things. I realized the twins were better off in Marblehead than in Cobleskill. They were thriving again. Having their cousin to hang out with and Rachel's positive influence helped tremendously. They enjoyed spending time with their grandparents, Memere and Pepere. Whatever happened, I wanted to stay in the area because I couldn't move them again.

Knowing that it was best for them made the decision easy for me. I had let go of my thoughts of returning to live in Alexandria. I knew that all that mattered was to focus on getting through this ordeal without allowing myself to become despondent about the future.

At the end of July, I got an email from one of my former customers.

Hi Kasey-
I was talking to our mutual friend Jenny about our Museum Fall Festival and asked about you. She tells me you are back in the States, in Boston, and this is and has been a very difficult time for you. Both Sarah and I are very sorry for the stress, worry, and the painfulness that you must be dealing with, considering the health of your husband and that you had to leave Canada. I know that you had high hopes for resettling here and launching

a number of possibilities, including the restaurant and a more active arts program. I am sorry that some of that did not happen. Alexandria is a very tough town to crack into and it is hard on newcomers. I speak from experience.

I understand from Jen that your spirit is good, considering everything. I do remember you as someone full of positive energy and, I suspect, able to rely on those strengths in difficult times. I look forward to your return here or success in some new adventure.

All the best,
Andy (from Sarah as well).

I read Andy's email a dozen times. I was so touched by the fact he had reached out to me, grateful that people reminded me that I meant something to them. It wasn't all part of my imagination, because there were times that my past life in Alexandria seemed like a lifetime ago.

The next day, I wrote back.

Hi, Andy-
Thanks so much for the kind and much-needed email. It always gives me a great sense of happiness to connect with friends in Canada.

While I must admit there is something that just doesn't translate down here about the pace and sense of well-being I had there, I have made a decision to embrace whatever life has in store for me, whether I am living here or there. I am trying to look on this as an opportunity to make some changes. I'm trying not to think of leaving Alexandria with the sense of loss or failure I initially felt. If nothing else, life certainly has a way of keeping me on my toes.

I am trying to find my "writer's voice" again, and although the moments I have to dedicate to this are few and far between, I have been managing to write a bit again. I had forgotten how much I love this, and it is something that has eluded me for some time. Writing for me is like scratching an itch, both are deeply satisfying.

Please let Sarah know I was thinking of her and send my warmest regards as well.

Onward and upward,

~ Kasey

In composing my response to Andy, it occurred to me that for a long time, other than the quick notes I wrote in my journals, I had stopped doing something that had once been a significant part of my life: writing. So many of the things that were once so important to me had been shoved aside years ago. Every once in a while, I thought about trying to start a new project or begin reworking an old one. However, I never found the time to act upon my goals. I knew that would have to change.

Regardless of my resolve to begin writing again, the events of the summer prevented me from doing much more than recording some thoughts sporadically. But in documenting even these tiny fragments of insight into the experience helped me feel heard, even if I was talking to myself.

Despite what Dr. Allison said, the treatment sometimes seemed to work because Phillip's blood tests were so good. These minor indications of stability kept his spirits up because he maintained a positive attitude outwardly. In this way, his ability to cope was a constant reminder that arguing with him would accomplish nothing because it hindered his frame of mind. So when he strayed into areas that raised my defenses, I fought to remain calm despite the desire to tell him to go screw himself. I wasn't always able to resist temptation.

Phillip and I agreed to get the kids to participate in more activities, so I looked into something I thought they would enjoy.

"Hey, I was able to locate a few places for fencing lessons. I don't want to promise something in case we can't afford it. But I reached out to the owners, and they can cut us some slack. What do you think?" I asked Phillip.

"Yeah, that could be good. I don't think Jack is enjoying soccer as much as I hoped he would. It could be his allergies. This is a terrible time of year for him," Phillip said.

"Maybe, because this is an indoor activity, he'll like it better? I'm going to see what type of discount they're offering and, if we can swing it, I think we should consider it." Phillip and I agreed.

"It's too bad you never enrolled them in more things like that when they were younger. Arianna is more advanced than they are with all her sports and dance," Phillip commented. I stopped myself from telling him that when the Beans were young, he told me those extra-curricular activities were too expensive.

Later that August day, things came to a head. It began with an innocent conversation with Rachel when I came out of the laundry room into the upstairs foyer.

"Oh, there you are. I was just going to go downstairs and tell you something," Rachel told me.

"What's up?" I asked her.

"My friend Laura is having a hard time selling her house. I think she might want to rent it. I don't know if I told you, but she got remarried, and her new husband is quite wealthy," she said. "It might be worth asking because it's just sitting there."

"That's interesting. I'll let Phillip know! Thanks!" I told her.

The brief conversation made me wonder if we were overstaying our welcome. Was this Rachel's way of seeing whether we could make other living arrangements?

Later that day, Phillip and I took the kids to the fencing lessons I worked out for them. I'd completely forgotten to tell him about my conversation with Rachel until we sat in the car chatting with the Beans. I turned to him and said, "Honey, I forgot to tell you, your sister said her friend Laura might be willing to rent us her house."

"What? We can't afford to rent a house."

"We don't know that we can't afford it because we don't know if she's willing to rent it. We can't stay with Rachel and Dennis forever," I joked.

"This is so typical of you. I'm always the last to find out."

"What are you finding out? Nothing has been done. I am relating a conversation Rachel and I had before leaving the house."

"You can't even understand simple math. We can't afford to rent a house," he screamed at me.

"Phillip, calm down. I never said we were renting a house. Rachel brought this up earlier. Now, I'm telling you about our conversation, that's all."

"You lie about everything," he screamed.

The entire argument came out of nowhere, and at that point he was screaming so loud, Lucy and Jack were crying in the back seat. I believed the suddenly explosive conversation was over when Phillip said, "Don't blame this on Rachel. You never take responsibility for anything. You know you're going to hell for all the horrible things you've done to me."

I lost it. "Oh, yeah? Just wait until we get back. Ask your sister who initiated the conversation. You're way out of line, and I'll prove it, not that it matters to you." I screamed at him.

The level of my rage at him surprised us both. The frustration of his unfounded accusation had me so angry, I couldn't contain myself. He got out of the car as if I were going to strike him and called Jack and Lucy to go with him. They reluctantly followed. If he wanted me to display my worst instincts, I didn't disappoint him. When I realized I'd played right into his hand, I was mortified that I'd lost control and began to cry.

I didn't want to show my tear-streaked face to all the parents watching their kids pretend to duel, so I sat in the van, wondering why Phillip had reacted so negatively. I replayed the scene in my head over and over again. Why was Phillip so threatened at the thought of leaving his sister's? I suspected it went back to his need for control. And what horrible things I had done? Was he referring to leaving him? Despite all the care and attention I lavished on him, it was never enough. I waited in the car until the Beans' class was almost over and then went in to watch the last few minutes. On the drive back, the twins chatted about their first fencing experience. While I drove, I fumed.

When we arrived back in Marblehead, we entered the garage to get to the laundry room. Rachel was taking a load of clothing out of the dryer. She had no idea of the horrible fight we'd just had. I was convinced that if Rachel set him straight about our conversation, he'd see how wrong he was about our argument.

"Hey, Rachel! I was just telling Phillip about our earlier conversation. You know, about your friend Laura's house," I said, looking forward to her reply.

"Oh, yeah! Did Kasey tell you?" she said, turning to Phillip. "Laura might be interested in renting her place. It's close to school, and maybe you guys can ask her about it?"

"Rachel, Phillip thinks I started this conversation," I said, feeling a bit self-righteous.

She made it clear to him that she brought up the subject. She looked at me as if to question why this was so important, but I didn't offer any additional explanation.

"Well, we'll have to think about it," Phillip told her as he disappeared into the kitchen for some reason.

I didn't wait for an apology because I knew one wasn't coming. When I was cold to Phillip later, he told me to "grow up and get over it." His words could still cut through me, and they were almost too much to bear. If I argued or fought with him, I risked doing more harm to him physically and emotionally, and if I kept it bottled inside, I was harming myself.

I told myself daily that I was not the person he portrayed me to be. I continued to reread emails like Sondra's and Andy's. I retreated into hot showers and went on more long walks with the kids and the dog. I got out of his way whenever I could. He kept telling his friends he was doing his best to survive. I wanted to say to him, so was I.

Chapter Thirty-Two

Grasping at Straws

By mid-August, Phillip was clearly declining. The only thing left to pursue regarding treatment was either a clinical trial at Dana Farber Cancer Institute or some sort of alternative therapy. His old boss, Barry, tried to help Phillip by slogging through insurance issues regarding the insurance company's willingness to pay for the expense of a clinical trial. At the same time, his best friend Kevin told him about an alternative treatment called vitamin C infusion. We were all doing our best to hold out hope that something could be done to save him.

Phillip was at his best when he dealt with friends like Kevin. He presented the side of himself that everyone adored. It was easy to see why he was loved and respected by his family, friends, and colleagues. That side of him is what kept me loving him all those years.

As angry as I was with him at times, I didn't want him to die. He was my children's father. I'd fallen in love with and married him because I enjoyed his company much of the time. I still didn't understand all the reasons why our relationship had unraveled. Still, I'd reconciled our problems with a greater desire for him to escape the unavoidable fate.

While Kevin visited one day late in August, he expanded on an earlier conversation with Phillip about a guy (in Canada, no less) who researched vitamin C infusion therapy and the impact on cancer with a strict alkaline diet. Kevin told us of his friend, John Bridgeton, who was involved in researching and developing treatment protocols using large doses of vitamin C given intravenously or orally. The information was coming from his own desire to help a loved one battling cancer.

After his visit, Kevin sent the information to Phillip, who wondered if this offered hope. At this point, Phillip seemed eager to try anything. After talking with Kevin's friend, John, the possibility of a new treatment offered us a sliver of hope.

Kevin forwarded the email his friend John sent, along with an article from the Canadian Medical Association Journal that discussed the use of vitamin C in the treatment of cancer. After reading it, Phillip told me, "I'm apprehensive about going down any path without Dr. Allison's approval. There might be some clinical trials she's aware of that I'm eligible for, but I know the protocols are rigid, and the timing must be right. But if she doesn't have any, maybe this thing Kevin's friend John is suggesting might be worth a shot. What do you think?" he asked me.

Suddenly, Phillip seemed anxious to hear my opinion. It was as if someone had waved a magic wand and pronounced that we were once again "Phillip and Kasey." Suddenly, he began treating me as an ally.

I wondered if part of his shift in attitude was because he wanted his friends to see him as they always saw him: as a great guy with a loving wife. Or, maybe when he saw me in the context of those cherished friendships, instead of the distorted image that lived somewhere in his head and deep in his heart, he realized I had some kind of merit after all. I cautiously offered my thoughts.

"Well, the doctor at Farber is about to go on vacation, so everything is very tentative with the clinical trial, anyway. I think the vitamin C therapy is worth considering," I told him. "In the meantime, why don't you reach out to Kevin's friend with questions regarding this alternative therapy? That way, when you do have a conversation with Dr. Allison, you can give her all the information." Later, he asked me to type out an email that related some additional questions about John's credentials. Phillip was open to trying this therapy because he regarded Kevin so highly.

I still wondered about the link between his diet and the cancer that had invaded his body. What I'd read made sense to me, but my understanding was limited. All I had to go on was what I found in books and online. I knew that what was out there on the internet wasn't always accurate. But we were desperate by this time, and Phillip looked at every possibility as time grew shorter. I didn't believe that changing his diet would save him. But my previous questions about cancer and sugar came to mind, and I was willing to do anything that could help him live longer and provide him with more strength.

There were other things to consider in his overall health; his neck's fragility and the discomfort it caused sometimes overshadowed his cancer. He anxiously waited for a follow-up with his neurologist at Mass General. The hope was that the targeted radiation had fused the mass on his C7 vertebra, stabilizing his neck. This appointment wasn't until the end of September, so Kevin's information significantly boosted his declining morale.

During this time, his old boss, Barry, also tried to help Phillip by using his resources to navigate the complicated nature of clinical trials. He even visited Phillip with one of his former colleagues in mid-August. I was in Canada dealing with the issues up there, so I never had a chance to thank them. While the visit was welcome, the news regarding the hopes of participating in a clinical trial was not.

> *Hi, Phillip-*
> *It was good to see you yesterday. Regretfully, it looks doubtful that a clinical trial will be covered. Glad you are surrounded by family and friends. Your courage, spirit and grace is truly admirable. Know you are missed at PII.*
> *Please keep me posted.*
> *~ Barry*

Barry might have been shocked to hear Blue Cross wouldn't cover expenses related to clinical trials. Our experiences back when Phillip was in the hospital in Albany had informed us early on of the healthcare industry's priorities: profit over patients.

Rachel helped Phillip return Barry's email.

Many thanks to both of you for the food! It was thoroughly enjoyed by all of us here. (We even decided to save some of the ice cream cake for my kids when they return.)

Also, thanks for your kind words. As mentioned, I truly appreciated the opportunity to have worked with both of you and hope things continue to forge ahead for everyone at work.

In the meanwhile, keep good thoughts for me. I plan on fighting as best as I can against the odds. Please stay in touch, and I will try and do the same.

Sincerely,

~ Phillip

While Phillip seemed outwardly optimistic, the realities were crushing him. He and I spoke by phone while I was in Canada with the Beans the last weekend in August. He broke the news he had little hope the costs of participating in the Dana Farber trial would be covered even if they accepted him.

I didn't know how to help him. I tried to sell everything I could while I was in Alexandria, but my time was consumed with cleaning out rental units. Without the funds necessary to pay for the costs of a clinical trial, our hopes were fading.

"What about the vitamin C therapy?" I asked him when we spoke.

"I'm just reluctant to begin following the regimented diet John's recommending," he told me. "The clinical trial options are still up in the air. I know it doesn't look good because of the latest rounds of issues with insurance. But Barry is doing his best to fight their decision, and he wrote to one of his former colleagues about the matter."

"Well, I hope they respond soon," I told him, then changed the subject. "Hey, Honey. Before I forget, I got an email from your friend Mike. I'm going to forward it to you."

When the Beans and I got home the next day, he asked me to type out a reply.

Hi Mike! Kasey forwarded your email to me. Many thanks for your concern. Currently, I am hanging in there with no pain...only fatigue, and a bit of nausea when undergoing chemo.

While my prognosis is still not good, I am doing my best to battle this disease as best I can. My last round of chemo at Mass General was not effective so I will hopefully be switching to an alternate therapy at the Dana Farber Institute. With all the chemo and radiation I've undergone, I'm learning cancer is like having a part-time job.

One positive note in this whole mess is to learn how truly fortunate I am to have the support of so many friends and colleagues. Your email is very much appreciated.

Please give my best to all, and continue to send all your good thoughts and prayers my way.

Sincerely,

~ Phillip

As I typed the email for him, I had to think that, for a person who is dying, waiting to learn if you qualify and can afford to pay for treatment options has to be the worst kind of hell.

Chapter Thirty-Three

Another August

While this was happening, I was in Canada. For a brief time, being there offered the Beans and me a much-needed reprieve. Being there kept reality at bay. So much had happened in the year since the farewell dinner at Jenny's house. Back then, I was desperate to stay in Canada. But I found myself eager to return to Marblehead, knowing with certainty that was where I should be. So, we left Alexandria earlier than I had planned.

Driving back, I found I wasn't as consumed with worry even though the panel on the dashboard of the van was still broken, and I couldn't gauge my speed and the amount of gas I had. I couldn't help but think about what Sondra said about 'letting go.' "Go with the present and always remember, 'all is exactly as it should be at this time," she'd told me. I smiled, thinking that maybe it was all sinking in and I was learning the valuable lessons my sage friend shared. None of the things I'd projected about the future had come true. Instead, I faced a loss far more devastating than I ever imagined. And yet, I was far more grounded in the present than I'd been in the past, and it helped me cope with the uncertainty.

I emailed Jenny to let her know we'd arrived in Marblehead safely.

Thank you so much for all your love and support. You are so important to my overall sanity. Even when I haven't spoken to you for weeks, I can think about sitting on your porch, having a glass of wine, and sharing some girl time with you and Carole, and it makes me smile. It is the oasis in my mind when I am depleted of my own resources and need to replenish my sense of hope and faith that life will offer me more than it does at the moment.

I will be in touch and keep you posted on this end.
Love you bunches,
~ Kasey

I'll never know what happened while I was away but, suddenly, Phillip was even more connected to me than when I had left. I accepted this with cautious optimism. Based on past experiences, I knew this wave of affection would not last. But because his remaining time was limited, I welcomed it. Perhaps he realized that all the stupid fighting was diminishing his remaining moments. Maybe someone said something that registered, and he also recognized I had reasons to be distraught. I didn't care. I couldn't bear the thought of our last days together being filled with acrimony. I was ecstatic when he began treating me more as a partner once again.

Phillip's friend Kevin and his wife Stephanie came for a visit over the Labor Day weekend. The fragility of Phillip's condition led us to stay inside to avoid the eighty-plus-degree temperatures. We all gathered around the dining room table. The loud hum of the air conditioner and the multiple fans Rachel placed around the room couldn't compete with the buoyant sound of our laughter and conversation as we ate the food and drinks they brought.

I marveled at the smile on Phillip's face and the ease of his conversation with Kevin. Their shared history gave them easy access to stories told in brevity because they knew the middle and end. It was so good to see him in the company of his friends, people he loved so dearly and who loved him equally.

While refreshing our drinks in the kitchen, I heard Kevin mention the idea of speaking with his friend about the vitamin C therapy with Phillip. I stopped what I was doing and listened as they discussed the matter. Weeks earlier, Phillip had shut me down whenever I brought up the subject, but now, he appeared open. This would have annoyed me before, but it didn't matter anymore. It thrilled me when he agreed to try the diet.

We spent the rest of the evening chatting, and I got to know Kevin's wife, Stephanie, a bit more. Before meeting Kevin, she'd been through a messy divorce and had two girls from a previous marriage. Some of her personal horror stories allowed me to put my relationship with Phillip into perspective. Even with all the insanity of the current situation, she was also a joy to be around. Her outlook made me laugh. While I didn't know her well, her candor was refreshing, as she stated things so matter-of-factly without an iota of judgment. When we found ourselves alone in the kitchen, she said, "This too shall pass."

At first, her frank remarks shocked me. I didn't want Phillip's life to end. Even after all the adverse reports on Phillip's health, the trips to the emergency rooms, and the visible wasting away of his body, I still held out hope that something could turn things around. The mere thought that there would come a day when my marriage complications and Phillip's illness would end stunned me. Even if the vitamin C therapy worked to slow the progression of Phillip's cancer, I needed to be prepared for what was inevitable.

The next day, Phillip got an email from Kevin.

Hi Phillip and Kasey-
It was wonderful to see you and the kids last night. Steph and I had a great time. I hope we didn't keep either of you up too late.

John is currently up in the Laurentians but will be back in Ottawa tomorrow. I plan to call him and let him know that you'll be phoning. And, as always, please let me/us know if we can be of any assistance.
We love you guys, and we'll see you soon.
Kevin

Kevin still thought of us as a couple acting in concert. His email touched me.

While there was little hope that this regimen would cure him, there was a hope it would allow him to live longer and stop wasting away. He was down from 195 pounds to 130 pounds. His face looked skeletal. He weighed less than our thirteen-year-old son.

John sent us a list of all the vitamins required and a list of dos and don'ts. The basic concept was aligned in many ways with the Anti-Cancer diet I had looked into months earlier. The idea was to starve the cancer and stop it from spreading. There wasn't much scientific data to support the results, but we reasoned that eating healthier wouldn't cause Phillip any harm.

All the foods Phillip ate now had to be pureed. He'd had two surgeries to stretch his esophagus so he could swallow. I used my culinary skills to make what he was eating palatable and found ways to incorporate berries and vegetables high in antioxidants into smoothies and soups he could still drink.

The added benefit of this project was it helped distract us from personal issues. It brought me back to the days we worked on film scripts or produced videos together. We discussed and planned our meals together because this diet was very regimented. I wondered if Phillip realized we behaved better toward one another when we worked as a team.

Once the Beans started school, I accepted a part-time job at a catering company. I wasn't happy to be away from Phillip, because I never knew what would happen while I was gone. But expenses were piling up, both in Marblehead and in Alexandria, and we needed to purchase the various items for this new diet. The money I earned helped in this way.

By actively participating in his health care, Phillip also seemed happier. Having radiation and chemo treatment was a passive method of treating his disease. With the vitamin C therapy, he could take part in the process. He was brilliant and enjoyed learning about things by searching the internet. We purchased a special pair of glasses that allowed him to read more easily because he didn't have to strain his neck. Still, it was difficult for him to hold his head in a comfortable position to work on the computer, so he started taking off his Aspen collar. This troubled me initially, but I could see how difficult it was to be in this contraption 24/7. I also wondered how much wearing it contributed to his foul moods.

A few days after he began the treatment, Phillip caught me off guard when he asked me to type out an email. He had several questions he had about each vitamin we were instructed to purchase. We needed more clarification about the amounts he was to take and sought recommendations about alternatives to some of the items John had listed. I just typed away at the keyboard and wasn't really paying much attention to this communication's mundane nature. What got my attention was how he asked me to end the email:

He asked me to type,

"Many thanks again, Phillip & Kasey."

I can't explain why asking me to sign both our names made such a difference. I can only tell you it did.

By late September, I wanted to pull my hair out. Problems in Alexandria continued to mount with no relief in sight. Then, Yves, who was once my coffee roaster, asked about leasing the entire building. I agreed since I'd no longer be responsible for the many issues involved in owning the property. We discussed a triple-net lease. Once I worked out the details, I forwarded him the information he asked for and kept my fingers crossed that I wouldn't be spending another winter dealing with the many issues presented with owning the building.

Between Phillip's needs, the building up north, the Beans' new school regimen, and my part-time job, there was no time for anything other than tending to the various things on my plate. Days passed with little progress on any front.

Phillip tried to hang onto the thread of hope this new diet gave him, and I supported him. However, even the healthier, pureed foods were difficult for him to swallow. Each night he reported his progress to John, it became more apparent that our efforts were fruitless. Even though both of us were doing our best, in my heart, I knew that Phillip's cancer had progressed beyond the point where even a promising new diet would help to stave off the disease that was ravaging his body.

As we approached the end of September, I realized that six months had passed since we learned of Phillip's illness. When we first learned about his cancer, we were told Phillip had less than two weeks to live. Then, at Mass General, Dr. Allison told us it was perhaps just a matter of months. When you're dealing with a fatal disease, these milestones have tremendous significance. On the one hand, it seemed like we were victorious. He'd survived well beyond what we were initially told in April. On the other hand, it was a reminder that little time remained.

Chapter Thirty-Four

A Bitter Holiday Weekend

In late September, Phillip had a follow-up appointment with his neurologist. It was a significant setback for him emotionally. He learned there was no improvement in the stabilization in his neck. I think he was also very insulted that his doctor didn't even attend this appointment. Instead, we waited for an hour to meet with his assistant. Phillip had hoped the radiation treatments had somehow fused the bones in his neck, allowing him to remove the uncomfortable Aspen Collar. From his silence on the ride back to Marblehead, I could tell that he was not in the mood to discuss having to wear the brace indefinitely.

The next day, I went to work at the catering company. I was so distracted during my shift, I couldn't focus on even the simplest tasks. Even though I'd only been there for a few weeks, I went to the manager's office, gave notice, and explained why I had to quit. He graciously agreed it was not a good thing to use sharp knives and hot surfaces when your mind is a million miles away.

When I got back to Rachel and Dennis's house, Jenny called. I was dumbstruck when she announced she wanted to buy the building. I believed I'd finally caught a break with the issues up north. She offered to take it under the same triple-lease arrangement I had offered Yves. Since the deal with him was still up in the air, I was thrilled at the prospect.

By Thursday, October 13th, I was so glad she was acting on my behalf to handle things up north. Life in Marblehead had become more difficult by the hour.

Jenny-

Since we spoke this morning, things have taken a turn for the worse. After countless telephone calls, I scheduled Phillip's appointment for the intravenous vitamin C therapy that John and Connor recommended. Even though he was part of that decision, when the moment arrived, he refused to go because we had not consulted with his oncologist, Dr. Allison.

Dr. Allison called me back after I spoke with you and said a feeding tube is no longer an option. She wants me to take him to the hospital on Saturday or Monday for hydration, and we're supposed to meet with her on Wednesday to determine how he can get nutrients, etc. She told me that the only way to do this may be this thing called TPN, which is an intravenous feeding that should be carefully monitored, and that may mean hospitalization.

He told me earlier that if that's the case, he wants to go into hospice care. He is talking about death in the next few weeks, and I do think he may be right, that he won't be able to hold on beyond that. He is weak and is depressed. I don't even have enough money to plan for a funeral.

If buying the building is something you want to go forward with, I would want to do things soon. I will make sure it is something that benefits us both. I just have so little left to deal with this.

Call me if you want to discuss details, etc. Call me on the home phone because I don't know if I'll have the computer on, aka magicJack.

Love you.

~ Kasey

I was utterly lost. Phillip's condition worsened by the hour. In subsequent calls to Dr. Allison's office, her nurse related the message that Dr. Allison wanted me to take Phillip into Boston to receive fluids. It was Friday of Columbus Day weekend. I was relieved he would get help but I was nervous about having to drive our van in holiday traffic. While I'd been fortunate for months on end, it still concerned me that it would break while I traveled with my extremely fragile husband.

On the 14th of October, we arrived at the treatment center late in the afternoon. With a heavy heart, the nurse told us that Dr. Allison said there would be no more hydration treatments after today, even though it was the only thing keeping Phillip alive. After giving him a saline solution intravenously, Dr. Allison stopped in, gave me a prescription for liquid morphine, then pulled me aside to give me some advice.

"Take him to hospice care. Find someplace comfortable. There's nothing we can do from here," she said and quickly left the room.

Ignoring jaundice in his eyes, I wanted to ask her, "Why was there hope last week but no hope today?" In that moment, it wasn't the cost of tolls, parking, gas or worry that the van would break down. Her dismissive tone lacked any compassion as she sent us out into holiday traffic at five in the afternoon. Why had she offered him months of treatment that robbed him of time with his family? It didn't matter to her because another patient would fill the void in her schedule tomorrow.

Once I filled his prescription at the hospital pharmacy, I got Phillip to the van. I promised God I would do anything if it didn't break down on the way back to Marblehead. The combined rush hour and holiday traffic made the situation worse. It took us three hours to get back. Just before arriving back in Marblehead, I pulled over. I couldn't drive another mile. I needed to release the overwhelming sorrow of knowing that my husband's life would soon be over. There was no more hope. It was the end of the line.

We sat, parked in a rest stop, and I sobbed uncontrollably. When I finally gained my composure, Phillip took my hand. I looked across at him, trying to stop the flow of tears.

"When we get back home, I want you to take the kids to the park or something," Phillip told me.

"Why?" I asked.

"I need to tell my folks what Dr. Allison said, and I have no idea how they'll react. You know how my mother is. It could be a real shit show," he said with a slight smile. "I need to ask them if it would be OK to be buried in their plot at Notre Dame. I want to be cremated, so it will only be an urn. I think that's best," he explained.

I didn't know what to say.

"Don't you want us to be together?" I asked him haltingly.

"Look, you don't know what will happen from here out. You're still young. Chances are you'll remarry. I don't want my ashes sitting in a closet somewhere. This isn't about us. It's about my last wishes, ok?" Phillip said matter-of-factly.

I hated him a little at that moment. He was forcing me to accept reality when I wasn't ready. I nodded, unable to argue with anything he said. I started the van, and we continued the trip back to Marblehead.

When we arrived back from Boston, Rachel took the kids out so he could tell his folks. I disappeared downstairs to make the necessary phone calls. I called dozens of places that provided hospice care, without luck.

"We're full," Life Care told us. I got the same answer wherever I called.

After Phillip told his folks, it seemed like he lost any strength to carry on. He came downstairs and went into his room, leaving the door ajar. I debated whether to go back upstairs so I wouldn't wake him as I continued to make calls. I tiptoed to the bedroom, where I assumed he was trying to sleep. I noticed the Aspen collar on the table beside his bed. He'd removed it so he could rest better. It was a startling reminder that his fight was nearing an end.

I sat in the next room, calling any place that might have an opening. Phillip's moans between doses of morphine kept me dialing. By a sheer miracle, there was a bed at a hospice center in Beverly that would be available the following morning. My good luck was only because of someone else's loss. I wondered who would be jumping for joy when my husband's bed finally became available.

Phillip wanted me to let his friends know the situation. He didn't want them to find out after he was gone. With great emotion, I wrote all the things I felt and believed about him, with complete honesty, because all anger had passed, and only compassion and love remained in my heart.

While he slept, I sent out emails.

Hi Everyone-

I just wanted you to know that my husband Phillip will be going into hospice care at a facility in Beverly tomorrow. He is gravely ill and not expected to survive beyond the end of the week. He asked me to let his friends know he loved you all, and to thank you for your love and support in his life.

At his passing, there will be a funeral Mass, but also a memorial service in a few weeks so people can gather and celebrate the life he lived.

He is a wonderful man, a loving father, and an exceptional husband. He will be missed beyond belief.

I don't know how practical it is for any of you to visit him. He is able to have visitors but it might be best to call ahead if anyone wishes to see him while he is still able.

I, too, want to thank everyone who has meant so much to him. It is unbelievable to me that he will no longer be here, but I have made peace with things, as he is in too much pain to want

him to remain here on Earth. His love and spirit will remain with
me until we can be together again.

> *If you need to contact me, please send me an email or call my*
cell.
Love to all
~ Kasey

I meant every word I said.

It was harder to speak to those who called to express their love and sorrow over the phone. After receiving the email, his favorite cousin, Rob, called. The words got caught in my throat when I heard the tenderness in Rob's voice. It was too much for me, so I hurried off the call.

I followed up with an email so Rob would understand I simply couldn't speak through the emotional turmoil.

Hi, Rob and Sandi-
I wanted to say something when you called the other day, but at that point, Phillip's folks were in the room and were not up-to-date, and I didn't want to say anything until he'd spoken with them.

> *Today we are bringing Phillip to a hospice facility so he will be more comfortable. He is experiencing more pain and is now not able to take in even fluids. I am so sorry to have to relate the news, but Phillip's end is very, very near.*

He was doing so well up until about three weeks ago and we thought he had much more time ahead of him, but a recent CT-scan revealed that the cancer has impacted his liver and other major organs. I can't even begin to tell you how sad this makes us all feel, and I know you share in our sorrow.

I am hoping you could relate this to the other members of your family because I simply cannot say the words. I am not able to speak of these things without emotion overcoming me and, right now, I need to bear up for the kids. I've wanted to visit your mom so often but knew it would be impossible to stay composed.

Please know that you mean so much to both of us. He loves you dearly, and you're not only his cousin, but a dear friend.

I don't know the time frame in which things will happen in the days to come, but the doctor doesn't think he has much time at all because he is not taking in fluids at this point. Call me or email me if you want to be in touch. We are most likely bringing him to the hospice facility sometime tomorrow morning or in the early afternoon.

Love to you both,

- Kasey

In the morning, I gathered Phillip's bags, Bible, and some pictures of Jack and Lucy—our Beans. I packed whatever I thought would bring him comfort. It was the longest seven miles I'd ever driven. We checked Phillip into the hospice center, knowing he would never return to Marblehead.

Chapter Thirty-Five

A Final Farewell

October 25th

Eleven days after he was brought to hospice care, Phillip signed the papers granting his caregivers permission to administer the drugs that would put him into an irreversible coma. During that time, he said his goodbyes to dozens of people who had traveled countless miles to see him. His best friend, Kevin, and his wife, Stephanie, had offered to take the kids overnight. I was glad, as it would distract them for a while. It was the first time in days Phillip and I were alone.

We sat together, holding hands, waiting for the nursing staff to come and give the drugs that would accomplish the end-of-life sedation. I sat with him, trying hard to hold in the waves of emotion. He still hated it when I cried. He looked down at his hand.

"I guess I won't need this anymore," he said, handing me his wedding ring. I slipped it on my thumb, afraid I would lose it. "I wrote the kids some letters. They're on a flash drive in the top drawer in the desk downstairs in the basement. Could you print them out on nice paper and give it to them on their twenty-first birthdays?" he asked.

"You bet," I promised.

"I also wrote down what I want put on my grave marker. Don't get anything fancy. I know you can't afford it. Just something simple, all right?" Phillip instructed.

I couldn't say anything, so I nodded.

"I'm so tired," he said, looking away. "I'm so sorry I hurt you," he said, squeezing my hand.

"Please don't. Let's just hold on to all the best things," I told him. An hour passed as we sat, recalling, with broad strokes, the most significant moments of our lives together.

"Remember that day we learned I was pregnant?" I reminded him, choking back tears.

"How about the night the Beans were born?" he responded.

We talked of joys we shared and the life we'd created together, for better or worse. There were so many memories. We reminisced over some of our twenty-seven years together, trying to forget the anger that had built up and led to our happiness going astray. I forgave him for being unable to recognize my deepest desire to bring him joy and happiness by giving of myself. I forgave myself for all the times I couldn't rise above my anger and deal with situations more calmly. I stopped myself from thinking about ever wanting to walk out on him months earlier. I pushed the thoughts aside, knowing that it was wasted time spent on things that no longer mattered as we reached the end of his journey. We held hands, and the love I had for him rebounded.

When the nurse came into the room, I turned away, unable to look as she put the drugs in his IV. I knew soon he would fall into a coma and never wake up. I nodded through tears, holding his fragile hand while he drifted off to an unending sleep. Before the Propofol took hold, I leaned over gently and kissed his mouth.

"I love you," he told me, blinking through tears.

I looked deep into his weary eyes and told him what was in my heart. "I love you too." He turned his head and closed his eyes. I sat down beside him and waited until he drifted off.

I sat in one of the lounge chairs in his room until he fell asleep. I looked over at him, lying a few feet away. He moaned. I wondered if he was dreaming. Was he haunted by his final goodbye to our twins, his sister, and his elderly parents?

Knowing the end was near, I remained in the corner of the darkened room, thankful Phillip's suffering would soon be over. But I was angry, too. I kept wondering if he'd received treatment earlier if it would have made a difference.

An entire spectrum of thoughts and emotions engulfed me and dominated the passing time. The magnitude of what was going to happen sunk in, and I knew I had to brace myself so I didn't fall into despair. I concentrated on the moments that could help me untangle the many lingering questions I had about my relationship with Phillip and how it went awry. Even then, the chaos of my mind and fragility of my heart didn't always provide the best explanations.

Some of those moments were spent willingly reflecting on all our days together. I tried to avoid backing down in facing the truth, as ugly as it sometimes was. Our relationship was highly flawed, but it didn't make either of us bad people. I was the fortunate one because I got to learn from the mistakes made along the way.

Throughout my life, I struggled to love the two men that meant the world to me. I thought of my dad and wondered why it never occurred to me before how much Phillip and my father were alike. They were both loved and admired by so many people throughout their lives. But those people saw only the wonderful qualities. It made those of us who witnessed their weaknesses up close question why no one else saw their true natures.

I suppose it was because, to the world, we all show our better selves. We trust that the face on display at work, church, or community is identical to that at home. But there, in our most intimate setting, we cast aside the masks we put on for the world, only revealing our underbellies to those who we believe love us the most. We hope those who are closest to us will love us regardless of how poorly we behave. We expect it. Sometimes we demand from our loved ones what we would never tolerate ourselves.

Phillip and I started out with some heavy baggage early on. Because we were often happy in those earlier years, it was difficult to see how much those issues infiltrated and shaped our relationship. Until I began to look back, I couldn't see how detrimental the lie about our first wedding was to our relationship. It had set the stage for future events and became the catalyst for the imbalance of power that drove a wedge between us.

I looked across the room where Phillip lay sleeping. His breathing seemed more erratic. His struggle to take in the air made me want to flee the room at times, but I could not move because I'd committed myself to stay to the end. Instead, I found myself assessing blame, and the what-ifs began to pile up.

I wondered how much my inability to confront the problems early on in our marriage contributed to how things played out? I knew I avoided confronting our problems head-on because we were apart so much of the time. By the time Phillip's patterns of behavior emerged, I was used to weathering the storms in our relationship. I waited things out until they were over so we could get on with life. His capacity to sometimes be so loving endeared him to me, and the cost of confrontation was often more than I could afford emotionally. That, too, played a large part in the dysfunction. I enabled his negative behaviors because I had little understanding of how destructive it was at the time.

But I also began to think about other things Phillip did and how those things contributed to the collapse of our marriage. There were clear distinctions between how Phillip and I approached our problems and how our attitudes toward one another led to things falling apart.

It wasn't hard to identify the largest shift in our relationship. While we had significant issues before having kids, Phillip's attitude changed significantly once I was no longer earning the income that supported us. In the early days of our marriage, Phillip was open to compromise, and I thought the praise he gave me was a sign of his love and support. But once I gave up my high-income job to stay home to raise the twins, my role as a mother and even my part-time work was dismissed as irrelevant. He acted as if his more significant role in our financial support gave him the ultimate right to make all the decisions, even though those rights were never granted to me.

There was a double standard in other aspects of our relationship as well. Long before we had the twins, Phillip also demanded control over all my time and energy. What I often gave freely was never enough to satisfy him. He worked hard in his career but failed to acknowledge that he wouldn't have had the time or ability to pursue his goals without my support. I still couldn't fathom how he justified making me beg for money toward the end of our marriage and seemed happy to humiliate me by requiring receipts for all expenditures. Thoughts roiled my mind at all the years he benefitted from my income and never once was asked to supply a receipt for the money he spent. My anger was stroked until I realized I couldn't hear Phillip breathing. I panicked for a moment until I found the courage to tiptoe over to the bed and confirm he was still alive. By the time I sat back down, I realized it was useless to keep reliving some of the most horrible moments of our marriage, and I tried shifting my thoughts to more loving moments.

I thought back to our move to Canada and how excited we were to reinvent our lives together. Within moments, thoughts of the loneliness I initially felt when he was absent from my lif,e when he left the Beans and me in Canada, came to mind. A wry smile crossed my face as I recalled how nervous I had been the first time a customer had entered the café. I couldn't remember why I was so scared, but I just remembered I was. But soon, I regained my confidence, and my self-doubt lifted. As I became more independent, Phillip's resentment grew. I looked across the room at him lying there dying and wondered what would have happened if he had stayed in Canada? I knew my life would be much different. I might never have realized how wounded I was. His unhappiness in Canada was brought on by his lack of control over me, and the independence I'd regained was reflected in his disdain of all I'd accomplished without him. I moved on from those memories because thoughts of those years weren't safe to reminisce about either.

I fought to stay awake and glanced at my phone to see what time it was. The night was slipping away, and so was Phillip's life. I finally admitted to myself all those negative thoughts, and even the positive ones, were all for naught. I would never be able to define why there was an enormous difference between my approach to addressing our problems and his; I just knew I was powerless to change the past. My only hope was to understand more when I wasn't as exhausted and emotionally distressed. I conceded this wasn't the time to thoroughly examine the past after all.

I reasoned that we had both changed as we aged, and it was hard to keep up, year in and year out. Our goals changed. Our interests changed. We had children, and that changed everything. We were two people who merely wanted to find happiness. In our earlier years of marriage, that was together. As time passed, it was not. To stay married to Phillip meant I would only be loved when he thought I deserved it. And even then, I'd always have to live in fear of when this momentary love would disappear. I couldn't accept that for myself anymore. Even though our marriage failed, I reminded myself that no one teaches you how to be married. We'd both come from families where patriarchal standards were the norm. We played into these notions without realizing how deeply they were ingrained. While we both believed we escaped the imbalance, it was there all along, hiding beneath the surface.

I also accepted that I would never know the depths of Phillip's struggles. For whatever reason, something skewed his perception of how others treated him. I admitted there must have been things I didn't know about his life. His perception of events was often quite different than what I witnessed. His accounts of his past, too, made me wonder about what was real and what was imagined. The questions that remained would never be answered. I recognized that it was probably for the best.

Sitting in the darkness, I realized I also had much to be grateful for. I acknowledged all Phillip had given me as my husband. He'd taught me many things in our time together. While working on projects together, I became a better writer, and he taught me how to edit film and audio. I learned how joyful and challenging it was to be a parent. Dealing with his illness made me a more compassionate person. It made me more resilient and more self-aware. I had a better understanding of the suffering of those with major illnesses and appreciated my health more. But I learned other lessons because our life together wasn't always easy or pleasant, as he didn't always teach me things through acts of kindness. I knew what betrayal felt like and how difficult it was to leave a marriage without financial security. I now knew what love was and what it wasn't. I hoped my painful experiences wouldn't be lost in bitterness. Ultimately, I only wanted Phillip to realize that I had enriched his life the way he had enriched mine.

I woke with a start as the nurse draped a blanket over me. I forgot for a moment where I was. Then, I heard the familiar sounds of the machines that monitored my husband's vital signs.

"He's still with us," she told me. "You should go home and get some rest. You can't be very comfortable in this chair. He might stay like this for quite some time."

I thanked her for the blanket, and she left the room. I was afraid to go. I wanted Phillip to know I loved him, even when I didn't like him sometimes. But, mostly, I wanted to be there with him so he wouldn't die alone.

I sat there for a few more hours, thinking about all the times we laughed together because those were safe moments, moments I could think about him and not be overwhelmed with grief. His keen sense of humor was one thing that drew me to him. It was the place I retreated to as his life slipped away. I remembered something I'd almost forgotten about. It made me smile and cry a little, too. It was one of Phillip's most endearing moments.

Our last significant renovation before listing the property in Blairstown was finishing some upgrades to the kitchen and laying some slate in the backyard to create a more finished patio. We had purchased some slate, and it was sitting in the yard under a blue tarp.

One Saturday morning in late April of 2006, Phillip went to work on the patio to install the slate when I heard him shout, "Oh, my God!"

I thought he'd had a heart attack! I ran out to see what was happening. He stood over the tarp with the edge lifted, staring at something on the ground.

"Are you okay? What's wrong?"

"Come here. Look at this."

I crossed the yard in seconds and marveled at four tiny kittens under the tarp. They were about 2-3 weeks old and mewing for their momma.

"Holy shit! What are we going to do?" I asked him.

"Well, we can't just leave them here."

By this time, Jack and Lucy were in the yard, and Phillip told them to go get a box sitting on the back porch and a towel from the bathroom. I wasn't sure if the mother cat had abandoned her babies, but the Beans had seen them and begged me to help the tiny creatures. I debated whether it was good to move them but was reluctant to take a chance they would still be alive if we waited to find out.

We gathered the four kittens into the box and brought them into the kitchen. Soon, I was calling every place listed in the phone book and online that rescued animals, only to find no one was available to take them. Each shelter I called was full. I called the woman who rescued our older cats, Duncan and Felicia. She offered a ton of information and suggested we prepare to feed them as soon as possible. I went to the pet store to buy kitten formula, bottles, and gear to save those little creatures.

Phillip's involvement really surprised me. He was more of a dog lover, and the only cat we ever had that he was attached to was Squirt. We took turns getting up in the middle of the night to feed them for weeks. However, what made me smile was thinking back to a picture I took of Phillip holding the kitten Lucy had named Milky. Phillip was holding the tiny thing in the palm of his hand while it sucked on the small bottle. He was so zoned out that he didn't even realize I had grabbed the camera and taken his picture. It showed a side of him that was gentle and kind. It warmed my heart, watching him half asleep, trying hard to help save the kitten.

Those were the memories I cherished as I sat in the chair. I recalled how tender Phillip could be and knew that side of his personality got buried sometimes. It hurt to think about these things, but I needed to feel the pain of losing him so I could truly appreciate what was being lost.

I finally dozed off, unable to stay awake any longer. The nurse came in again, and I could feel her pull the blanket around me. I opened my eyes and smiled in appreciation.

"Maybe he's holding on until you leave," she said. I was famished and needed to eat, and I wanted a shower desperately, too. I finally let her convince me my vigil was unnecessary.

I left about 2 am to shower quickly and change my clothes. As I rushed back to Marblehead, a cop pulled me over to give me a speeding ticket. He let me off with a warning when I told the officer why I was going 30 miles per hour in a 20-mile-an-hour zone.

"Really?" I thought as he ran my plates. I slowed down for the remaining trip and made it to Marblehead. I was just grabbing some clean clothing when my new cellphone rang. The night nurse at the hospice center told me that Phillip had passed moments ago.

He died alone after all.

I showered and dressed, then returned to the hospice center to say my final goodbyes.

When I arrived, the nurse told me I could spend as much time as I needed with Phillip. But that meant being alone with his corpse, and I was frightened to enter the room. I stood looking in momentarily, trying to muster the courage to approach Phillip's cooling body. I walked guardedly to him, finally reaching out and touching his smooth hand. It was cold and lifeless, and I accepted that Phillip was really dead. The gray stubble on his shrunken, unshaven face made him look so much older than his fifty-two years. I quickly looked away and closed my eyes. I didn't want my last memories of him to be of this shell of a person. I wanted to remember him the way we first met, the handsome man in the elevator who made me blush. I tried to forget all the pain he'd caused and the fear I felt that because now I was alone after being married for twenty-five years.

As tears fell, I thanked him for all the love we shared. I told him I wished him peace on his journey. When I could finally compose myself, I opened my eyes and rushed from the room. I went to the nurse's station to hand over the vial of morphine that had remained in his room in the basement at his sister's. I didn't need that hanging around. They took the vial and placed it in a baggie with a seal.

As I left the place, I could see my weary reflection in the door's glass and smiled through my tears when I noticed what the writing on the tee shirt I was wearing read: Free Agent. I must have grabbed one of my brother-in-law's shirts by mistake. The irony wasn't lost on me. I left the hospice center, knowing that Phillip's story was over. Still, my journey would begin with an ever-changing epilogue.

AN UNPREDICTABLE CURSE

.

SEATTLE

Truth is subjective, as is the experience of how we live and navigate our lives. While this personal reflection does not highlight the best of all those mentioned in these pages, these events are how I perceive the threats and traumas that influenced my life. I may still feel the sting, but I hold no grudges. Well, only toward the serious lack of dragons in this story.
~ K. J.

December 23, 2022

Nothing jolts a parent from a dead sleep before 5am like the blood-curdling scream of their child. My body reacts before my brain, pulling me from the warm covers into full alert mode. It's my eleven-year-old daughter, Willow. She paces back and forth in a panic sobbing, "Daddy fell. Daddy's hurt."

I race down the stairs, fearing the worst, only to be met with silence.

Heavy breathing follows. Finally, I hear his voice. "I'm here."

It's the night of the worst ice storm the Seattle area has seen in a decade. My husband stepped outside to smoke a cigarette before work. He slipped on the deck, now a solid sheet of ice, and landed on the rail for the sliding glass door.

My husband is half in and half out of the house. The door's open to the frigid air as he tries to drag himself off the sliding door rail. I drop to my knees next to him, yelling for my daughter to grab the phone so I can call 9-1-1.

"I don't need an ambulance," my husband mutters. "I'm fine. We can't afford it."

Cursing under my breath because we'd had this conversation thousands of times, I look him over. There's so much pain on his face he's trying to hide. "I just need a minute to gather myself."

Bullshit. My husband might be a southern man with farmer's blood in his veins, but he can't hide his anguish from me.

I have to trust my instincts because we'll never make it to the car. His leg is turned at an awkward angle, and I know he has a broken bone.

It's two days before Christmas.

As the EMTs carry him through the snow and ice to the ambulance, I can't help but wonder why the universe has kicked us again. It seems to be the cycle of our marriage—claw our way to stability and a manageable debt, and then catastrophe kicks us right back into the abyss.

My husband and I often joke about how we just can't get ahead, but I'm fairly certain I'm the one who brought this curse into his life.

It's a pattern. An echo of something that continues to ripple the waters of my life. As I usher my kids into the kitchen for some hot chocolate to help ease their worries, our three dogs curl up at my feet. They need my attention, too.

Our border collie, Harley, is an older dog—my little shadow. He follows me everywhere and has been my companion for over ten years. We know he has cancer, but we could never afford the surgery to get his tumor removed. The vet quoted us at upwards of $3,500. We like his care team, but they always underquote, and that price is only for the surgery, not the medication he'll need during and after the procedure.

Our other two dogs are pups—livestock guardians we purchased from a farm going out of business. They need a herd to guard, but we live in the suburbs so I guess we're it. We really can't afford both of them, but the farmer convinced us the pups who don't find a home would be sent to an animal shelter. We can't bear the thought, so here they are.

As my kids and animals all look to me to make the world right again, I know the ambulance—and likely a forthcoming surgery—for my husband will put another huge dent in our finances. We'd just started to stabilize, but this always seems to be the pattern. I can't stop this curse and my whole body aches every time it happens. It means more conversations about money, a topic I loathe in the depths of my soul. It feels like lead in my heart while my mind buries the anxiety. If I don't think about it, maybe it will all go away.

December 24, 2022

It's good news and bad news. My husband's hip is broken. All I want to do is grab my kindle and curl up in a chair next to his hospital bed to offer him comfort and support. This man is the love of my life and I want to be with him, but I've got five children—if you count the dogs—that I can't leave alone.

The kids beg me to take them to the hospital. All they want is their daddy and it breaks my heart that I have to tell them no. As much as my husband wants to see them, our kids love climbing on their father. We both know they'll throw themselves across him for hugs and might end up injuring him worse. That "no" brings tears and heartache, and there's only one other way to fix it.

I pick up the phone and call my brother. We've been planning to spend Christmas Eve with him and the family, so I don't feel like I'm putting them out. No guilt today for me, but my kids need a distraction. A big one.

A holiday is just the trick to do the job. Once my kids are safely at my brother's house, I can breathe. I don't have to worry about any more last-minute gifts or spending the last of our money. We're already tight, living paycheck to paycheck and crossing our fingers we have enough to cover our bills.

But it's the same every year. Once October hits, we're scraping together every cent and holding our breath until January when we'll be pulling coins out of penny jars.

It makes me hate the holidays and this year's stress is now too much to bear. I continue to push the anxiety into the darkest corners of my soul, because once the medical bills begin rolling in, our credit will tank (again). My husband has insurance, but we have no idea how much they'll cover. We'll be lucky if the cost of the surgery and hospital stay is in the low six figures.

It wasn't.

On Christmas Eve I sit alone with my dogs and watch *Firefly*. It bothers me how calm I feel about suffering another financial hit. Somehow all of this is my fault, I'm sure of it. There was some part of my life I was doing wrong.

I was unable to tolerate most people because I'd spent years in customer service jobs. Clients were great to talk to, but too many bosses and constant critiques about how I handled my workload whittled away at my self-worth.

All I wanted was the space to feed my creativity and work on the projects I loved—without judgment.

I became a freelance web developer several years before we married. It came with its own challenges, but I was home for my daughter, Iris, when she got sick, and I could set my own hours. It was a liberating career move and offered me the freedom I needed, but it was a constant struggle just to have the basic necessities.

So maybe my job was the problem—I wasn't "contributing" enough.

This was an argument my husband and I had many times early in our marriage. I didn't make nearly as much money as he did, and needed to get an office job. His logic was that I'd make a higher wage than him with my skill set, and we could double our monthly income.

Nearly five years into our marriage and we were barely surviving. Our second daughter, Willow, was a toddler, and I was pregnant again. But he wanted me to "go back to work and get an office job" so we'd have two incomes.

I gave serious thought to running him over with the car, but instead I slapped down a piece of paper and wrote out every dollar we'd have to spend to get our household ready for that kind of transition.

Groceries for bag lunches every day, daycare for two kids, a second car, more car insurance, a weekly allowance of fuel, money for coffee and lunch, etc. I kept writing it all down along with the dollar figures until it finally sunk in. If he wanted me to go back to work, it was going to cost nearly ten thousand dollars to get into a position where I could.

It was the second worst argument we ever had. No one won, but I made my point. Besides, I already had a job. I had a growing list of clients, a particular niche of work that fit my skill set, and I was writing my book *Bloodflower*. I clung to these like a lifeline. They were the only parts of myself I had left amid a sea of children, dogs, household chores, and some disturbing new health issues I had no insurance for.

As I lie on the couch Christmas Eve watching my favorite starship crew, I think about all the clients waiting on me for work to be done. Websites, book covers, bookmarks—design projects that allow me to explore new facets of creativity and feed my soul. They are all a part of me as much as I am of their projects, and the future looks bleak.

I have no idea what to do with my husband when he returns from the hospital. He won't be able to sleep in our bed. It's too much of a risk that the dogs will jump on his leg. They'll want attention and won't understand that daddy can't play with them.

The same with the kids. They'll want to snuggle their dad, but their squirms could cause more damage. My husband needs a quiet space to rest and recover for the foreseeable future. His surgeon chose to repair the bone with titanium pins, which means a much longer recovery.

Running the house, the kids, doctor visits, all driving, all cooking, everything. . .it's all on my shoulders now. My job always seems to come last in our house, and now I see the future like a tunnel. The few hours I had for myself, work and the new book I've already promised readers will disappear.

I'll have no more income, and neither will my husband.

It's a certainty, and as Captain Mal from the TV show *Firefly* swears by his pretty floral bonnet, I feel the tears sliding down my cheeks. It's mine— my job and my stories—and without them I'm nothing.

Just another housewife.

Just another mother.

Just another faceless woman who's lost herself in a world of chaos.

December 29th, 2023

My husband has been home for two days, and the kids are on their way home from my brother's house. They've had a wonderful time and they're so excited to see daddy and know he's okay.

All the money I thought we'd save from the kids spending Christmas elsewhere is now gone. My husband needed a recovery lair, so I had to go out and purchase a new bed, sheets, and medical equipment to help my husband stand up a few times a day to help strengthen his leg.

I've made him a space in the basement and even brought down his big TV and Xbox. He's going to be home for at least a few months, and he'll need something to keep himself occupied. It's time for another round of his favorite game, *Witcher.*

I spend my time that afternoon cleaning the house, and the kids tell me several times that our pup, Loki—now six months old—keeps growling at them.

Loki is a Turkish Kangal, a livestock guardian. His tawny fur and black muzzle are genetic marks of his bloodline, which originates in the Anatolian region of Turkey where dogs like him protect flocks of sheep by fending off wolves. It's why they're nicknamed "wolf killers."

We're Loki's flock until we buy a farm, something we've been working toward for almost fifteen years. So when the kids tell me he's been growling at them, I suspect they might be hearing a "leave me alone" grunt, something our border collie, Harley, often does. But I keep their concerns at the front of my mind as I walk into my bedroom to grab more cleaning supplies.

Loki blocks the way to the bathroom, his tail curled high and his tongue hanging out. A happy stance, so I have no concerns. He's always such a happy dog and loves to lay across my lap. Still, I can't discount what my children have said. This anomaly concerns me and I need to understand exactly what they're witnessing.

I drop to my knees to grab a rag. Loki's happy pant turns to a deadly growl and his jaws slam down on my hand. He might be a puppy, but his fangs bite deep as he shakes his head with my hand still caught in his mouth.

I barely have time to register the shock when his jaws release my hand, and he dives for my throat. My back hits the floor as I scream for help. With one hand holding Loki's throat, I try to kick him off. His fangs tear into my jaw and neck.

One thought is crystal clear—if I don't get him off, he's going to kill me. I fight to push his jaws off my neck so I can scurry out from under him.

I never have the chance. Loki finally releases my throat, but he's not finished. His jaws grab my arm in a death grip, and he shakes his head hard, sharp teeth tearing through flesh. He's trying to rip it off.

All I can do is scream and kick and punch. I refuse to die like this, and as soon as I get him off me, I'm going to kill this dog.

I don't know why the fight stops, but Loki finally releases my arm and races out of the room. Adrenaline has me now and he's not going to touch my children.

Covered in blood with my arm and neck torn open, I bolt after Loki. He sits in the living room, happy panting as if it's a normal evening.

My eight-year-old son sits ten feet away on the couch.

Not today, you fucking demon dog. I grab the leash and slip it around his neck. It only takes a minute to drag his ass outside and slam the sliding glass door shut. It's the same slider that broke my husband's hip.

I hate our home

Loki scratches at the glass slider trying to get back in, wagging his tail like nothing is wrong. My husband shouts in panic from the basement, desperate to know what the screaming is, and my son is now in a panic, flapping his hands (an autistic behavior) as the blood drips down my arm.

Livestock guardians are supposed to protect their herd, not attack them. The ones that do get shot before they kill the rest of the flock.

I don't even know what to do at this point. I'm in so much pain I can feel my brain trying to block it. I have to tell my husband what happened. Partly so he'll stop shouting, but mostly because that dog has got to go.

I hold my arm, the torn open flesh spilling out of the wound. It's hard to tell exactly how deep his teeth ripped, but the flesh spilling out of my wounds isn't skin. I need to go to the hospital, but as I walk down the stairs to my husband's recovery space, I have to figure out what to do next.

It's gonna cost us another ambulance ride, another medical bill we simply can't afford.

My husband takes one look at me and he's ready to shoot Loki, except he can't move. I've never said these words in my life—animals are family—but I can defend myself, my kids can't.

"Get rid of the dog," I say to my husband, guilt lodging itself deep in my gut. I know when the city comes to take Loki away, they're going to kill him.

He's only a pup.

I don't know what I did to trigger the attack, but I can't bear the thought of killing a puppy. It would be like killing our own children when they fuck up.

"Call Charlie," I say. Charlie's a dog trainer. We would have hired him to work with our dogs, but he's so damn expensive. Regardless, one of Charlie's friends has a farm where she works on corrective behavior with dogs. I tell my husband that Loki needs to go there so he can have a chance at life, but he can never be in this house.

Without waiting for an answer and ignoring the "are you okay, Mommy" pleas from my children—no I'm not fucking okay, read the room—I grab the keys to the truck and drive myself to the hospital.

Everything hurts, my heart is broken, and now I'm worried that our other livestock guardian, Freya, will attack us, too.

At least I saved us a forty-thousand-dollar ambulance ride.

I step out of the elevator and don a mask with one hand. Covid regulations haven't relaxed yet, so I breathe into the cotton and shuffle into the emergency room.

It's packed. Wall-to-wall, every chair and space to stand are filled with others who cannot heal their own injuries. We're all in need of help, and my neck is killing me now. I can feel the blood dripping out of the puncture wounds as I step to the counter.

I stand in the waiting room for more than two hours before my name is called. It's another two hours before a doctor will see me. Loki is still at the house howling to be let in. The city can't pick him up until tomorrow. And my husband just got off the phone with the breeder. "Oh yeah, we were gonna shoot that dog. He kept attacking our colts."

The breeder, knowing we had children, released this dog into our home.

The anger I feel when I hear these words battles my adrenaline. My mind races as the doctor sews up my arm and neck. I drive home from the hospital with half a dozen stitches in my arm, more in my neck, but my kids are safe. It's all that matters.

My husband and I will figure out the rest, but it's going to be a long, shitty road, and all I want to do is curl up in a ball and block out the world.

January 10ᵗʰ 2023

It's only been a few weeks and I'm losing myself. With my husband unable to walk, I have to take care of everything in our house, including hand-delivering every meal to his bedside. I love my husband with all my heart, but I'm not cut out to be a caregiver. I'm caring for him, my children, and Freya is grieving the loss of Loki. I have no time to work on client projects and I shelve my book. It won't get done before any deadline, so I'll just have to write it next year. Or the year after. Or maybe in 2042.

My husband has to sign up for family medical leave, which only pays out a portion of his wages. Our combined incomes aren't nearly enough to pay the bills, so I have to make calls to everyone we have a bill with.

I can't do it. My chest is starting to tighten and I can feel all the gates and walls and barriers in my head slamming shut. I hate it. I'd rather be attacked by Loki again than make these calls. My whole body is shutting down, and all I can do is clutch the phone while I freeze up.

My skin tingles like it's filled with thousands of needles and my throat starts to close up. It's hard to speak and along the inside of my mouth, words recoil back into my skin.

Sometimes it will take me a week to brace myself enough to pick up the phone and make a five minute, "I'll be late with your money" phone call.

It's a curse.

It triggers panic attacks.

I will do anything to ignore those phone calls.

Avoidance is one of my superpowers. That and making salsa.

With a deep, stabilizing breath I pick up the phone to call our landlord and let them know my husband and I will be late on rent (again).

My fingers won't press the buttons.

A heavy weight bears down on my chest, and I can't breathe. I wish I had a better excuse than 'we're waiting on FMLA to pay us.'

I can't do it. There is an emotion welling up inside me that I don't have a word for. It's a sense of judgment that I can't act like an adult mixed with the shame of my inability to have a financially stable life. I've done something wrong along the way and now I'm acting like a coward as I lay next to Harley and take comfort from him. He doesn't yell at me or tell me what an absolute joke of a human I am. Harley doesn't judge me when I can't do a simple task. All he does is snuggle up next to me like I'm the best human he's ever known and calms my aching heart.

Which I desperately need.

A few years ago my therapist diagnosed me with post-traumatic stress disorder. I didn't quite understand why she would give me that diagnosis until she asked me to write down a timeline of my life as if I was writing a story. Only the moments that left an impact—it didn't have to be a deep dive.

I only got as far as my senior year in high school. My list hadn't even hit the big traumas, but it was all right there in black and white—all the events I'd buried that left scars on my soul.

The next time we spoke I told her I couldn't do it. I couldn't even write a timeline without a pain so deep in my heart that I couldn't get out of bed.

She asked a few questions, and I dodged every one of them. I wanted to talk about derelict starships, the weather, the trail of an ant through the pine needles. I didn't fucking care, she just needed to back off.

My therapist guided the conversation to easier topics. She did it with such grace and I'm forever grateful, especially because she never asked me to write that timeline again. I still won't touch it.

I tell myself every day that it's a mild case of PTSD, that I was never in a war so it's only an airbrushed diagnosis. Until the pain in my chest freezes me. Or I walk away from a conversation because I don't want to talk about it. Money, religion, my mother, my father, my exes, life in general. Sometimes I hate talking about real life, because all it does is bring up memories, emotions, and traumas I've buried deep in my soul and I don't want to face them.

My life *is* a war.

I'm constantly dodging those topics that will tear me open like a bullet to the chest. I'm always fighting, so my body has to find new and creative ways to get the pain out.

It gives me severe migraines, which in turn trigger seizures. I'm fully conscious when they happen, but I have no control over my body. The seizures didn't start until I got pregnant with my son, but my PTSD has been around since childhood when my father used to pin me against a wall and yell in my face about whatever I'd done wrong. I was so terrified I'd start crying, only to get screamed at for the tears on my face.

I spent years forcing myself not to cry, so I'd freeze like a deer until the yelling stopped. In these moments as I stood silently with my back against the wall, the weight of shame would settle on my shoulders. I was nothing. I was worthless. That knowledge would tighten my chest and prickle all the emotional sensors in my head. I needed to cry, but I didn't dare.

My father never physically struck me, but his words cut deeper than a knife. The ability to freeze correctly and hold my tears in became a narrative that peeled away the layers of my self-worth and set the stage for a life of fear and self-deprecation. When I would discuss this childhood ideology decades later with my brother, he didn't believe me.

"Dad never did that," he said. He never witnessed these events and for many years he seemed to block out experiences that weren't his own. It took a long time, and many heartfelt discussions, before he really began to understand the depth of what I experienced with our father and how it was so very different from his own experience.

June 5th, 2023

It's my birthday today.

I haven't been excited about my birthday in over a decade, so I always try to do small things for myself to at least have three-minute-long happy moments sprinkled through the day. Usually these come in the form of closing the bedroom door and taking a very deep breath without kids and dogs hanging off me.

But this year is extra "speshul"—intentionally spelled this way to inject some extra sarcasm there.

It's mediation day.

This means it's the oh-so magical time when my husband and I (the peon humans) get to sit down with our billion-dollar corporate housing company, and their lawyers, to have a "conversation" about our housing situation.

My husband's leg isn't healing as well as it should be, and he's *still* struggling with mobility. Both of us curse his surgeon for not replacing his hip, which would have been a much shorter recovery. But his surgeon decided to bolt my husband's bones together until they fused. My husband should be fully healed and walking by now. Instead, we're seven months post-surgery and he limps around worse than the TV character Dr. House. He can use a cane, but most days he's all-aboard a rolling walker as he stands behind a counter and kisses people's asses while they yell at him about their cars.

I don't know how he does it. I'd be a soulless shell of nothingness if I had to do his job.

Every day my husband comes home from work in a boatload of pain as he battles exhaustion and his ambitious drive to drag us out of crushing debt.

We haven't been able to pay rent in months. It's our fault, at least that's what the anti-siren song that lodges itself in my head assures me. We're working our asses off to scrape our pennies toward every critical bill while others fall into collections.

Ten years ago, we'd have been kicked out of our home with a police officer's knock on our door, but during Covid the laws changed to protect renters against evictions. While we're both grateful for this, it's also terrifying to watch the amount of money we owe our landlord in rent and fees stack up, and yet we can't escape.

Wages from FMLA have run out, my husband has just barely returned to work, and I still have no time to focus on my clients.

To make matters worse, my son has begun having seizures and the doctors can't figure out why.

Every week we have half a dozen doctor appointments in my family, and I'm the one who drives everyone around. Exhaustion has turned me into a robot—I just do the thing, no questions asked, while ignoring all those dollar signs glaring at me to pay up.

As I sit down at my computer for the zoom call that's been giving me panic attacks for weeks, all I want to do is ostrich myself in the ground. If I can't see the lawyers, they can't see me, right?

We're supposed to have a state-appointed mediator sit in on the call to keep things on track, but that doesn't give me any comfort. Some people have a way of smiling at you while spewing poisonous, condescending words, and that's what this housing bitch was about to do to us.

Waiting in the zoom call for the housing company, their lawyers, and the state mediator to log on, it takes every ounce of strength to hold the broken fragments of myself together.

My husband and I don't want to live here anymore, but we have to work out a payment plan to keep a roof over our kids' heads. I should be able to handle this. Hell, I never should have fallen into this situation in the first place.

If my father could see me now. I'm absolutely certain both disgust and disappointment would be frozen in his ice-blue eyes. He would shake his head because he wouldn't believe his daughter was still making stupid mistakes.

That would lead to the guilt I always felt—that I can't do anything right. Something is obviously wrong with me. A long time ago, I didn't lose this badly at life all the time. I miss the feeling of a win, of the happiness and sense of accomplishment I once felt, long ago, before my life was railroaded onto a different trajectory.

At five years old, I was a gymnast. I might have had a chance to be a mediocre one if I'd ever gotten over my fear of broken bones. Although my love for the sport was strong, every time my feet touched a balance beam a silent terror gripped my heart. I was absolutely certain I'd slip and break my arm, and that was the most frightening thing I could think of at the time.

Overcoming my fear wasn't necessary though as I was forced to quit after four years. I suffer from Osgood-Schlatter's disease in my left knee, and it hurt all the time. Constantly jumping around and stressing the limb only exacerbated the pain.

The devastation was difficult to bear. I hid out in my room and read. I discovered science fiction and fantasy books by Andre Norton, Anne McCaffrey, Mercedes Lackey, Julie E. Czerneda, and C. J. Cherryh. I devoured their stories, their fantasy worlds, their alien characters. All I wanted was to keep returning to the library and searching for more dragon stories, or more alien worlds.

Along with my passion for fantasy worlds, I also loved the outdoors—hiking, fishing, horseback riding, and playing football with the guys. This was where I found my joy, and I was damn good at all of it. I rarely got along with girls in my younger years—they were far too petty and only cared about makeup and popularity. I wanted to get dirty.

In junior high I itched to play sports again. I loved field hockey, broom hockey, and soccer. I was decent, but as a skinny whip of a kid, I really didn't belong near a ball or with a weapon in my hands. Maybe folks thought I was too frail, I'm honestly not certain. I just didn't belong.

Then I discovered Track & Field. During gym class we raced each other on the dirt track. I was faster than all of the girls and most of the boys. Every class it kept happening—I'd beat them all.

When we learned high-jump, I could bend my body in wicked ways thanks to my years as a gymnast. I was invited to join the Track & Field team. All I needed was for my parents to say yes.

Thank the great plaid fireweasel atop the mountain high™ for my mother. Dad wanted me home and focused on my grades. I was bored with school, but "sports will force her to keep her grades up." At least that's how my mother pitched it.

I belonged on the track, and it was a few more hours of the day I didn't have to be home and get yelled at.

After one week of training, all of us track kids raced in a meet against one of the other schools. I won two medals that day. For the first time in a long time, I felt a strong sense of pride in myself.

When I made the transition to high school, I told myself that to get on the varsity team I'd have to spend the next two years training hard. I wanted to be that kid who made the varsity team in her sophomore year.

I was on the junior varsity team. After one local track meet, the coaches switched me to varsity.

Yes, I was that fast.

Despite the elation of becoming a freshman varsity runner, it always felt like I had to prove myself to other people. No matter how many races I won, or how many medals I took home after each meet, in the back of my head I just wasn't good enough. I wanted to get all the way to the state championships, and I wanted to be invited to the Arizona Track & Field meet, a prestigious, invite-only event where high school students from half a dozen southwestern states competed against one another.

When sophomore year started, I still sucked at school. I didn't want to do it, so I did the absolute bare minimum until my grades became Ds. Then my father would stand over me at home and yell until I finished my homework, constantly telling me how horrible a kid I was for not having better grades. He would do this until I was up to a B in my classes, then he would ignore me, and I would slack off again.

As a kid, I really loved my father, but I did everything in my power to escape his notice. I was terrified of him, of getting in trouble, and of the degrading, narcissistic speeches I'd have to endure every time I did something wrong.

So each day I'd arrive at school two hours early to work out in the gym, then stay three hours after school to train on the track. That's how I got nicknamed 'Rabbit.'

And no, nothing dirty—I was a good girl. (nauseatingly good) Foxes and Rabbits is a game used to help sprinters increase their speed. The Rabbit (me) would start fifty yards ahead of the other runners (the Foxes). Once the gun fired, the foxes had to catch the rabbit.

My team always tried to catch me, but only one person ever did, a senior football player who was fast as hell. The sheer joy of never getting caught by anyone else kept me working harder than ever for one of those invitations to the prestigious Arizona meet.

In my junior year, I was breaking records and winning gold medals at almost every track meet. Strong, fast, and determined to become an Olympic runner, I finally received my invitation to Arizona. I was thrilled.

This was the pinnacle of my high school career—at least my sixteen-year-old mind told me this. The best part was that I'd never seen any other state, so traveling out of California was going to be a grand adventure.

Three weeks before the trip, I went on an outing with my youth group. We traveled to an ice-skating rink and spent hours beating each other up in broom hockey or racing around the rink in a game of *Tag*.

During one of the rounds, I grabbed onto a rail and my fingers slipped. One bad spin later and the ice skate blade slammed into my tailbone, shattering it.

The pain is something I can't begin to describe. I couldn't breathe, couldn't think. There was a sensation of such overwhelming agony that my mind blocked it on one level and froze me completely on another.

Our game day was over—I'd ruined it, and destroyed my chance to travel to Arizona.

That was the last youth group outing I attended.

On the injured list now, I couldn't compete and Arizona slipped through my fingers. I was absolutely devastated and more determined than ever to get that invitation next year. It would be my last chance.

My senior year I joined the cross-country team for extra endurance training. We ran far too much that summer (and distances far too long for a sprinter), but before school even started, my family uprooted our entire lives and we moved to Colorado.

I was ecstatic. It wasn't Arizona, though we were really close at one point in our travels, but I'd finally get to see a new state!

From a school of three thousand to a school of five hundred, it took me all of thirty seconds to make new friends. Colorado people are different from Californians. They're laid back, intensely smart, and I swear all of them have a deep love for *Rocky Horror Picture Show*.

Right away, I felt that sense of belonging and fell in love with my new life. More determined than ever to make it to the Olympics, I joined the track team and immediately broke several school records. There were a lot of great athletes on that team, and the end of the season saw us to the state championships. Although I never made it to the Arizona meet, winning several medals at a state championship left me with an unshakeable sense of accomplishment.

But it was about to be shattered in a way that would trigger a rage so deep, I still battle it today.

During the state track meet, scouts from multiple colleges were in the stands, searching for athletes to add to their school rosters. Before I stepped on the bus to go home, I was offered a full-ride Track & Field scholarship to a 4-year college.

This was the dream, and I was ready for it.

Although I wasn't deeply in love with my classes, it was a free education and I'd get to run for their track team. It was an opportunity to advance my sports career.

It was an escape. I could finally show my family I was more than just the kid who always got in trouble. The competition in college would be more intense, but I craved it. Competition meant growth.

A few days before graduation, my father sat me down at the kitchen table and ordered me to sign a stack of paperwork an inch high. The creamy white paper had so much tiny black text on every page it was almost painful to look at. I never read the documentation, but then I didn't need to. Dad made things very clear from the beginning.

He was ashamed I wanted to attend a state school and not a university. I needed to attend a prestigious university so it would reflect well on him, a man who never even graduated from community college. Don't worry, he had some pretty stellar accomplishments in his life, this just wasn't one of them.

My father had called the college sports committee at my new school to refuse the scholarship and my admission. As if he was the fucking boss of me.

There are no words to describe the utter devastation and rage coursing through my veins that night. I was still seventeen, not yet an adult, and terrified that I'd lose the coolest opportunity I'd ever received, just as I'd lost Arizona.

I fought, maybe for the first time in my life. I desperately wanted to leave home, to keep running, and more importantly, I wanted to get the fuck away from my father.

His anger exploded that night and it turned into a screaming match. I kept my back to the open air so I wouldn't be cornered against a wall, but it didn't matter. Before long, I was a deer in headlights, too scared of my father's anger to resist. I already carried the weight of wrongness that defined who I was under the family lens, and I was tired of the shame.

So tired.

All the fight went out of me, and I collapsed in tears. He won, and he knew it. He forced the pen into my hand and methodically flipped to each page that needed my signature.

Shell-shocked and on the wrong side of *his* law, I signed the papers, which included large student loans. I now had a federal debt that brought a suffocating weight.

In my later years, I learned of the fight my parents had that night. My mother yelled at him for hours, but in the end Dad won. Just like he always did. After all, he was the head of the house and had control over every big decision. If it wasn't for the family—translation: for *him*—it wasn't happening.

But maybe I could salvage the situation. The next day, I called my intended college several times, telling them I still wanted the scholarship, and that my father had spoken out of turn. It didn't matter. By the time I put in that first call, the college had already given my scholarship to someone else. If I still wanted to attend, I had to take out more student loans to pay for tuition and housing.

The devastation hit me like a speeding train.

I'd lost, and there was no way out.

A week later my father accepted a job in Atlanta, Georgia, 1,500 miles away. Before he left, he made sure I understood that part of my enrollment in the university was because I needed to stay here (in Colorado) and take care of my mother and brother. They were perfectly fine, by the way, and didn't need me, but somehow I was responsible for them now, and I had to keep up my grades.

It was a manipulation tactic to keep me under his control. It was now my duty to get a job and help with bills, to attend school in classes with over three hundred students (per classroom), to keep my grades at a B or above, and to keep the family together.

Off to Georgia he went, leaving behind a legacy that would both define and destroy my future.

I hated him.

For the first time in my life, I really hated my father. The emotion festering with rage is something I've carried throughout my life. I had no control over anything, and the things that made me unique—that might have been fostered—were stepped on and smashed into the mud.

My life was on his terms now and I despised him for it, falling into a depressive routine of school, work, and survival. I loathed the campus, which was spread out over several miles, and many of the classes had more than three hundred students. I couldn't learn anything. Hell, I didn't even know what was going on half the time because I couldn't hear the professor.

All of my friends were now up in Laramie, Wyoming, and I didn't know anyone. In my spare time I loitered in public spaces hoping to meet some new friends, but all I experienced from that was greasy pizza, the crippling weight of a debt I'd never be able to pay back, and the worst comedy show on every planet in the solar system. Seriously, the Vogons would have been impressed.

I registered for the cross-country team to keep up with my training, and to find some spark of happiness in my misery, but because of the school's immense population, no one could join the team that wasn't dedicated to the long marathons, and I was a sprinter.

When I tried to sign up for track, I spoke with one of the assistant coaches about my running career so far.

Less-than-impressed is an understatement.

The guy looked like I was reading the cable guide to him. I might have gotten a more positive response if I had. He handed me a stack of paperwork and told me I had to try out, but not for several months, and I couldn't use the school gym for workouts until I was officially on the team roster.

This coach had zero interest in watching me run—or exist for that matter. All I could think was *why bother*? I'd lost my shot at a college team, and I knew walking out of that office that the coach would never let me run track for the university. I briefly considered a local city team to keep up with training, but the only one that existed was mostly senior citizens. I needed competition—runners who were stronger and faster—to help me train.

My first (and last) year of university I failed gloriously. If it was a competition, I might have medaled there, too. I tried to find any thread I could tug on to bring me back to the sport, but it was the end of my career. Applying to another college meant more loans and more debt, something I couldn't afford for a sport that didn't pay a salary. And honestly, the university had jaded my perception of college. I didn't want any part of college life anymore.

Powerless and frustrated, I took a year off (i.e. dropped out) and went to work full time at a local grocery store, which didn't pay more than minimum wage.

I found a new group of friends and developed a new attitude: fuck those loans, my father could pay them off. I hated him now anyways. He didn't live with us anymore, and my mother was happy for the first time in years. That happiness resonated to me and my brother, and all the eggshells I'd been walking on in life slowly began to disappear.

I spent my time working, driving every other weekend to Estes Park because the roads up the mountains were so curvy, and watching Marx Brothers movies with the dearest friend in the world. For a time, I was almost happy.

The absolute sense of worthlessness and "you're always wrong" resurfaces years later, as I shift on the couch, trying not to throw up during the worst zoom call of my life.

This horrid woman who speaks with such a sweet voice and a lying smile on her face while threading subtle condescending phrases through the discussion holds absolute control over our housing situation.

I want to give her the middle finger and walk out of our home, tossing a lit match behind me. My husband and I try to negotiate with calm, intelligent logic, even owning our part of the blame and empathizing with their side of the situation, but we're two peons up against a billion-dollar company. There's a huge power imbalance, and we all know it. Without a lawyer of our own, we don't stand a chance of negotiating anything.

That woman and her lawyer keep pushing back until we have no wiggle room left. Either sign their agreement or vacate the property and be labeled the rest of our lives as 'evicted.' We can't afford to buy a home. We have to keep renting, so in the future that eviction status will block us from more than seventy-five percent of rental properties.

I convince myself that a successful negotiation leaves both parties feeling like they've lost. I know it's a lie. Once I can hide away in the shower, I sob for over an hour. Even with the "negotiated" agreement, we still can't pay, and we can't leave. It's not the first prison I've been in.

Happy fucking birthday to me.

July 4th, 2023

Independence Day, my ass.

My husband and I are still within our grace period for this month's rent, but we have barely enough money to feed ourselves until payday, and our kids desperately want fireworks. We have no excuses for why we can't do fireworks, and telling the truth would only stress them out about money. I've stressed about it enough since childhood, and I don't need my kids to carry that heavy weight.

Our lives feel like we're one step away from death. It reminds me of the movie *Monty Python's Holy Grail* where John Young's character doesn't want to go on the cart because he's not dead yet.

We're not dead yet either, but we are dying a slow death.

Sitting on the back deck on yet another holiday I wish I could ignore, I watch my kids jump on the half-baked trampoline they've nearly destroyed.

The same idea keeps circling my thoughts: my family and I need a fresh start. A reset. We can't pay for a new home, we can't escape our current situation, and it's only a matter of time before we're dragged through litigation with more lawyers, judges, court fees we can't pay, and that dreaded 'eviction' status that will follow us until death.

I'm old enough to know better, to not have to deal with this shit anymore, so how the fuck did I get here? Why am I nearing my 50th birthday and still dealing with the same cycle of rent, rinse, repeat?

A storm settles over my head, whipping my thoughts around but refusing to rain and rinse all the grime away. It pulls me back to Colorado and the dark clouds that followed me, triggering another fresh start.

During the year my father was gone from our lives, my mother, brother and I were happy. It's something no one wants to hear, that people are happier without you around, but in our case, it wasn't because we didn't love my father. Well, them... I held no love. It was because we could make our own decisions without him swooping in to control the outcome.

Then, my father came home.

It was like a dark cloud scuttled over the house and dared us to call upon the sun. None of us were happy about it, because he wanted the whole family to move to Georgia with him. Looking back on this moment, I often wonder why my mother stayed with him and made the move. The answer has changed over the years. I'm not sure if it's because she changed too, or that she was slowly unpacking her own trauma and discovering the language that described her plight.

I was nineteen, a full adult now, and had no desire to be on the same planet as my father, let alone the same house again. After making plans to move in with one of my mother's friends until I found an apartment, an instinct grabbed hold of my senses that I couldn't ignore.

My life was in Georgia.

The idea prickled my skin. I didn't want to believe it. I hated that instinct, but it grew stronger every day. Finally, I caved and accepted my fate. If I wanted to have control over the decisions in my life, I needed to trust *my* instincts.

Within a week of moving, I had a new job. I'd never lived below the Mason-Dixon line, so it took all of my strength not to giggle through the interview. Yes, I'm a brat. I'd only learn later that week that the boss's accent was barely a lilt next to my co-worker, who grew up deep in the Ozarks.

Even with my athletic career down the toilet, I was proud of myself for getting a job so quickly and becoming the dutiful part of society every daughter should be. I had my own car, could afford my own gas and clothes, and even some food. This would help take any financial burden off my parents until I could move out.

I never quite knew how much of a shield my mother was to all of us until she left for California to take care of my dying grandmother. The house felt empty without her, but I worked a full-time job, made my own money, kept up with my household chores (mostly), and would creep quietly in the door when I came home from work so I didn't wake my father, who could hear a mouse fart three states away from a dead slumber. And once he got woken up from sleep, he was an absolute ass to everyone and would constantly reinvent the rules about how noise was used in the house.

He worked a typical nine to five job. I often didn't start work until four in the afternoon, so our schedules always clashed. I understood his sleep disorder and was beginning to make friends, so every night after work I'd stop at the top of the neighborhood, hang out with Denmark and Douche-Waffle (trust me, this is the nice name for him), then drive home.

Before I hit the last curve to the house, I'd turn off the car and coast silently into the driveway. After taking off my shoes and spending twenty minutes creaking open the car door and nudging it shut, I'd tiptoe to the side of the house, pull out my keys, and spend another ten minutes holding my breath as I silently unlocked the door, inched across the entry, and held the knob twisted all the way tight to close it with a whisper.

I'd moved myself into the basement too, so I never had to travel upstairs to sleep. All the noise would be downstairs, on the other side of the house, and far away from my father. Stepping around every cricket and cockroach, shoes held in one hand, keys in the other, this whole process would finally get me tired enough to fall asleep so I didn't toss and turn on my creaky pull-out couch.

I did this every night for months.

But the shield known as my mother was in California taking care of my grandmother, who was dying from cancer. That's when my father started calling me names.

Whore.

Slut.

Thief.

Drug addict.

For reference, I was still a virgin and had never been in the same room as any (non-legal) drug, and the only thing I ever stole was a pocket full of candy at six years old, which my mother still laughs about today.

Every time the slurs slid out of my father's mouth, I tried to defend myself, but a daughter can only take so much.

I packed up the car and moved in with my boyfriend and two best friends. The four of us split the rent, the food, and we never missed a day of work. I might have been poor, but I wasn't completely broke. For the next two years I worked, partied, and tried to forget the life I could have had. My father's words had tainted me, so I began sleeping around, getting high, and I lost every ounce of self-respect I had.

Only work gave me a sense of pride. It was something I could do right, and my boss saw how smart I was. It's why when she got promoted to another store, she took me with her.

I lived an hour away and I didn't love the new store, but it was a paycheck and I'd started to slow down the partying. Apparently there's more to life than booze and dancing. Who knew?

Even though I tried to straighten out my life, the universe threw me a curve ball I never saw coming: one with a uniform and a badge.

I was twenty-one the first time I had to face the law. I'd forgotten to pay a traffic ticket (or three) because I was so busy working, partying, and hating my father for all the years of humiliation he'd put me through.

I worked as an assistant manager for a grocery store Drug/GM department, something I'd done for three years. My schedule constantly shifted around, sometimes working days, other times overnight. It always depended on the season, what sales were going on, and when store management decided to spring inventory on us.

One night I'd just gotten home from work after a twelve-hour shift. Every part of my body ached with exhaustion, so I ran a hot bath and poured myself a drink.

Then I got a call from my boss—I still had the truck key in my back pocket.

"Fuck," I muttered into the phone. Work was an hour away and I didn't want to go back until I'd had some sleep. "Can it wait until tomorrow?"

"We have to clear out the truck tonight so they can run the next haul," my boss said. I loved her like a sister, and I could tell by her voice that she heard the fatigue in mine. She was using her nice voice. Trust me, you didn't want to hear her angry voice. That woman could toss a stock cart across a warehouse when she was angry. I'd seen it happen.

"All right. I'll be there in an hour." After hanging up the phone, I shut off the bath, put my drink in the fridge (with no intention of touching it again because my new roommate was an ass), and climbed back in the car.

Even without traffic, it still took me an hour to drive back to work. As I put on my blinker and turned into the parking lot, red and blue lights flashed behind me. My body went on full pins-and-needles alert.

No big deal, I was probably speeding. Even though I couldn't afford it, I would just eat the ticket fine. As I pulled into a parking spot at the back of the lot, I looked to the front of the store and there was my boss on break, with a cigarette between her fingers. Next to her were the Grocery/GM manager, the assistant store manager, and the store manager. All the top bosses. I laid my head against the steering wheel and cursed the fucking universe. Sometimes I really hated this planet.

I rolled down my window to hand my license to the officer when he said, "Did you know there's a warrant out for your arrest?"

"WHAT!?"

I went into freeze/panic mode, begging the officer that he must have the wrong person. He asked me a series of questions, then told me about a new law that passed which stated that all people with unpaid tickets (didn't matter what for) were to be arrested.

I barely had enough money to cover gas in my bank account, but I would be paid Friday. "Can't I just pay the ticket now?"

Anything to avoid this horror show.

Nope. He had to arrest me.

Once those handcuffs were on, my boss ran over to grab the truck key from my back pocket. I was so mortified and humiliated I just hung my head. I couldn't even look her in the eyes. A fucking unpaid speeding ticket, that was all, but it felt like I'd murdered someone.

I was taken to jail, and the bail was a lot higher than the ticket. The price of everything together turned out to be twenty times higher than the original speeding ticket, and that didn't include impound costs.

That night was the last time I ever saw my car.

My parents arrived the next morning and we had to talk with a thick glass pane between us. I don't remember my mother saying much, but my father yelled at me then said these exact words: "You screwed yourself in, you can screw yourself out."

This from the man who was arrested twice in his teens, and *not* for minor infractions I might add. I won't divulge the nature of his crimes, but his father (my grandfather) bailed him out both times within a matter of hours. I digress.

The moment my father walked out of that room, a bitter resentment lodged itself in my heart, festering with a rage that honestly has never quite evaporated. He has no idea how much that moment still fucks with my head.

I spent a week in jail. While it wasn't the worst facility, it fucked me up in ways I still carry today. After my bail was paid (with my own paycheck I might add), the officers told me about a second unpaid speeding ticket. And yeah, off to jail number two. I was only there for four hours this time. My boss told me she took care of the bail. It was only years later when I learned that she'd used her home as collateral. I am so grateful for that woman, but every time I think about what she did for me, it comes with a wave of guilt. I was never good enough to earn that level of kindness.

August 30th, 2023

Summer is almost over.

I desperately want to believe our nightmare is about to end too, but fall in Seattle brings the Iron Curtain of Despair™ that hangs over the Northwest like a dark god. The sunlight can't get through that thick cloud layer, and the drizzle it brings never ends.

My husband and I don't want another cold, wet season. His hip still hurts and the pain in my knee has returned. Every month we're sending the housing company thousands of dollars, but it's still not enough, so my husband keeps working fourteen-hour days on straight commission to boost up his paycheck. My PTSD has gotten so bad I've developed some new twitches, and I'm lucky if I can get in ten hours of work a week.

I haven't run for years, and I still ache for the smell of the track, for the explosive ease at which my body moved through life. The only sport I'm good at anymore is sarcasm. I can't even walk my dogs because Harley is getting sicker. His last days are close, and I can't bear to lose another dog.

Then Covid hits our house like a freight train.

My kids have been in school for only three days, and now they're sick and crying and puking. At the foot of my bed is a small, cheap folding couch that I lay flat so they can sleep next to me. I'm trying to keep myself from getting sick. If I do, they'll expect me to keep on cooking, cleaning, and all the other jobs I do around the house. Plus I've just signed work agreements for two large website redesign projects, and I have no time to work on either.

I've quarantined myself with the kids so my husband doesn't get sick. My poor kids are suffering from extreme body aches as the sickness rolls through them. All they can do is cry and cling to me.

Halfway through the day, my husband stumbles through the door with a 102-degree fever. Now he's got Covid, too. We can't win. We just can't fucking win.

As I hold onto my son, not knowing that this is only the first round of what will turn into months of continued sickness for my family, I try to stop the twitching. It's a new symptom in my never-ending cascade of illnesses that keep my mind and body locked in an invisible war.

We need an exit strategy. A fresh start. It's not the first time I've felt this way either.

During the year that followed my arrest, life spun out of control in a way I couldn't rein in.

I returned to Colorado, and within the first year I got pregnant by my old friend Douche-Waffle. In a religious household, this is the ultimate act of betrayal. My family already criticized me for so many things, including sex before marriage, and with this new revelation, the whore daughter had finally committed the ultimate shameful act.

I'd already had three doctors confirm I was barren and couldn't have children, and I was even on medication for what was believed to be stomach ulcers because I couldn't stop puking stomach bile.

When we finally figured out I was pregnant, I was twenty-seven weeks along. My father ostracized me and sent a very long-winded letter about what a shame to the family I was, a shame to his religious beliefs and all his friends, and that I wasn't fit to be a mother. He ended the letter by telling me to get rid of the child and dump her into the foster system—that she'd be better off.

That man could go fuck himself. Douche-Waffle, too..

News of the pregnancy hit me hard. Getting ostracized from my family devastated me. And when I called Douche-Waffle (the sperm launcher) to let him know I was pregnant, he stopped all communication with me while his family declared me a gold digger. Apparently they're wealthy—something I had no knowledge of.

I'd become the cancer in everyone else's lives, but I knew one truth in my own: no matter how hard I had to work, I would care for my daughter so she would always know how much her mother loved her.

Iris was born at 11am in the morning. I'd been barely squeaking by as a single woman, so with a daughter to feed now, life pushed us into poverty.

The only way to feed my daughter was to fill out the mountains of state paperwork to get her on WIC so she'd have milk and diapers. Yippee for paperwork.

We moved into low-income housing alongside other single mothers, all of us with children to feed after the men vanished from our lives. All of us mothers were left to financially fend for ourselves, but here's the kicker: none of us could get state benefits for ourselves, only for our children. We all made too much money—meaning we worked. If we'd all quit our jobs, we might make more money than our current wages, which is still a huge problem in social services. Moving on.

When Iris was two months old, my mother came to visit. She instantly fell in love with her granddaughter and regretted her role in the events that took place since I'd declared my pregnancy. To this day, my mother and Iris are joined at the hip. They have a bond that's so strong and beautiful, and a happiness together that lights up the world.

At eight months old Iris got croup. I didn't sleep for two weeks, terrified she would stop breathing.

Not long after, I needed surgery. During my recovery I was fired. The reason? "You're taking too much time off work."

Seven words that hold a deadly poison to single parents, often followed up by "you need a better support system." I could write a whole book on the absolute heinous nature of these words and how they're weaponized against single parents whose children have no other protection and comfort aside from their one parent. Because of these venomous words, single parents are pushed out of jobs, passed over for promotions, and constantly chided like children by bosses who have spouses, families, and support systems that allow them to hold positions of power. Just in case you're dying to know why I stopped working corporate jobs and began freelancing.

For me, it meant it was time for a change again—a fresh start.

I was so exhausted with poverty and scraping together every nickel and dime just to eat. My daughter deserved better, and somewhere in my fucked-up brain I still needed to prove to my family that I was someone they could be proud of.

This time I wanted to live in a place with no family to stand over me and put on their judging eyes. Not until I'd gotten control of my life.

Somewhere in my adventures I met a code-tester at Microsoft who we're going to name Code-Tester. He was charming, laid back, and tons of fun to be around. Plus, he made a decent wage at his job, and I could maybe (just maybe) start having real dates (not the "let's just stay in and watch a movie" kind of date). i.e. The *all I want is sex* date.

Code-Tester lived in Seattle, and he'd been hinting at a more long-term commitment together. I was absolutely in love with him and knew the only way to make a firm decision on this was to live in the same area. Plus, I loved Seattle—it felt like home.

Iris, now eighteen months old, and I packed up our meager belongings and headed to greener pastures. We moved in with Code-Tester, who lived in a very dark one-bedroom apartment under a highway.

Now that I re-read that line, it sounds like the beginning of a horror movie. It kind of was.

I didn't have to pay for rent or food, and I'd spent my last year in Colorado as a technology teacher at a local elementary school. Honestly, I think the only reason I got the job was because I knew how to write DOS code, which is a fun irony since the school ran on MACs.

I wanted to find the same job again, but the only opening available was for helping special needs children at a school located three bus rides away.

Three.

Bus rides.

Away.

Although Code-Tester had a car, I didn't. We were still working out the nuances of living together, and his job lay in an entirely different direction than mine, so he drove to his work while Iris and I took the bus (a two hour ride each way).

The school didn't pay much, but it was enough to keep Iris and I fed. Most of our time spent together was on the bus, snuggling amid a sea of strangers. And if we missed our connection, one of two calls would have to be made: I'm gonna be late for work, or I'm gonna be late for dinner. The second one was usually much easier.

As the weeks passed, I noticed odd behaviors in Iris. She seemed tense all the time, cried around candy, and had developed a fear of the vacuum cleaner. It would be months before I finally figured out that Code-Tester had been tormenting her because, according to him, "she wasn't a real person yet."

I should have kicked him in the balls when he said that.

Meanwhile, Code-Tester was getting more controlling, more manipulative. He also had a pent-up rage that came out in spurts, usually when we were playing board games. If he was losing, he'd roar in anger, throw the game across the room, and storm out, squealing out of the parking lot in his ridiculous mustang. It would be hours before he'd return home—if he did at all that day.

I was starting to get nervous about the relationship, and where I would find the funds to get Iris and I our own apartment.

Then Code-Tester's parents came for a visit.

They were such lovely people, right up to the moment they started pressuring me to marry their son. At the point that they were practically spelling it out, I made it very clear that I would never marry their son. I didn't like his unpredictable rage spurts. Plus, I was already working on an exit strategy.

A few days after they left, Code-Tester and I got in a huge fight. I can't remember what started it, only where it ended—my back against the wall and him screaming in my face. Just like my father used to do.

This was followed up by Code-Tester punching a hole in the wall next to my head. When I glanced down, my daughter stood behind him, witnessing the event.

I held her in my arms and stayed silent until he left for work. Once he was gone, I packed up our bags and hopped on the first bus to freedom. He could keep the crib and anything else left behind. I would do anything to keep Iris safe, and that meant running.

That afternoon I cashed my paycheck, rented a car, and drove to Oregon. We had friends there, and with one call we had a place to crash for a few days. I turned off my phone and spent the weekend as an emotional wreck. Iris, on the other hand, laughed and ran through the fall leaves until she couldn't keep her eyes open.

She was safe, that's all that mattered, but I still had to figure a few things out. I was expected to be at work Monday morning. We had nowhere to sleep, and we were never going back to Code-Tester's house.

We were homeless now. I couldn't call my family. I couldn't bear the shame, or the judging words once more assuring me that I was a trash-fire human. Proof of it came into focus the day Iris and I entered the domestic violence shelter.

I didn't want to be "that woman," the one who ended up in a domestic violence shelter because she kept going back to her abuser. But I also didn't want to enter a shelter because I didn't have physical bruises or a black eye. I didn't want to take a bed away from someone who needed it more than I did.

And yet, all it took was one glance at my daughter and that logic changed. I didn't understand at the time but I already *was* that woman. I embraced my new "that woman" status to make sure Iris had a roof over her head and food to eat.

Our names were changed during our stay, and we were placed in a discreet hotel far away from Code-Tester and close to work. One fifteen-minute bus ride away.

After our stay at the DV shelter, Iris and I were accepted into a homeless shelter. When we arrived, I was certain that we'd just be on a cot in the middle of a warehouse, but we were given our own small apartment. It was a three-hour bus ride from work, but I didn't care. I curled up on the bed and cried for hours while my daughter took lipstick and painted all the walls right about ankle level until the final streak swiped sideways to the carpet. That's where I found her asleep with lipstick clutched in one hand and her kitty in the other.

We had $0.67 in our bank account and three cans of green beans in the cupboard. I finally debased myself and called my mother to tell her what happened, begging her to let us come home. I would take my father's abuse with a smile on my face if it meant my daughter got to eat.

"You can't," she whispered into the phone. "I love you both with all my heart, but if you come back, your life will be over. Dad will make sure of that."

She didn't even have to explain what she meant—I already knew. My father would destroy me, and he would make sure my daughter was shoved into a foster home where I couldn't touch her.

Something in me died that day. My daughter and I had nothing left. Those haunting words erased the last bits of my self-worth while I clutched the phone in my hand. I'd been a winner once, but all I could hear now was my father's voice. *You're an unfit mother. You need to give your daughter away.*

I almost believed it, until my mother whispered one more thing into the phone. "You'll find a way out. I believe in you."

She hung up the phone.

I just stood there with cold, numbing prickles all over my skin. Dropping the phone, I returned to the small apartment and stared at the curtains for hours. My daughter knew her mother loved her, but it wouldn't be enough. Not for her.

That was Tuesday.

The next morning someone knocked at the door. When I opened it, there stood an empty hall and a laundry basket stuffed with a giant turkey, boxes of stuffing, cranberries, green beans, potatoes, pies, and enough food to feed a family for a week.

It was Thanksgiving weekend—I'd completely forgotten. I don't think I've ever been more thankful for anything in my life.

That Thanksgiving I cooked all day for us. We received another knock on the door with a second basket stuffed just like the first. More food that would take us weeks to eat.

We ate until our stomachs hurt and laid around watching cartoons until bedtime. It was a beautiful day with the most wonderful daughter. She laughed and played and snuggled against me, oblivious to all that was wrong in our world. Her hugs and smiles erased the destruction in my soul. At least for a little while.

On Friday a social worker visited to go through all the items they had to check off their list for families who ended up in a homeless shelter. There were mountains of paperwork, several hours of lectures on how I ended up there, housing applications to fill out, and job applications to submit.

"I have a job," I said to the social worker.

"Miss Harrowick, you ended up here for a reason." The judgment was back, this time in the eyes of the tweed-suit man sitting across the table from me. "You need to fill out and submit these job applications. Do you have any special skills?"

I wanted to punch him.

"Sir," I said with all the southern respect I could muster. "I teach technology classes for adults, I work with special needs children, and I have health benefits for both me and my daughter. I have a job. Two jobs, actually."

"We'll get to that in a minute," he said, clearly meaning to berate me about the health of my daughter. It was a miserable afternoon. The only way to make it stop was to fill out his stupid paperwork so the bastard would leave.

Throughout the rest of the interview, he continued to talk over me as if I was the trash of human society. I let it roll off my back. After all, I'd been told this most of my life, so one more person telling me how I wasn't good enough wasn't going to make a difference.

October 15th, 2023

A storm brews on the horizon, and it has nothing to do with Seattle's dreary weather. Every day my husband and I sense it coming—the final eviction notice, the summons to court, the point of no return, and no escape.

As I sit at my computer with the first spare time I've had in nearly a year, an email slides into my inbox. The sender: *Housing Company Extraordinaire* (not really). The subject: *Move out Agreement*.

I'm terrified to open it. The housing company hasn't sent an email like this before. It's the end of the line—the "get the fuck out now" final notice as we march the plank to our death.

I want to jump, the ocean swells be damned, but there are sharks in the water.

It's a new contract agreement that they haven't discussed with us. My husband is back at work—everyone finally deCovidized—and he can't bear to open it either.

We stayed when we didn't want to. We tried to make it right. The other side of that email will be against lawyers and judges and all the things that terrify me, and I just don't have the strength anymore.

I've been in this position before—so many times it's like rote. I fucking hate this feeling of absolute degradation that I can't escape. My finger hovers over the mouse as I will myself to open the stupid email. To rip off the band-aid.

I click the mouse and hold my breath. Words pop up along with an attachment. Through my tears I read everything multiple times to understand what's happening.

I'm wrong about the email. And I'm right.

The housing company wants us to get the fuck out and stay out. I understand, and I would feel the same way if our positions were reversed, but seeing the words set against me and my family trigger an anger I can't contain

All the alarms in my head shoot off. All the flags I've collected over the years raise high and flash red.

It has to be a trick. It's a contract to move out in two weeks—completely out—and in exchange they'll erase the entire debt we'd accrued.

The bitch from the local office calls it a clean break for us (as if she or the company have our well-being in mind).

I can't take it anymore. For all the things I've experienced in my life, this one is entirely brand new, and I don't know how to navigate it.

I pick up the phone and call Kasey, a trusted friend who is dealing with the same thing—but she's on the other side of the equation, attempting to coax a tenant to move.

"It's not a trap," she says. She keeps her voice calm. Kasey has known of our plight for a long time, of how hard we fight to set things right. "You have to think like a rich person. They need you out because they're not making any money. The company can write off your debt like they've lost ten dollars. If you can do it, take the deal and get yourselves out of that mess."

When I first met Kasey, on the gameshow Wordcrash, it felt like we were two women living on different planets, and yet there was an easy connection between us. The more we talked, and the deeper our conversations got, we discovered so many similarities in our lives that reflected and threaded our individual struggles together. It didn't take long before we talked for hours every day on the phone as we navigated life's ruthlessness.

She's right. I don't know how to think like a rich person—I've never been one. In fact, if you look at my ancestry, my family hasn't had any form of wealth for at least sixteen generations. We worked—farmers, store clerks, apple pickers, mechanics, alcoholics (it's more of a sport, I guess)—this is my family legacy. I can't think like a rich person because I always have to worry about money and be hyper-aware of every dime I spend.

I trust Kasey, but I need more than one voice telling me this new contract agreement from the housing company is legit. I call 2-1-1 and explain our situation. I'm immediately connected with a local lawyer. He makes it very clear that he's sorry we've ended up in this situation and that I'm not his client, after which he promises to look over the agreement and get back to me with thoughts in a couple of days.

We have 48 hours to sign the agreement or it will be revoked. It's already taken me 20 hours to get to the lawyer, and now the clock is ticking.

My husband and I have to make a decision, and our instincts are all over the place. This type of thing is not in our experience database, nor is it a superpower. We want to trust that signing the agreement will work out, but if life has taught us anything, it's that nothing can be trusted, especially a deal too good to be true.

It isn't the only deal that seemed like a dream. For nearly all of Iris's childhood, we lived in homes that had no yard, a giant asphalt hill that led straight into oncoming traffic, or cement stairs that were supposed to serve as a playground.

We'd slowly been making small adjustments to improve our lives and it was time for another. I found us a new place, a home in the country with a top floor apartment in a farmhouse by the river.

The farmhouse was a giant madhouse, in the best of ways.

The single father who lived in the bottom levels had five kids he was trying to raise alone. His children were all around Iris's age, and I'll never forget the day we moved in. We pulled into the driveway and Single Father's kids were all swimming in this huge pool. They saw Iris and were so happy to have another kid around that they all yelled at her to come play.

She bolted from the car, and I didn't see her the rest of the day.

Iris now had three acres to run around on, a pool to swim in, our sweet dog, Sadie, to play with, and her two ferrets. While we lived there, she even got to see kittens born and go on her first (and last) snipe hunt. Seriously, I think she's still pissed about that one. I know my nephew is.

We were still poor as shit, but finally I could check off another thing I'd done right. I'd gotten her out of the city and into a home with a yard, and she was *happy.*

Once a week, Single Father and I cooked dinner together for both families. There was absolutely no romance between us, but as parents we had a healthy respect for each other. Plus that one night a week gave us a chance to swap family recipes and learn how to cook some new meals.

In fact, I was exhausted with trying to date as a single mother. It was absolutely the worst, and I could write a whole book about the complexity of dating and parenting.

I was working, running an online RPG forum, and picking at the early stages of *Bloodflower's* world.

Then I met my husband. Well, re-met. We'd known one another in Georgia and had a strong bond of trust, but we hadn't spoken with one another in thirteen years. He'd become a professional pool player, had a daughter, and lived a full life.

All it took was one phone call, and I knew I was gonna marry him. Within a few months he moved to Seattle and into our crazy house. Meanwhile, Single Father started dating a single mother with six kids.

Three adults and twelve kids later and the house was absolute chaos at all hours of the day and night. I couldn't sleep, couldn't think, and even Iris started to fracture at the seams.

We needed silence, so we rented an old hunting cabin with a working gravel pit. Eighty-six acres of wilderness, coyotes, a rogue mountain lion, a bear that didn't exist (according to local rangers, despite the photos we had), a heating bill that almost destroyed us, and a stray bullet from the owner's son that nearly took my daughter's head off. It was both a dream and a nightmare.

My husband's parents lived in Texas, so it wasn't long before we packed up our lives, our dogs, our cats, and our daughter, and off we went into the sun. It was the first time we moved to Texas.

I remember coming out from under Seattle's cloud cover and into the sun that day. By the time we got to Yakima it felt like we'd stepped into a new, better life.

My husband and I often talk about returning. As I glare at this new agreement with the housing company, all I want to do is sign, sell off all our shit, and run back to Texas. The land is beautiful and the sun is almost always shining. We'd go if we could, but my husband's job is here, and we still don't have the money to go anywhere.

August 17th, 2023

Signing that contract agreement destroys a part of me I'm not sure I can ever get back, or even explain in words. I hate doing it because I don't trust it, but the housing company won't give us any extra time to speak with the lawyer, and not signing leads to a far worse fate.

It takes weeks for my husband and I to recover from signing that document. Part of me still wonders if the agreement is still in circulation with the company lawyers or if it's been tucked away in a closed file. We don't know, and we don't want to call and accidentally instigate a revival.

Once it's a done deal, our despair turns to chaos. I have to put all of my wonderful clients on project holds (again), keep the kids out of the way, apply for new housing (which we still can't afford thanks to Seattle's ever-skyrocketing prices), and explain to every teacher and school counselor why the kids still aren't in school.

It's also the day Harley dies. The light left his eyes the day we received the agreement, and the day we sign I have to put him down. He's shadowed my every movement for over a decade, and when he's gone, I can't make myself leave the vet office. He isn't gone—he's still there. The essence of who Harley is won't leave, and I can't walk away until he does.

His loss devastates me, but I've learned to live with the emotional chaos of my life. It's just another day and my pain can wait.

I already know what it's like to be homeless. The ticking deadline has me nervous, but it only occupies a small part of the days I spend ripping apart our lives.

We continue to look for homes we can afford now that we no longer have to pay out most of our income to the housing company. We're not picky and we want to downsize and simplify our lives so this nightmare never happens again. There are small apartments far off the beaten path that nobody else wants. We make enough to at least afford that, even if it's a huge adjustment for all of us.

Application after application we receive the same answer: your credit rating isn't good enough.

Of course it isn't—we've been fucked so many times I'm surprised they even use numbers for us. I don't know when this credit rating bullshit started when it comes to housing. We make enough to afford the tiny places. It doesn't matter though—everything changed through the Covid years, and our current housing company has absolutely annihilated both our credits.

When the last door closes on our house, we're homeless. It's a hard reality to face. I blame myself for all of it, and I know my husband does the same. Beating ourselves up won't change the situation, so we've got to figure something out, and we've got to do it for our kids.

November 5th, 2023

One of my dearest writer friends always says, "You need to get out of Seattle. It's a Hellmouth."

She's right. It may not be for everyone, but it has been for us. My husband and I still talk about moving south again, but we can't afford it. Too bad, because our stuff is already in storage. All we need to do is toss it into a truck.

We've been living in a hotel now for about three weeks, which is about the same price as a house. At least utilities are included. We've gone from a four-bedroom house with a yard to a single room. I still haven't had time to grieve Harley's death, and our other dog, Freya, is apathetic. She's grieving, and I can't seem to pull her out of it, despite daily visits to the dog park.

She still misses her brother Loki—the dog who attacked me—but she really misses Harley. The kids and I try to play with her, and sometimes it works, but I can see her aching need for something just beyond her reach.

Kasey's keeping me sane. She helps me keep myself stitched together while I sit in that hotel room every day, always on a Zoom call with a client or my therapist.

My PTSD is coming out in spurts again—twitches, convulsions, or hour-long sessions of time where I stare off into space. It will be a few more months before I discover that the staring spells are migraine-induced seizures. I call them silent migraines because they sneak up on me and I can't feel a lick of pain.

I need to work, but it's hard to focus on creativity when your office is a five foot by ten foot kitchen. My kids are always hungry, so they're constantly shuffling behind me, opening the fridge, cooking, and slamming cupboards. It's hard to concentrate and get anything done.

I still can't write. I haven't even thought about it in months, though I feel the ache to dive back into my dark and delicious worlds.

The schools call every day asking about my kids. They know the situation, but we live nearly an hour away now—if you count traffic—and I don't even know where we're gonna land. We might be living in a hotel for the next six months.

Nights are the hardest. Three of us suffer from insomnia while my son can fall asleep with a snap of fingers. My daughter, Willow, struggles the hardest. She rarely sleeps. Her doctors are aware, but there's not much they can do to help. It doesn't help that my husband snores either. There are nights where Willow and I watch TV on our phones in the bathroom just to keep the noise to a minimum.

It's been hard. Each of us has made accommodations to help the situation, but I know that every day we struggle for a little alone time.

I think it hit my husband the hardest. He fought every day to find us a new home, but I can tell he's done with Seattle. He doesn't want to live here anymore. And honestly, I have one foot out the door as well.

As I try not to think about our finances, if the housing company is going to renege and drag us into court, and how we are ever going to find a home again, I sip my coffee and try to get my head on straight so I can tackle the day.

That's when I receive a surprising call. It's my husband, and his company is relocating us to Texas.

November 9ᵗʰ, 2023

My husband's company has one small hitch to their offer—we have to be in Texas in ten days.

I want to both kiss and slap somebody. We finally have a chance to move south, but the timeline is ridiculously tight. The only thing crossing my mind is thank the great plaid fireweasel atop the mountain high™ that the company didn't transfer him last month—we'd have been fucked.

Our possessions are already in storage, so all we have to do is rent a trailer, if our truck can handle the weight. Then there's the sticky little problem of finances. My husband's company doesn't want to help us with the move, they just want us to get there.

Sigh.

My wonderful husband keeps the dialogue open and finally they agree on a small stipend, which they insist we pay back on the other side. I mean. . .they're a billion-dollar empire, and that's on the conservative side. I guess rich folks can't think like poor folks either.

We scrape together every dime we have, sell our second car, leave half of our belongings behind to save on trailer costs, and after a quick, tearful goodbye to family members, we're on the road four days later.

During those first hours as we race for the Oregon border, the dark clouds of doom weigh us down. We can't shake the idea that we'll just keep driving until the world disappears around us.

I stare out the window into the graying dawn, desperate once again for sunshine as we inch our way toward the Columbia River. My husband

and I originally planned to travel our previous route to shave off some time, but the winter storms in the Rockies and high Utah deserts push us to travel through California until we reach the southern states.

The moment we hit the Oregon border, my husband and I both laugh and cry in one breath. We're finally out of Hellmouth. We're free.

I glance up at the sky to find the sun, but Oregon is host to an overcast gray. The black clouds over Washington state are reaching their long fingers over the Columbia River into Portland's skyline.

The Hellmouth is calling us back. It's a dark monster refusing to release its grip on us. But this is our escape, worthy of an epic fantasy book. The highway leads us south of Portland before Washington's dark claws retract and the sun breaks through the clouds. It's a sight I'll never forget.

The trip takes five days with long stretches of driving broken up by my son's desperate need to visit every single rest stop along the way.

By the time we hit the white sands of New Mexico, the dark clouds of the past year finally begin to release their hold. The kids are laughing and smiling in the sunshine, and even our dog, Freya, is finally shedding the last threads of her grief.

Along the way, my husband finds a home he falls in love with. It's a single landlord, an old rancher, and he approves us as renters before we hit New Mexico.

When we arrive at our new home, none of us can believe it's real. It's an old, converted barn in the middle of a large cattle ranch. The rent is manageable, the cost of living is lower, and as I hold onto my coffee and step onto the porch, I'm greeted by a herd of cows napping beneath the tall oaks.

My father's manipulation and control stole a future I desperately craved but will never possess. Perhaps in another dimension, or on another timeline, that future has played out. Maybe it's better, maybe not, but the decision was ripped from my hands by his ability to incite a terror that took me decades to overcome.

At times it still feels like I have no control, that what I want is always eclipsed by a world I don't feel I belong to. But in the words of Captain Malcolm Reynolds from TV's *Firefly*, "We have done the impossible, and that makes us mighty."

My husband's leg is finally healed, and the limp is gone thanks to the endless walks along the ranch that have helped strengthen his muscles again. The kids have lost a year of school due to all the fiascos we've suffered—more than half of them which aren't listed in this narrative—but every day they smile and tell me how much they love the country.

As for me. . .nothing in my life has been easy. I suppose all I can do with the time I have left is to seek out the sunlight in this world. For anyone who knows me, that means a deep dive into dark spaces where I can pour my soul into derelict starships, insidious villains, and alien worlds worthy of all the science fiction and fantasy authors who came before me.

EPILOGUE

When life started to settle down, Kasey and I talked more about our shared traumas. The emotional and financial abuse we experienced at the hands of our domineering fathers wasn't the only thread that connected us. We've both struggled against the healthcare crisis in this country—or lack of healthcare available to our husbands—and we both missed out on attending the colleges of our choice because of decisions our fathers made against our consent. Me with my athletic scholarship and Kasey with a full music scholarship her father made her turn down. We both realized we could have a positive impact on others by sharing our stories.

Kasey had been working on a project about this very subject matter for a while called *I Know Why She Stayed*. As we worked together on other projects, we began collaborating on ideas and it was as if the stars began to align. We brought out the best in one another and provided tons of support in both our professional and private lives. Thus, I was ~~dragged~~ woven into the project.

While life isn't perfect for either of us, we're committed to furthering the mission of the *I Know Why She Stayed Initiative* with the hope of helping others escape from financial abuse.

Or better yet, avoid it altogether.

If you're interested in learning more about the initiative, you can visit the website at www.iknowwhyshestayed.org.

I know why she stayed

I N I T I A T I V E

We also would like to thank those who have been so supportive in our efforts to make this a reality. Besides our families, who have given us unending support, we'd like to acknowledge Vicki Lowry, Dave (db) Dennison, and Justine Manzano for all they've done to help us. They have been our rocks and offer their support in multiple ways. From the bottom of our hearts, we thank you all.

ABOUT KASEY ROGERS

Kasey Rogers spent much of her earlier career working in the commercial film industry in New York City by day and writing a musical in-between film projects. After the birth of her twins, she switched gears to pursue another passion, cooking. That passion led her and her late husband to turn a vacation property in Alexandria, Ontario, into a restaurant. For several years she owned and operated The 2Beans Café and Tearoom in Ontario before moving back to the U.S. Since then, she has written the memoir *Our Better Selves: From Secrets and Lies to Healing and Forgiveness*, along with a work of literary fiction, *The Color of Frost*. Along with writing, Kasey is an outspoken advocate for women and speaks about the connection between domestic and financial abuse. Learn more about the *I Know Why She Stayed Initiative* at:

www.iknowwhyshestayed.org

Visit Kasey's website: https://kaseyrogers.com

Sign up for her newsletter: https://kaseyrogers.com/#footer

ABOUT K. J. HARROWICK

K. J. Harrowick is a fantasy and science fiction author with a strong passion for twisted stories blending grimdark worlds and futuristic technology. She's the co-founder and CTO of the *I Know Why She Stayed Initiative*, a repeat panelist for the WriteHive Annual Convention and the Weeknight Writers Convention, and she's appeared twice as a contestant on the gameshow Wordcrash!

Her novel *Bloodflower* has captured readers' hearts by casting a grimdark lens on what happens when a colony ship turns against its own passengers. With an unhealthy obsession for dragons, tacos, cheese, and beer, K. J. also works as a freelance web developer and graphic designer on a broad range of client projects.

Visit K. J.'s website: https://kjharrowick.com
Read more of her grimdark stories: https://kjharrowick.com/books
Check out her studio: https://kjharrowick.com/inside-the-studio/
Subscribe to her newsletter and receive your starship *Hàlon* digital crew patch: https://kjharrowick.com/newsletter/

ACKNOWLEDGEMENTS

Writing a memoir is hard. Neither one of us realized the full depth of what exposing your life and vulnerability feels like when you type out those words until we faced this challenge.

Writing this book was not a solitary adventure. After penning the first draft, several friends read the work and offered advice and encouragement to keep moving forward. Along the way, we've had so many people help us, support us, and give us the courage to keep going.

We are very grateful to them all, so a special thanks to: Danna Bonner, Jeni Chappelle, Lynda D'Amico, Dave (db) Dennison, Shelly Icardi, Kathy Inman, Astrid Julienne, Russell "Pirate Man" Leggett, Vicki Lowery, Justine Manzano, Loretta Meredith, Amy Myer, Lesley Orr, Chris Roffey, S. M. Roffey, Mary Anne Slack, Cheryl Smith, Betina Spathis, Swan, and of course K. J.'s wonderful rescue dog Roger.

We also want to add a special thank you to Megan Alnico of Wordcrash! If she hadn't invited us as guests on her game show, this book wouldn't exist.